Dublin's Industrial Heritage

Dublin's Industrial Heritage

From Sandymount Strand to Crumlin Road

ROB GOODBODY

WORDWELL
in association with Dublin City Council

First published 2025 by Wordwell Books, in association with Dublin City Council

www.wordwellbooks.com

First edition

Wordwell Books
The Wordwell Group
Suite 5
Hub 17
17 Corrig Rd
Sandyford Business Park
Dublin 18, Ireland

The Wordwell Group is a member of Publishing Ireland,
the Irish Publishers' Association.

ISBN: 978-1-916742-13-0 (paperback)
ISBN: 978-1-916742-25-3. (ebook)

British Library Cataloguing in Publication Data. A catalogue record for this book is available from the National Library of Ireland and the British Library.

Typesetting and design by the Wordwell Group
Printed by SprintPrint

Comhairle Cathrach
Bhaile Átha Cliath
Dublin City Council

An Chomhairle Oidhreachta
The Heritage Council

This publication was part-funded by the Heritage Council

Contents

Preface

In 2007 a comprehensive survey of the South-East Area of Dublin, initiated by Dublin City Council's Heritage and Archaeology sections in collaboration with the Heritage Council, surveyed 315 industrial sites and structures. The survey, part of the Dublin City Industrial Heritage Record (DCIHR), revealed that many of these sites retain significant industrial remains, reflecting the city's once-thriving industrial base, although nearly half show no visible remnants and 57 of the sites were on the city's Record of Protected Structures.

Central to Dublin's industrial expansion were its waterways, including the Liffey, the Dodder and the Grand Canal. The rivers acted as arteries for industrial growth, supporting the transport of goods and facilitating water-dependent industries. The Dodder, in particular, was once home to 45 watermills and various factories by the late nineteenth century, though few remain today. Bridges, embankments and flood-control measures along the Dodder survive as vestiges of the area's industrial past. The river also played a critical role in flood control, especially after devastating events, prompting significant infrastructure changes over the centuries. Efforts to manage the Dodder's flow, such as the construction of reservoirs in the nineteenth century, helped to regulate water-supply and limit the effects of flooding.

The Liffey, described as the 'spiritual heart of Dublin', has been a vital lifeline since the city's earliest settlements. The river fostered trade routes during the Viking period and, after the Anglo-Norman invasion, saw the construction of the first bridge in 1215. Dublin's orientation shifted dramatically during the late seventeenth and early eighteenth centuries, when the development of quays along the Liffey transformed the river into a key urban space, promoting commerce and industry. By 1700 numerous quays and bridges had been built, and the city expanded eastward towards the Docklands, where industrial development flourished. The construction of the Grand Canal in the late eighteenth century further enhanced Dublin's industrial capacity by linking the city to the Shannon River system, allowing for greater movement of goods and people.

The Grand Canal, completed in 1796, enclosed Dublin's south side and connected the city with its rural hinterland, significantly influencing industrial growth. Industries such as brewing, tobacco-manufacturing and laundries flourished along its banks. The canal served as a vital transportation route for goods, and its water was used by industries well into the twentieth century.

Dublin's transport systems, particularly the tramway and railways, were also integral to the city's industrial heritage. The Dublin United Tramway Company, formed in 1881, ran one of the largest and most efficient electric tram networks in the world by the early twentieth century. The expansion of tramlines facilitated the movement of people and goods, supporting both industrial and residential development. The Dublin & Kingstown Railway, Ireland's first, opened in 1834 and provided a crucial link between the city's industries and the port at Kingstown (now Dún Laoghaire), further accelerating industrial activity in the city and the suburbanisation of the coastal areas.

The Docklands area, which has been a hub of industrial activity for over 300 years, represents another critical element of Dublin's industrial past. From its early days as a site of fishing and boat-building, the Docklands evolved into a centre for warehouses and milling complexes, driven by the construction of the Grand Canal Docks in the late eighteenth century. Although the area declined in the nineteenth and twentieth centuries, the recent regeneration has transformed the Docklands into a major commercial and residential district while preserving some of its industrial heritage. The adaptive reuse of industrial buildings for alternative uses, such as the former Boland's Mills complex of buildings by Google, or the former Bewley & Moss Sugar Refinery building on Grand Canal Quay, now part of Trinity East (formerly the IDA Enterprise Centre), or the Barrow Street gas-holders (converted to apartments in 2005), show how industrial heritage buildings are eminently adaptable to new uses, contributing to urban renewal while retaining a sense of place.

Public utilities, including water-supply, gas and electricity, were instrumental in shaping the urban landscape of south-east Dublin. In the nineteenth century, the construction of mains drainage systems and public gasworks addressed public health and urban infrastructure challenges. The first recorded gas-powered street lighting appeared in Ringsend in 1825, and the electrification of Dublin began in earnest with the opening of the city's second power station, the Pigeon House Power Station, which opened in 1903 (a power station on Fleet Street, which opened in 1892, was the first). The South Docklands area, once an industrial powerhouse, now hosts some of the city's most significant modern developments, reflecting the continuous evolution of Dublin's urban landscape.

About the Series

This richly illustrated limited series of publications aims to showcase Dublin's industrial heritage, often overlooked in architectural history, and is organised into three volumes, one focusing on the South-East area, one on the South Central area, and one on Dublin's Central, North-West and North Central areas. This series will provide readers with an overview of the rich legacy of industrial heritage in each of these areas, both past and present. The present volume shows how the area's rivers, canals, transport systems and utilities have played crucial roles in fostering industrial activity and shaping the economic development of the city. While many industrial sites have been lost, those that remain, such as bridges, canals and former factory buildings, provide invaluable insights into Dublin's industrial past and the workforce that sustained it.

Charles Duggan
Heritage Officer

Acknowledgements

This book would not have been possible without the support and assistance of Dublin City Council. I wish to thank Charles Duggan, Heritage Officer of Dublin City Council, for commissioning this series, and Abigail O'Reilly, Graduate Heritage Officer, whose research provided many superb images.

I wish to acknowledge the support of Dublin City Council's Chief Executive Richard Shakespeare; Assistant Chief Executive Anthony Flynn, Acting City Planner Emer Ui Flatharta and Deirdre Scully, the former City Planner; Máire Igoe, Executive Manager; Malachy Bradley, Deputy City Planner; and Rhona Naughton, Senior Planner for Conservation and Heritage.

I am grateful for the support and guidance of Dr Ruth Johnson, City Archaeologist, and her team, including Assistant City Archaeologists, Niall Colfer, Seán Finlay Scott and Louise Callan; and Mary-Liz McCarthy, Executive Architectural Conservation Officer.

This work has been the culmination of many years of collecting information about Dublin city in general and industrial heritage in particular. Many people have assisted me over the years in a large range of colleges, libraries and archives, as well as colleagues in Dublin City Council, the Royal Irish Academy Historic Towns Atlas project, the Industrial Heritage Association of Ireland and various historical societies. In view of this protracted period, it is not possible to list all those who have helped and encouraged me, but you know who you are—though I should mention Fred Hamond, who generously passed over a number of his unpublished reports on certain sites.

The team involved in completing the Dublin City Industrial Heritage Record, developed by the City Council's Heritage and Archaeology Sections between 2004 and 2009, includes Dr Ruth Johnson, Donncha O'Dulaing and consultants, including Mary McMahon, Industrial Heritage Consultant, and the staff of Carrig Conservation, including Eimear O'Connell, Mary-Liz McCarthy and Cora Coleman.

Sincere thanks to Lorraine McLoughlin and the staff of Dublin City Archives; James Harte and the staff of the National Library of Ireland; Vincent Buttner and the staff of the National Archives of Ireland; the staff of UCD Digital Library; Ciarán Cooney from the Irish Railway Record Society; Seán Mooney from the National Gallery of Ireland; Rebecca Cairns and the staff of the Royal Irish Academy; South Dublin County and Laois County Libraries; Beatrice Okoro at the National Maritime Museum, Greenwich; Stephen Weir and the staff of National Museums Northern Ireland; Tailte Éireann; the Digital Collections team and the Map Library at Trinity College Dublin;

Stephen Knight of the Colne Valley Postal History Museum; Tanya Keys and the staff of the ESB Archive; Seán Walsh of the Irish Photo Archive; and Brendan McCarthy and the staff of Messenger Publications.

I am grateful to the individuals and organisations who licensed or gave permission to reproduce the images that appear in this text. This is noted with each individual image and in the list of illustrations at the back of the book.

This book is an action of the Dublin City Strategic Heritage Plan 2024–2029 and received County Heritage Plan Grant Funding from the Heritage Council.

In the more immediate production of this volume, thanks are due to Ronan Colgan, Nick Maxwell and the staff of Wordwell for their usual encouragement, diligence and production skills in bringing this work to its final form.

Rob Goodbody

1.
Introduction

This text is an introduction to the industrial heritage of the south-east area of Dublin city. The area covered runs from the Grand Canal at Goldenbridge, south of the circular line of the canal, through Crumlin and Kimmage, Terenure, Rathmines and Rathgar, Ballsbridge, Sandymount and Ringsend. To the north of the Grand Canal, it takes in the area to the east of Winetavern Street–Patrick Street–Clanbrassil Street and south of the Liffey. This was an area that had substantial amounts of industrial heritage of all types, from mining and quarrying, through watermills and windmills, to railways and trams, roads and bridges, docks and harbours, shipbuilding, iron-founding, distilleries, breweries, factories, utilities and much more—not to mention the canal itself.

The sheer breadth of the industrial heritage is such that it would not be possible to include everything, though it is hoped that the principal elements have been included, whether surviving or not. The examples included should be considered to be a sample of the entire industrial heritage of the area.

Throughout the text the street names that have been used are the modern ones, which is simpler than repeatedly explaining where Brunswick Street Great was, though for the most part the street names have remained fairly constant over time. Some figures have been expressed in litres or metres rather than the original measures to accommodate a contemporary audience; this has not been applied consistently throughout, however, and it is hoped that no confusion will result.

In many cases sections of text commence with descriptions of the background to a particular category of industrial heritage, and it is hoped that this is helpful.

It will be noted that there is an apparent bias in the location of heritage sites discussed, with the majority in the area enclosed by the Grand Canal and the Liffey and extending to Ringsend, while there are fewer sites in the Kimmage–Crumlin–Dolphin's Barn–Goldenbridge area. This is partly due to the greater availability of sources of information for the inner city but is mainly a result of the longer period of urbanisation in the city centre. The western section of the south-east area to the south of the Grand Canal was mainly agricultural through to the twentieth century and so it had its fair share of non-urban industry, such as mining, windmills and watermills, but fewer industries overall.

The structure of the text divides industries into broad categories; the older industries are described first, followed by the industries introduced in later times through to recent decades, although the emphasis is more on traditional industries.

2.

Mines and quarries

The geology of Dublin

The bedrock under the entire extent of Dublin city is limestone, while beyond the city boundary to the south and south-east the Leinster granite area begins, running southward through Wicklow and beyond. To the north-east Howth Head is predominantly quartzite and greywacke with some limestone.

Limestone was formed through the deposition in warm seas of calcium carbonate, which over the millennia consolidated into stone. The Dublin limestone, however, is of a type known as calp, which has a certain amount of mud mixed in with the calcium carbonate, resulting in a stone of poorer quality. The proportion of mud is inconsistent and so the quality of the limestone varies significantly, even within a single quarry.[1]

Dublin calp limestone was the traditional material for masonry walls in the city and was used for early structures such as the two cathedrals and churches and the city walls and gates. Even with the advent of brick in more recent centuries limestone remained in use, and most Georgian houses had walls of stone at basement level.

Another use for limestone was the production of lime. This had many applications, not least for agriculture, but within the city the principal uses would have been the production of mortars, plasters and renders, and limewash for use as a decorative and protective covering for walls and as a disinfectant.

Some minerals occur in this limestone and have been mined, the most significant being lead and copper, known to have been found within the south-east area of the city.

Overlying the limestone in the city are riverine deposits of sand or gravel and deposits resulting from the Ice Age or the period immediately following it.[2]

Bricks

Clays suitable for making bricks have been quarried in various places around Dublin city and its environs over the centuries and have also facilitated other ceramic works, such as roof tiles, floor tiles, flowerpots and crockery.

An early reference to brick-fields in Dublin dates from 1599, when the city granted a lease for four acres of the strand to the east of the River Stein 'for the use of a brick house'.[3] Townsend Street then ran along the shore line and this land would have been in the area to the north, around Tara Street and Moss Street. At the end of the seventeenth century brick-fields in the Ringsend–Irishtown area were noted on a map.[4]

Within the south-east region the significant area for quarrying clay and for brick-making was in the low-lying land at Merrion and Sandymount, and there are numerous references in the Fitzwilliam estate papers and maps from the beginning of the eighteenth century.[5] In the mid-eighteenth century this area was noted as providing potters' clay.[6] John Rocque's map of Dublin Bay, published in 1757, shows the extent of these brick-fields, with the caption 'Lord Merrion's Brick Field's [*sic*]' stretching along the coast from around Newgrove Avenue to Merrion Gates (Pl. 1), while extensive areas of water scattered over the area south of Sandymount Avenue seem to indicate the presence of brick-pits.[7] The village of Sandymount was named 'Brickfield Town' on that map.

Brick-making in this area came to an end with the passing of an act of parliament in 1771 that banned the making of bricks within two miles of the city.[8] The brick-

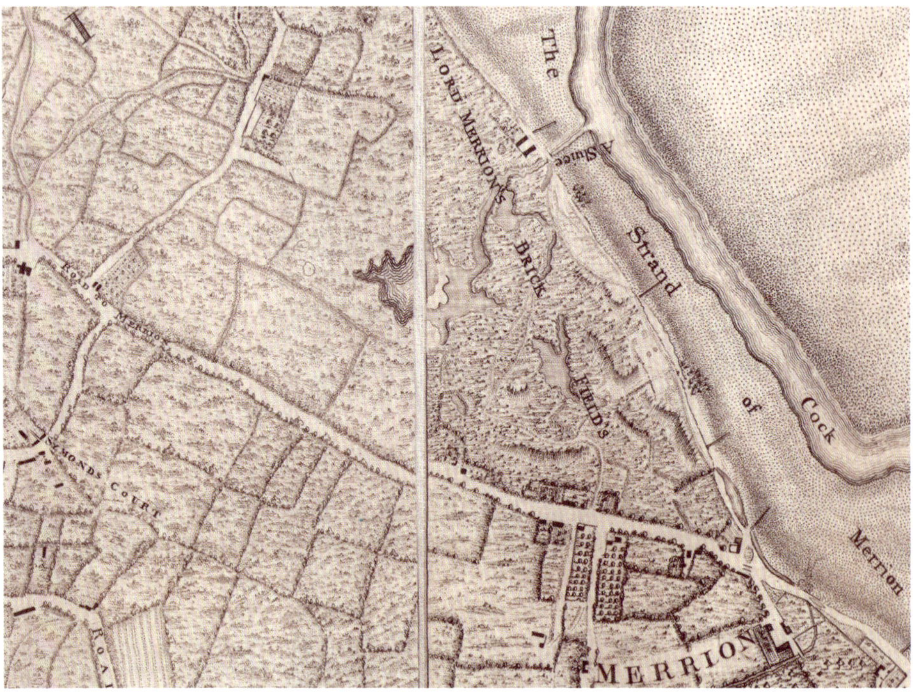

Pl. 1—Merrion brick-fields, seen on Rocque's map of 1757. These covered the areas now occupied by St John's Road, Sydney Parade and St Alban's Park.

pits at Sandymount and Merrion have disappeared from the landscape and no trace remains in the south-east area of any brick-making industry.

Wilkinson recorded in the 1840s that bricks were made at several places about four miles from Dublin but failed to specify where these were.[9]

The Mount Argus Brick & Tile Company was established at Harold's Cross in the mid-1880s, on the site to the north of the monastery at Mount Argus now occupied by Eamonn Ceannt Park. In 1900 the Dolphin's Barn Brick & Tile Company was established at Crumlin Road, with an additional site on Davitt Road. This company quarried brick clay from an extensive area around the brickworks and produced yellow stock bricks with 'Dolphins Barn' stamped into the clay. These two companies merged in 1921, together with the Rathnew Brick Company, to form the Dublin Brick Co. Ltd, which ceased operations in 1940.[10] By then the brick-fields at Mount Argus had not been in use for some time and the brickworks had been demolished, not being shown on the 1936 Ordnance Survey map. The site is now Eamonn Ceannt Park. The brickworks on Crumlin Road is now the site of the Sunshine Estate business park, while the clay-pits are now laid out as Brickfield Park.

Another large brick-clay quarry and brickworks was developed in the later nineteenth century to the north of Crumlin Road on the site now occupied by the Crumlin Shopping Centre. A smaller area, but still significant, was quarried at the rear of Harcourt Mills on the site now occupied by Good Counsel GAA Club, on the western side of Slievenamon Road, and there was a brickworks on that site.

GRAVEL-PITS

Nothing remains of the gravel-pits that formerly existed in the south-east area. A number of these quarries were depicted on the first-edition Ordnance Survey map, published in 1843. They were concentrated in the Simmonscourt area, with two between Anglesea Road and the Dodder, one to the east of Serpentine Avenue, another to the south of Simmonscourt Castle and a more extensive pit at Shrewsbury, between Merrion Road and the DART line. None of these were depicted on the second-edition map, published in 1871.

LIMESTONE QUARRIES

Being the principal building stone in Dublin, calp limestone has been quarried around the city for more than a thousand years, though most of the quarries have disappeared without a trace.

An early record of extensive repair works to Christchurch Cathedral in the mid-sixteenth century refers to stone being quarried from the bed of the River Dodder at Milltown, Clonskeagh and Rathmines.[11] The beds of limestone are visible in the river, particularly in the vicinity of Packhorse Bridge at Milltown, where the river bed has been quarried below the original level of the bridge, leaving the central pier perched on a pillar of stone, now encased in concrete. The stone appears to be of a higher quality here than at some other locations around Dublin.

In 1707 the city assembly granted a lease of a slip of land adjacent to Temple Bar and which was 'formerly part of the lane leading to the city quarry'.[12] Where that quarry was located is not known, but an old quarry was found by James Gandon's work crew when constructing the portico of the House of Lords, facing College Street, in the 1780s. The quarry was 5.75m deep and had been backfilled with rubble, and the foundations of the portico had to be deepened to reach firm ground.[13]

Rutty described a quarry at 'Smith's Mills, situate on Stubbin's land by the river Dodder', which was a very ancient quarry of a hard black building stone, deemed the hardest of any in County Dublin. He states that the old spire of St Patrick's Cathedral was said to have been built with it.[14] It is not certain where this quarry was or whether it was even within the present city boundaries, and it is possible that it was the quarry in the river that had been used in the reconstruction of Christ Church in the sixteenth century.

The first-edition Ordnance Survey map of 1843 shows a quarry on the northern bank of the Dodder to the west of Clonskeagh Road; this was not marked as a quarry on Taylor's map of 1816, but that map does show a limekiln, indicating the presence of a quarry. The 1865 Ordnance Survey map shows an engine-house adjacent to the river; this was not shown on the 1843 map, suggesting that the quarry was still in operation. By 1878 the Ordnance Survey noted it as 'Old quarry', indicating that it was no longer in use. This is now the open space between Ramlegh Park and the Dodder. There was also a substantial quarry at Donnybrook, on the site of Donnybrook Bus Garage, close to the Dodder. Marble is a metamorphic rock, formed from limestone through high pressures and temperatures. In the quarrying business, however, any limestone capable of being given a high polish is referred to as marble, and John Rutty referred to a number of quarries in the Dublin area having marble-quality limestone in the eighteenth century, including one on the bank of the Dodder to the east of Clonskeagh Bridge.[15]

Away from the River Dodder, quarries were located throughout the south-east area, some of them substantial in area and apparently also in depth. Several of these

Pl. 2—Rathgar Quarry and its windmill by George Petrie, 1831. The quarry was on the site now occupied by Rathgar Park, off Orwell Road.

had windmills on the edge of the quarry, which would have been used to pump water from the quarry (see Chapter 4).

Rutty referred to a quarry on the east side of St Stephen's Green; this reference would relate to the original extent of the Green rather than the present extent, as the quarry was located on the northern side of Baggot Street Lower, at the western side of the junction with Fitzwilliam Place. Rutty stated that it had been opened in about 1751 and had produced flagstones and hearthstones, with limestone at the lower levels.[16]

A large quarry at Rathgar was located on the present sites of Rathgar Park and Rathgar Tennis and Bowling Club (Pl. 2), while to the north, on the site now occupied by St Enda's Road, was another substantial quarry. The first Ordnance Survey map marked an 'Engine house' at the lip of the quarry, suggesting that it may have had a steam engine for pumping water out of the quarry.

Further to the west there were extensive quarries at Kimmage, on either side of Kimmage Road Lower, around the area now occupied by Kimmage Grove and St Martin's Park and Drive.

At Goldenbridge and Crumlin there were more limestone quarries on land now occupied by Glenview Industrial Estate, Old County Glen, Pearse College, Loreto Senior Primary School and Templeogue Synge Street GAA Club sports ground. Rutty described the stone from these quarries as being blackish and supplying hearthstones, flags and headstones.[17] In addition, there were about eight quarries to the south of Crumlin village on land that is now partly green space and where the former use is recalled in names such as Quarry Drive and Limekiln Lane.

Limekilns

As has been noted, lime can be produced from limestone for use in mortars, plasters and renders, as limewash and as fertiliser on fields. A number of the quarries in the Dublin area are known (mainly through the evidence of maps) to have had limekilns associated with them for this purpose. On some maps the words 'Lime kiln' appear, though in many cases on the Ordnance Survey map they are merely indicated by a small circle with a black dot set just inside the circumference. It is more than likely that these kilns were built of stone, 5–6m in width and 3–4m in height, with an arch at the front to facilitate the removal of the lime.

The earliest known limekiln in the south-east area was uncovered during an archaeological excavation in Fownes Street and is presumed to have dated from the thirteenth century.[18] In the eighteenth century there was a limekiln in the Grafton Street area, while another in Fleet Lane, to the south of Aston Quay, is shown on maps drawn in the 1790s.[19]

A number of limekilns are depicted on Ordnance Survey maps during the nineteenth century. Some of these were limeworks, where lime was the primary product, such as one on Grand Canal Dock at Barrow Street and the Baggot Street Lime Works at the northern end of Eastmoreland Place, which remained in use from at least as early as the 1830s through to the late 1880s. William Sweeny established a limeworks on the northern side of Long Lane in about 1820, and it continued under a succession of proprietorships until the late 1870s. A little to the north of this, J. & P. Conaty had a limeworks in the 1830s at New Street. Later in the century this works was acquired by the Cullen family, who had the Kildare Lime Works in Clane; the works in New Street continued under that ownership until the 1960s, when the land on the eastern side of New Street was required for road-widening. The site is now occupied by the houses at Cathedral View Court. Another limeworks was established in King Street South by Edward Egan in the late 1820s and this continued in use until about 1890.[20]

Pl. 3—Limekiln at Rathgar. The kiln is in the park to the south of Orwell Road, close to the Dodder and the footbridge leading over from Dodder Road Lower.

Other limekilns produced lime as part of another industry and four examples were found to the north of Grand Canal Dock. The Ordnance Survey maps of the 1880s show three chemical works at the eastern end of Sir John Rogerson's Quay, each of which had one or more limekilns on the premises. Adjacent to the south was a cokeworks on Hanover Quay, also with a limekiln.

A limekiln survives near the Dodder in Rathgar Park, close to the footbridge over to Dodder Park Road. This appears to have been repurposed as a store; it has a door to the front and a concrete roof (Pl. 3).

No traces of any of the other kilns survive.

LEAD MINES

Several lead mines were operated around the Dublin area in the eighteenth century and possibly earlier. All of the lead veins were discovered in limestone, as limestone

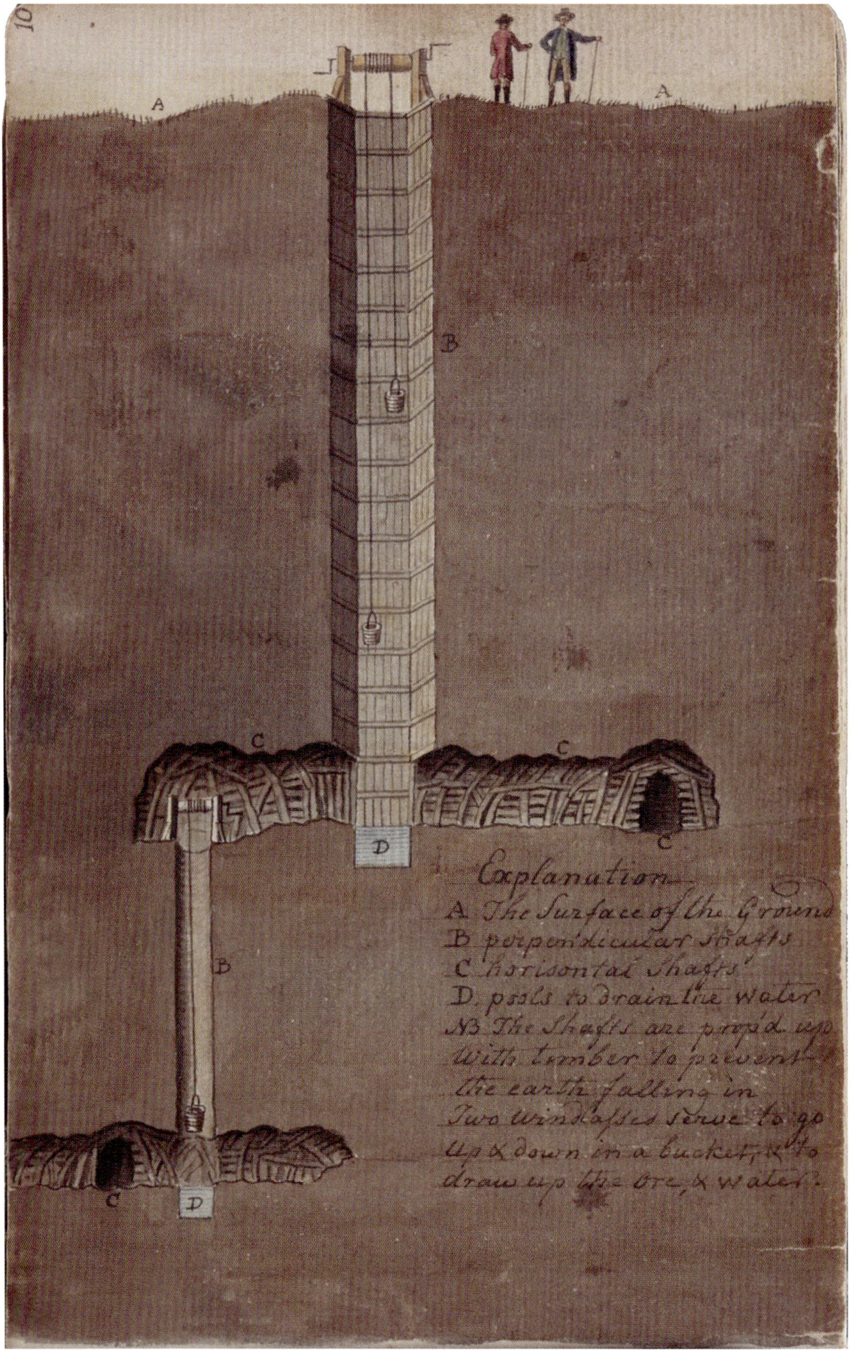

Pl. 4—Lead mine at Dolphin's Barn, by Gabriel Beranger, 1770s. It is not clear exactly where this mine was located, but it was probably at a limestone quarry on the site now occupied by the Glenview Industrial Estate.

is the only rock beneath the city, and it is likely that they were discovered by chance when the main object was the quarrying of building stone.

In the eighteenth century, John Rutty noted a reference to a lead mine between New Row and New Street, immediately outside the boundary of the south-east area, though he gave no indication as to the date of his source. He also mentioned that lead had been found at the quarry near St Stephen's Green on the road to Blackrock; this refers to the quarry on the northern side of Baggot Street Lower at the junction with Fitzwilliam Place.

A third source of lead ore was at one of the quarries at Dolphin's Barn, where lead had been found in sufficient quantity to justify the erection of a smelting furnace in the vicinity.[21] The quarry was to the west of Herberton Road and was visited by Gabriel Beranger, who executed a watercolour showing a section through the mine, based on his own descent into the workings (Pl. 4). It is not clear when he visited the mine, but in the 1770s he recorded that 'the mines have been abandoned these several years'.[22]

No trace remains of these mines.

3.

Land reclamation

Today the Liffey runs through the heart of Dublin, contained between two walls of granite. The river varies in width as it passes, frequently spanning about 40m and expanding to approximately 65m at Grattan Bridge, before narrowing again on its way downstream. Eastward from Butt Bridge the river widens, reaching about 130m where it meets the mouth of the Dodder.

A thousand years ago the landscape was very different. At the area now occupied by Grattan Bridge the river is estimated to have been about 250m wide, downstream from which the southern bank had the wide estuary of the River Poddle; after that the land projected out toward the river again, before the river broadened on its way to the sea. The river-bank was somewhere close to College Green, with an island on which the Vikings had erected a landmark known as the 'long stone' somewhere in the vicinity of Pearse Street Garda Station.

The present southern bank of the river was not all laid out in a single operation but occurred gradually, with each separate section reclaimed in its turn as the city moved eastward from its beginnings within the medieval walls.

The archaeological excavations at Wood Quay and Fishamble Street showed how the city and its quaysides gradually moved into the river, expanding the city and narrowing the waterway. This occurred in nine stages from about the year 900 through to the construction of a stone wall on the river-bank about 400 years later.[1] The present river wall along Wood Quay is still further into the original river, and in all approximately 110m of the river were reclaimed.

Significantly for what was to occur downstream, the city charter gave the city the rights over the area covered by water. This meant that Dublin Corporation could grant leases of land within the river, the estuary or Dublin Bay on the basis that it had a commercial value if reclaimed. These lands were part of the city estate, and the city benefited from rents paid for the land while the tenant organised and paid for the reclamation.

The south-eastern sector of the city was not the only location for reclamation, which also occurred upstream to the west and to a significant extent on the northern side of the river.

WELLINGTON QUAY TO BURGH QUAY

As noted, to the east of the medieval city walls the River Poddle flowed into the Liffey with a broad estuary. Downstream from this the land initially projected towards the river before the latter widened again. As a result, the area now occupied by Wellington Quay was originally part of the river, with the shore line a little inland along Parliament Street. Speed's map of Dublin is somewhat diagrammatic in this location, suggesting that to the east of the Poddle estuary the shore line was straight as far as the later location of Westmoreland Street and that it was walled. This is not quite accurate.

In 1606 the city fathers granted Jacob Newman a lease of Isolde's Tower, the easternmost tower of the medieval city, adjacent to the Poddle estuary, together with land to the east stretching for some 250m as far as the present Temple Lane. The lease specified that the northern boundary of his holding was the low-water mark, thereby allowing for the reclamation of the land above that line.[2] By 1620 he had reclaimed the land along the river frontage, creating the area that was to include the site of the Custom House and its quay, together with Essex Street, Essex Gate and the lower parts of the streets to the south.

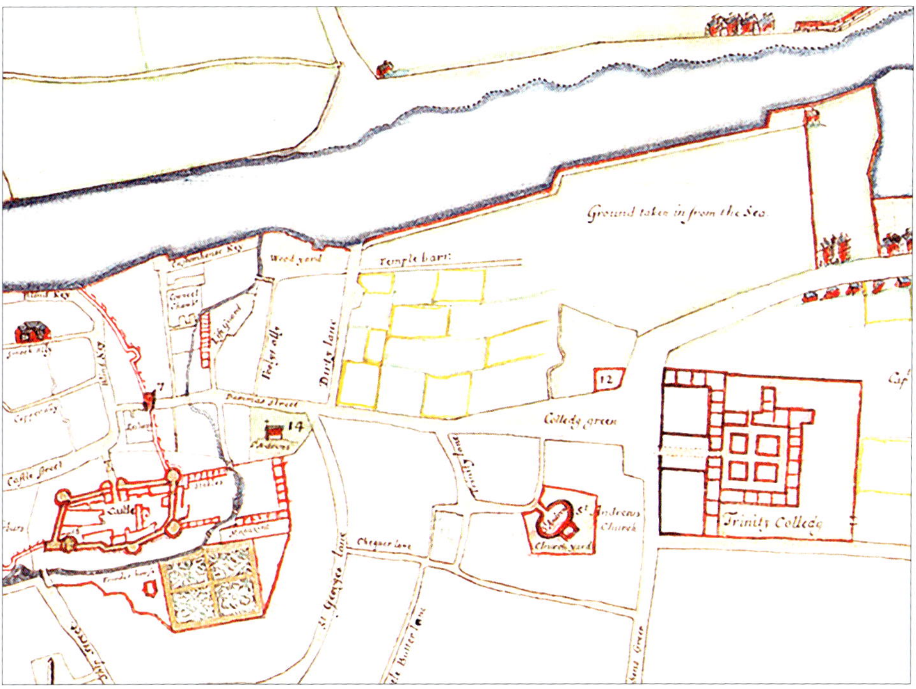

Pl. 5—Bernard de Gomme's map of Dublin city, 1673, showed the land around Temple Bar and eastwards to the Tara Street area as ground taken in from the sea.

In 1656 Dublin Corporation granted Sir John Temple a lease of land to the north of his house and reaching to the Liffey.[3] This was the area along what was then the south bank between Temple Lane and Fownes Street.

In 1662–3 William Hawkins built a wall along the river between Temple Lane and Burgh Quay, allowing for the reclamation of the land now enclosed by the wall. Sir John Temple availed of this facility north of his land to reclaim an area and laid out the street known as Temple Bar.[4]

Bernard de Gomme's map of Dublin, produced in 1673, shows the results of this reclamation (Pl. 5), with 'Customhouse Key' shown on the site of the backfilled Poddle estuary and a woodyard to the east of the Poddle, while further to the east Temple Bar is labelled and William Hawkins's wall is clearly shown; the land east of Sir John Temple's holding is shown blank between the wall and College Street and is labelled 'Ground taken in from the Sea'. This area terminates around Hawkins Street and Burgh Quay.

The river margin as shown on de Gomme's map is not the current line; further reclamation has consolidated the present line of the river, particularly to the north of Temple Bar, while Custom House Quay was later extended to form Wellington Quay after the Custom House moved downstream in 1791.

George's Quay and City Quay

John Mercer, a merchant, had a dock in 1712 to the east of Burgh Quay, while other land was held on lease by Phillip Croft, who was in arrears with his rent. Mercer sought a lease from Dublin Corporation of land along the river to build a new quay, and it was agreed that Croft's lease would be terminated and Mercer granted a lease.[5] Mercer began to build his quay but died in 1718 before it was complete. Dublin Corporation found that the unwalled section was creating a nuisance through rubbish being thrown into it and being washed into the river by the tide. The city took the land back and decided to complete the work by direct labour before leasing it on. For this reason that section of the river frontage was named City Quay.[6] The quay was completed in 1720.

Sir John Rogerson's Quay

Sir John Rogerson, an alderman of Dublin Corporation, held a lease of part of the land on the southern side of the Liffey. In 1713 he approached the corporation with a view to getting permission to wall in a substantial area south of the river channel

Pl. 6—A detail of Charles Brooking's map of Dublin, published in 1728, showing the Liffey enclosed between Sir John Rogerson's Quay and North Wall Quay, with the land behind the quays still under water.

to reclaim it; he offered as part of the agreement to use dredgings from the river as the material for filling the land. This would ensure that he could reclaim land from the sea to avail of its commercial potential while also improving navigation in the port. An agreement was reached that included how much he would pay the city per ton of dredgings.[7] The area held by Rogerson ran from Creighton Street and Sandwith Street in the west to the Dodder in the east, with Grand Canal Street as its southern boundary. This amounted to about 800 hectares, with a frontage to the river of more than a kilometre. Rogerson began to build a wall or quay along what was to become the southern margin of the river channel, consisting of two retaining walls with a fill of river dredgings between them. By the early 1720s he had completed the wall along the Liffey and turned it southward to run along the western bank of the Dodder.[8]

Reclamation of the land enclosed by Sir John Rogerson was a slow process and its pace would have been governed by the demand for land, the income from leases being used to fund further reclamation. Charles Brooking's map of Dublin, published in 1728, shows a panoramic view of the city, with Rogerson's Quay clearly visible while the land behind it is under water (Pl. 6). John Rocque's map of Dublin Bay, published in 1757, shows very few buildings on the land, while the greater part appears to be marshy and partly covered by water. Well into the nineteenth century much of the land was still undeveloped. By the end of that century, however, it had become a thriving commercial area with a major focus on port activities.

The present quay is a nineteenth-century structure and from time to time Sir John Rogerson's original quay is uncovered during archaeological investigations prior to development.

The Dodder

In the eighteenth century the River Dodder spread out into several channels downstream from Ballsbridge. Shelbourne Road formed the western shore of a marshy area, with the eastern shore around the Tritonville Road area. Rocque's map of Dublin Bay (Pl. 7), published in 1757, shows a road called Irishtown Road crossing these various channels along a line more or less coinciding with present-day Lansdowne Road and Newbridge Avenue. The area was narrowed towards the north, where Sir

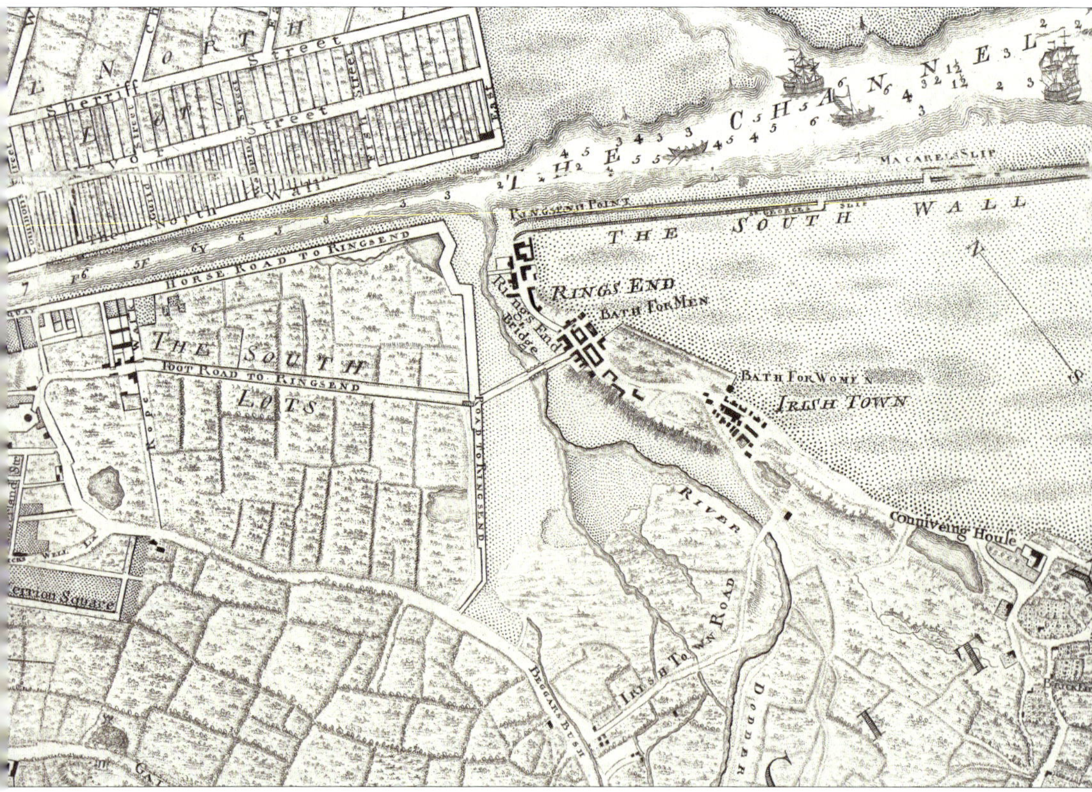

Pl. 7—Detail of John Rocque's map of Dublin Bay, 1757, showing the Dodder spreading out into a number of channels downstream from Ballsbridge.

John Rogerson's land came close to Ringsend.

In 1792 the Ballast Board granted permission to William Vavasour to enclose the Dodder between two walls and to reclaim the lands outside that channel.[9] This work was completed by 1798 and shortly afterwards Bath Avenue and Londonbridge Road had been laid out, with a wooden bridge crossing the Dodder. Development was slow within the area; as late as 1843, when the first Ordnance Survey map of the area was published, there were a few buildings along Bath Avenue–Londonbridge Road and very little elsewhere within the reclaimed land.

RINGSEND AND POOLBEG

The reclamation of land to the east of Ringsend occurred during the twentieth century, other than the triangle of land between Cambridge Road and York Road that was reclaimed by the 1860s and a small area alongside the South Wall that was reclaimed later in the nineteenth century. By the early twentieth century this latter land had been reclaimed sufficiently to site the Rathmines and Pembroke sewage pumping station on it, along with a coastguard station and an isolation hospital. The causeway built to contain the sewer leading to the pumping station cut the western part of this land off from the sea, and that area was reclaimed as Ringsend Park, beginning in 1900. After this time the area to the east of the sewer causeway was used by Dublin Corporation as a landfill site and was later developed for housing, Irishtown Stadium, an industrial site and GAA playing fields. Further along the South Wall, land to the south of Pigeon House Harbour was reclaimed as industrial land, and to the east of the Pigeon House the ash from the coal-burning power station and other material brought in built the land up and formed the basis for the land reclamation on which the Poolbeg power station was built.

SANDYMOUNT

In the seventeenth and eighteenth centuries much of the land between Ringsend and Merrion Gates was in use for brick-making and quarrying for brick clay. The only significant road in the area shown on Rocque's 1757 map was Sandymount Avenue, while the rudiments of Serpentine Avenue–Tritonville Road could be seen, as well as a road leading along the coast at the Merrion Gates end.

The lands of Sandymount and Merrion formed part of the estate of Viscount Fitzwilliam and in the early 1790s the Fitzwilliams commenced the construction of a wall to protect Sandymount from the incursion of the sea.[10] The wall is more like a dyke or embankment; similar to Sir John Rogerson's wall, it resulted in the creation of a roadway that was raised above the level of the sea and which is now Strand Road. Along much of its length the embankment is raised above the level of the land behind it, as may be seen in the slope down from Strand Road into St John's Road.

Part of the sea wall is still visible, though much of it is now concealed behind the area that has been reclaimed from the sea in more recent times alongside Strand Road.

4.

Watermills and windmills

Industrial processes began as home-based enterprises and many examples have been uncovered in archaeological excavations in Dublin and elsewhere, including shoemaking and other leather-working, pottery-making, weaving, milling and baking. As the number and type of industries increased, some processes tended to be sited away from the home, particularly those that were location-dependent such as mining and quarrying and the processes associated with them, like lime-burning and smelting.

The development of the watermill added further specialisation in specific locations, determined by the availability of a suitable supply of running water. Similar to this was the use of windmills for various processes, particularly pumping and flour-milling, and this was also location-dependent, needing to be placed where there was steady wind, not affected by nearby buildings and other obstructions, although some later windmills opted for height so that they could be located in urban areas while keeping their sails well above nearby buildings.

A significant factor in these windmills and watermills was their environmental impacts, which were low in comparison with later industries. While the development of steam power in the eighteenth century and its expansion into industrial uses in the nineteenth century brought about significant improvements in the economy and in many aspects of society, it was at a significant cost to the environment that has persisted to this day, and the development of the internal combustion engine in the late nineteenth century brought further deterioration.

In the mid-nineteenth century Robert Kane carried out a detailed analysis of the potential for water-power to provide Ireland with industrialisation on a much greater scale than was then in operation.[1] This was in the context of the smaller reserves of coal in Ireland as compared with the more industrialised Great Britain. Far from resulting in an increase in the use of water-power, circumstances led to the decrease over time, although, as is noted below, water-power continued to be used in mills such as the Greenmount Spinning Mill in Harold's Cross well into the twentieth century. Perhaps there is still great potential for this environmentally friendly source of power to be exploited more effectively, in addition to the wind power that is al-

Pl. 8—An old mill on the River Poddle at Dolphin's Barn, photographed in 1893.

ready coming back into use.

The introduction of steam power from the end of the eighteenth century brought about a significant change in the pattern of industry. Some of the earlier industrial uses of steam were for supplementary power in times of low water flow at watermills, though steam engines quickly provided a power source that was independent of the riverside locations.

MILLING

Flour-milling was probably the first mechanised process, replacing hand-turned querns with water or wind power. It is more than likely that there were flour mills in the south-east area almost as early as any mills in Ireland, though the first evidence does not appear until the later Middle Ages. Records show that there were mills in Palace Street and Patrick Street in the twelfth century, in Ship Street, Dublin Castle and College Green in the thirteenth and in Dame Street in the fourteenth.[2] Beyond the city boundaries, in the fourteenth century the de Meones family of Rathmines

Pl. 9—Rathgar Weir, with Orwell Road Bridge and the Locke & Woods sawmill at rear. This picturesque weir is still in place, a little downstream from Orwell Road.

were recorded as having a mill near the Dodder, while the Brigg family had a mill at Milltown.[3]

In the seventeenth century a number of mills are noted in the city centre, at Wood Quay, Townsend Street and in St Bride's parish, while some of the earlier mills still survived.[4]

The principal motive power prior to the nineteenth century was water-power and hence the larger mills were located on the rivers, particularly the Dodder and the Poddle but also on the city watercourse and other streams. These are discussed below in the sections on watermills. With the advent of steam power it was no longer necessary to locate mills alongside rivers, and new sites were found closer to towns and cities. From the mid-nineteenth century imports of grain from abroad, such as from Canada and the United States, encouraged the location of mills close to ports, minimising the cost of transporting coal and grain between the port and the mill. It may be assumed that any mill that had neither windmill nor flowing water for water-power must have had at least one steam engine.

In the early 1820s James Conolly established the Dock Mill in Barrow Street at Grand Canal Harbour and operated it until his death in 1830.[5] After a period of vacancy the mill was occupied by Hastings & Carter, who expanded the mill in the 1860s and again in the 1870s. In the late 1890s the mill was occupied by the Dock Milling Company and the premises were expanded again.[6] In 1926, however, the Dock Milling Company went into liquidation owing to difficulties in the flour market resulting from imports, and the milling concerns in Barrow Street were offered for sale.[7] The new owners established a new company, the Dock Milling Company (1928) Ltd, and used the mill for the production of animal feed.[8] As a result of the economic war with Britain in the 1930s, legislation was passed to protect the Irish flour industry and the Dock Mill began to produce flour again in 1934 under new management; a new company, the Dock Milling Company Ltd, was launched on the stock market in 1939.[9] In 1987 Boland's, Dock Mill and Davis-Mosse merged, and Dock Mill was operated by IAWS under the Boland's name until 2001.[10]

In 1848 Pim Brothers acquired a former shipyard at Grand Canal Dock, on the southern side of Ringsend Road, and on it they built a steam-powered flour mill.[11] It was six storeys high and was provided with a 60hp steam engine driving fifteen pairs of millstones; the premises also included a six-storey store and a two-storey store. Over the next 28 years Pim Brothers added new buildings at the mill.[12]

Pl. 10—Dock Mill, Grand Canal Dock. Now converted to apartments, the mill building is a picturesque site on the waterfront.

Pl. 11—Boland's Mill on Ringsend Road alongside Grand Canal Dock. Originally built by Pim Brothers, the mill became a substantial enterprise and was acquired by Boland's in 1876.

In the early 1860s Patrick Boland inherited a bakery in Capel Street from his father and he expanded his business very rapidly on the original site, while also acquiring other properties in Grand Canal Street and Dún Laoghaire. In 1876 he acquired the mill on Ringsend Road from Pim Brothers (Pl. 11). He did not live to see the success of his enterprise, however, dying intestate in 1877, following which his wife, Mary Boland, took over the running of the business until her untimely death in 1882.[13] The complexities of the business following the deaths of Patrick and Mary Boland took some time to resolve, and it was not until February 1888 that the affairs were ironed out through a judgement in the Court of Chancery, following which Boland's Bakery, with its assets including the mill at Grand Canal Dock, was floated on the stock market.[14] By this time the mill had been converted to the use of rollers rather than millstones. Some changes were made to the mill in the ensuing years, the largest being the addition of concrete grain silos in 1954, 1956 and 1960.[15] Boland's was acquired by Barrow Milling in 1976; in 1987 it merged with Dock Mill and Davis-Mosse, as noted above, but closed in 2001.

WINDMILLS

Dublin may not seem like an obvious place to find windmills, but the city had a number of them in the past and a large one still survives in the Guinness brewery

Pl. 12—Windmill at Windmill Lane and the Dublin & Kingstown Railway, 1840s. The train is heading for Westland Row station, now Pearse Station. The ships in the background to the left were on the Liffey, and the smoking chimney in the background is the gasworks at Grand Canal Dock on the site now occupied by the Bord Gáis Energy Theatre.

site off James's Street. It is no surprise that there was one in Windmill Lane; this was another substantial windmill, similar to the one in James's Street, and it survived until as late as 1971. The site of the windmill was archaeologically excavated in 2015 prior to redevelopment, and this revealed that the windmill measured 8.5m wide at the base.[16] It is not known when it was built, but it was certainly there by 1828 when the firm of Robinson & Taylor occupied the site.[17] This firm, previously Robinson & Fayle, had moved to the site in about 1820 and it is possible that the windmill was built at that time.[18]

There had been windmills in what was then a more rural area outside the built-up part of the city in the eighteenth century, though when they were built is unknown. A windmill is recorded at Orwell Road in the mid-eighteenth century, probably used as a corn or flour mill. Many of the windmills would have been used for pumping water to keep quarries dry, and there was one such mill at Baggot Street Lower until the 1760s.[19] Two more were to be found at quarries in Kimmage, one at Terenure and another at Rathgar, all at the edge of quarries and all disused by the time that they appeared on Ordnance Survey maps from the 1840s; Archer's survey of Dublin in 1801 did not list any windmills in the south-east area, suggesting that none of them were working at that time.[20] A windmill shown at a quarry in Goldenbridge on Duncan's map of 1821 was gone by the time of the 1843 Ordnance Survey, as was another at Harold's Cross. The 1843 map showed another near Crumlin village that may have still been in use at that time. Windmill Road in Crumlin takes its name from a windmill on the site now occupied by Swan Leisure; this survived through much of the nineteenth century as a stump of the tower. There was another windmill at Donnybrook, just north of the village; this was in ruins by the 1840s and had been shown on Rocque's map of County Dublin in 1760. It is possible that there was a quarry at that location that no longer survives, though it is noted that there was a watermill adjacent to the windmill. Nothing now remains of any of those windmills or of the quarries or mills that they served.

WATERMILLS—DODDER

The vertical water-wheel was introduced into Ireland in the early medieval period and proved to be extremely versatile. Over the years it came to be used for more than just the grinding of corn. Iron mills were developed in the sixteenth century, paper mills in the seventeenth century, and from the latter part of the eighteenth century there was a massive increase in the mechanisation of the textile industry.

Watermills could function on relatively small rivers and so they were widespread. An 1801 survey of Dublin listed the mills in operation, with a large number in the south-east area.[21] These included thirteen mills along the Poddle, of which five were at Kimmage and eight at Harold's Cross, though at least one of the mills at Kimmage was beyond the present city boundary. The survey listed twenty mills along the Dodder, with two at Rathgar, two at Rathmines, three at Milltown, three at Clonskeagh, four at Donnybrook, three at Ballsbridge and two at Beggar's Bush. A further two were located at Dolphin's Barn. The numbers listed relate to machines or water-wheels rather than operators; for instance, the two woollen machines at Rathmines were operated by Robert Belwood and were on the site now known as Dartry. The list includes a wide variety of materials processed, such as paper, wire, cotton, iron, woollens, oil and bark, as well as the inevitable corn and flour mills.[22]

Rathgar Mills

Not far downstream from the bridge at Rathfarnham there is a weir which was constructed to provide the water-supply to the Rathgar Mills. These mills were at the bottom of Orwell Road and may be seen on John Rocque's map of 1760, which quite clearly shows a sizeable building with a mill head-race and tail-race. The occupier at this time was a miller named John Kean, and the premises had two watermills

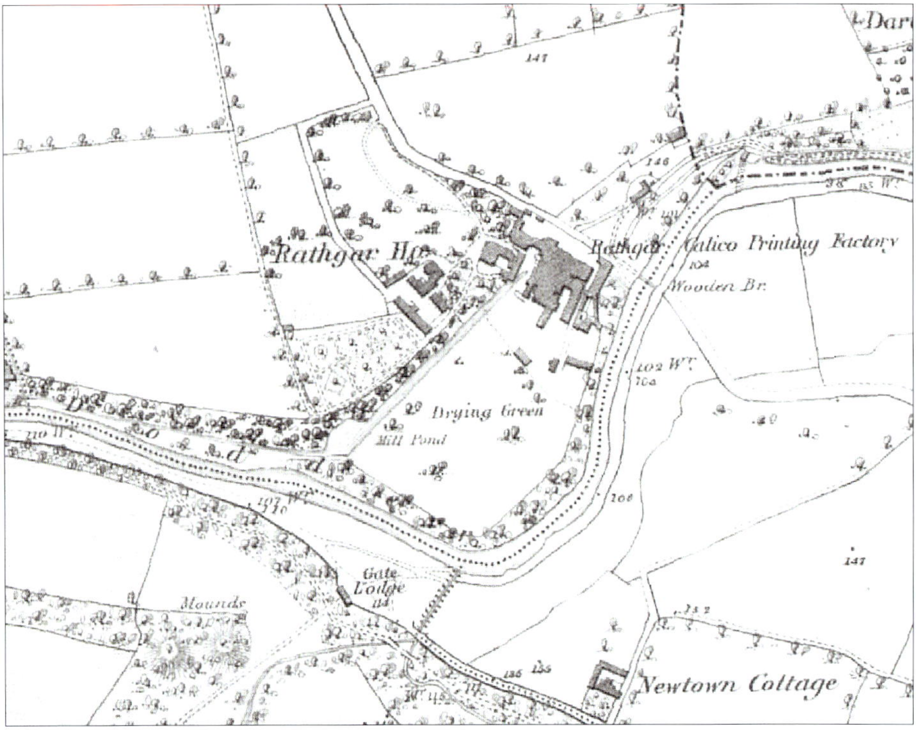

Pl. 13—Rathgar Mills as depicted on the 1843 Ordnance Survey map. Orwell Road is seen above the mill, which stood on the site now occupied by the tennis courts at the High School.

as well as a nearby windmill. In 1793 the mills were acquired by Gerard Osbrey, who converted them into a calico-printing mill with an extensive bleaching green along the river's flood plain. The works was acquired in 1833 by Laurence and Patrick Waldron, who printed muslin, calicoes and silks. They had a 30hp steam engine in addition to the 30hp water-wheel, and accounts of the number employed range from 100 to 300. The works closed in the mid-1840s, and the extensive buildings were taken down in 1846.

For a number of years afterwards, until the late 1890s, there was a sawmill on the site, while the old bleaching green was quarried. The sawmill is now a private house, while the bleaching green is partly a public park and partly the playing fields for the High School.

The tail-race from the Rathgar Mills seems to have gone on from here to serve other mills downstream, until they provided their own watercourses. The first of these was at Dartry.

Dartry

This was another mill that was already in use by 1760, the building and the mill-race being quite clear on John Rocque's map of that year. At that time it was run by Andrew Hughes. In 1800 a clothier named Robert Belwood took a lease on the property, and he was succeeded in 1826 by William Willans, who ran it as a woollen mill. Willans had a number of mills in Dublin. His mill at Dartry had a 20ft-diameter water-wheel that drove six power looms with 840 spindles, and a tuck mill with thirteen fulling stocks. The water was sufficient to run the mill for six months on full power and on somewhat less than full power for four months, while little could be done in the driest two months of the year.

The mill closed in about 1845 and was converted to a laundry run by Thomas Bewley, before reverting to use as a cloth mill in the 1860s until 1880. It lay vacant for about ten years before being repaired and opened as the Dartry Brewery in 1890, run by Stoer & Sons. This enterprise brewed lager and, being nearly a century ahead of its time as far as the Irish drinker is concerned, it did not last long. The mill was acquired by the Dublin Laundry Company in 1894 and opened as the Dartry Dyeing and Cleaning Works in the following year.

The weir belonging to this mill lies not far below the bridge at Rathgar, and the line of the mill-race can still be traced behind the railings bordering the adjoining park. The mill-wheel could still be seen into the second half of the twentieth century. Some houses associated with the mill survive, but the mill itself has been replaced with a modern structure.

Milltown

A mill on the northern side of the Dodder at Milltown stood on the land now occupied by apartments to the east of the nine-arched bridge that carries the Luas.[23] In the late seventeenth century, a tuck mill on this site was in the hands of Alderman William Fownes. By 1708 it had been converted into a paper mill and was leased to John Waters, a paper-maker, and his son Edward, a printer. Edward Waters seems to have been keen to improve the property and borrowed £150; he overstretched himself, however, and in 1730 the mill was sold by the High Court of Chancery. James Hamill ran the mill for more than twenty years until his death in 1753, when he left it to his daughter Jane. Jane Hamill leased the mill to John Eustace and subsequently to Michael Geraghty, who converted it into two corn mills, borrowing £80 to do so. Within ten years Michael Geraghty was gone, and the mill was let to a merchant named John Classon.

Classon invested heavily in the mill, spending £600 on it in the late 1760s and more in the early 1770s, when he constructed a new mill-race. He converted the property into a logwood mill, which contained a large pair of stones for grinding wood for making dyes and a metal press for manufacturing oil. Business seems to have gone well for him, and he constructed the bridge that bears his name, although it is now almost invisible under concrete. In 1791 he took out a further loan of £500, but this time he had gone too far and was unable to repay. He was declared bankrupt in 1793 and the mill was sold.

The new owners were the business partners of Rainsford, Mullen & Burke, who paid £160 for the mill and used it for the same purpose as before, as well as including a tuck mill. Their business seems to have boomed, to judge by the price of almost £1,600 which Walter Burke paid in 1798 to buy out his partner William Rainsford's share, and the £3,000 he paid for Barnaby Mullen's share in 1807. In the following year Burke entered into partnership with two of his sons, William and Christopher, as Walter Burke & Sons, Clothiers, Dye Stuff and Oil Manufacturers, but within a few years Walter Burke had died and two of his sons were bankrupt. His eldest son and partner, William Burke, took over the mill, whose extensive machinery was driven by three water-wheels. To supplement these, William installed a steam engine and in April 1823 he took out a loan of £1,400. By December he was deemed to have failed in making good the payments, which is not surprising as he had died in August.

The mill was then taken over by a Maurice Harnett, who concentrated on the cheaper end of the market for cloths. He kept it going until the late 1830s, after which it was run by Samuel Moore. The concern was less extensive than in William Burke's day and was run by a single water-wheel without the backup of a steam engine. This meant that in winter the factory worked for twelve hours a day, while in summer it was down to six hours a day. It was probably because of this that by the mid-1850s the mill had been closed and was becoming dilapidated, and the machinery had been removed.

In 1856 the mill was acquired by Patrick Gibney, who converted it into a flour mill. His family ran the mill in conjunction with a bakery in Dublin's Patrick Street until the late 1880s, when it was acquired by the Dublin Laundry Company and was converted into a laundry. The company invested in a number of improvements to the premises, including the installation of a 30hp steam engine, though water power continued to be used occasionally. The Dublin Laundry closed in 1982.

The Red Mill

On the northern side of the Dodder at Clonskeagh there was a mill that had been converted into a paper mill in the mid-eighteenth century. This was acquired in 1800

Pl. 14—Thomas Roberts's view of the weir at Clonskeagh in the 1770s, with a paper mill at the right-hand side and Clonskeagh Bridge in the background. The paper mill was later replaced by an iron mill and later became Smurfit's factory.

by Hugh Jackson, son of Henry Jackson, who had established a large iron mill on the southern side of the Dodder at Clonskeagh. It was a condition of the purchase that Hugh Jackson and his partner should spend £500 on improvements, and he spent more than £4,500 in converting it into an iron mill. The mill was acquired a few years later by William McCasky, and after a brief interval of use as a dyestuff factory in the early 1840s it was afterwards a spade factory run by Thomas Henshaw & Company.

This was one of the last mill sites on the Dodder to be used for industrial purposes and the last one to take water from the river. In the later twentieth century it was converted for manufacturing corrugations for cardboard by the Smurfit Group and remained in use until the end of the century.

Pl. 15—The paper mill at Clonskeagh that was seen at the edge of Thomas Roberts's painting of the weir (Pl. 14). This image, executed in 1797, suggests that the mill was in poor condition, and shortly afterwards the site changed hands and was rebuilt as an iron mill.

The hat factory

A little downstream from Clonskeagh Bridge there is a waterfall on the Dodder which has been adapted as a mill weir. The water-supply from this weir was used at a hat factory that stood between the river and Eglinton Road, at the end of Harmony Avenue. The factory can be seen on Rocque's map of 1760; it is labelled 'Hat Factory' on Taylor's map of 1816 and on the first edition of the Ordnance Survey map in 1843, though it had closed in the late 1830s, when the business moved to Mespil Road. Beaver Row, on the opposite side of the river, owes its name to this factory, as beaver fur was a favourite raw material for the manufacture of felt for hats.

The mill-race from this factory went on to serve three other mills through Donnybrook, then on to the calico-printing works which was later to become the site for Johnston, Mooney & O'Brien's bakery at Ballsbridge, before finally leading to a flour mill at Lansdowne Road.

Donnybrook

It seems likely that there was a mill at Donnybrook from an early date, given that Donnybrook is a medieval settlement. John Rocque's map of 1760 shows a mill-race running from the Dodder through the southern part of the village and, while he doesn't note the presence of a mill at that location, in 1756 a Mr Ashworth, a linen-printer at Donnybrook, was presented with a premium of £500 by the Dublin Society.[24] Taylor's map of 1816 notes the existence of a printworks at that location, to the west of the main road through the village. By 1843 it was a sawmill, noted on the first-edition Ordnance Survey map. It was then converted into a flour mill; the miller, Robert Lynch, was declared bankrupt in 1857, the mill subsequently being run by M.A. McCann.[25] The site was later acquired by the Sisters of Charity, who used the water source to power a laundry. A steam engine was later added at the laundry, on a more elevated site away from the watercourse. The laundry closed in 2006.

Donnybrook Flour Mill

A mill-race from Donnybrook to Ballsbridge crossed the main road and passed close to the windmill to the east of Donnybrook; Rocque's map of 1760 shows a building close to the mill-race, probably representing a watermill. Both Taylor's map of 1816 and Duncan's of 1821 show an extensive range of buildings on the site, suggesting that the watermill here was of some significance. Both maps carry labels that run from this mill to the one downstream at Ballsbridge and read 'Calico Print Works' and 'Print Works' respectively. The 1843 Ordnance Survey map shows the building and labels it 'Bleach works', and shows an area to the north that appears to be a bleaching green. The alterations to Griffith's Valuation, published in 1848, record that this bleach mill was occupied by John Nixon, under John Duffy, and it is noted that John Duffy was the proprietor of the calico-printing works at Ballsbridge, as described below. Nixon converted the premises for use as a flour mill under the name Donnybrook Flour Mills, and in the 1860s it was run by George MacCann before being taken over by Johnston & Co. in conjunction with that firm's larger flour mill at Ballsbridge (see below). The Donnybrook Flour Mill was in ruins by the end of the nineteenth century and Herbert Park Mews now occupy the site.

Ballsbridge

The mill-race shown on Rocque's map leaving the Dodder at Donnybrook continued downstream and through Ballsbridge. It is uncertain how early there was a mill there, though in 1750 a linen-printing works at Ballsbridge run by a Mr Grant was presented with a premium of £500 by the Dublin Society.[26] While the site of this works

Pl. 16—James Arthur O'Connor's painting from about 1820 showing the view up the Dodder towards the linen-printing works at Ballsbridge, which stood on the site later occupied by Johnston, Mooney & O'Brien and now by the Herbert Park Hotel. Ball's Bridge may also be seen.

is not stated, it is certain to have been on the northern bank of the Dodder to the west of Ball's Bridge, as by the early nineteenth century John Duffy was operating a calico-printing works on that site, where he employed 400 workers.[27] His operation had begun in 1792 as a partnership known as Duffys, Byrne & Hamil, established 'for the purpose of manufacturing and printing cottons and calicoes &c on an extensive scale from their works at Ball's Bridge'.[28] John Duffy junior was taken into the partnership in 1802, when the business was operating as the Ballsbridge Printing Company.[29] Duffy's printing works remained in operation until 1850, when it was taken over by Robert Johnston and converted into a bread and biscuit bakery.[30] This later became Johnston & Co., and in 1889 this company went into partnership with T. O'Brien of Leinster Street and John Mooney of Clonliffe Mills as Johnston, Mooney & O'Brien Ltd.[31] Johnston, Mooney & O'Brien continued to bake on the site at Ballsbridge for almost a century, owned by Odlums from the 1950s. In 1988 the former Irish Hospitals Sweepstakes site at Ballsbridge was sold and Johnston, Mooney & O'Brien decided to test the market by offering their site for sale.[32] The result encouraged the firm to move; it was announced that it was to build a new bakery and that the site in Ballsbridge had been sold, with an agreement that Johnston, Mooney & O'Brien would lease it back pending the construction of its new plant.[33] However, owing to a bread price war the company ran into difficulties and in 1989 it was put into liquidation with the loss of 485 jobs.[34]

Shelbourne Road

This potential mill site is elusive, and its existence is based on map evidence that may be imprecise. John Rocque's map of County Dublin, published in 1760, shows a building adjacent to the mill-race at Shelbourne Road and this may have been a mill. Taylor's map of 1816 shows buildings at that location, and these are labelled 'Paper mill', while extensive buildings are shown on Duncan's map of 1821. No mill is depicted on the first-edition Ordnance Survey map of 1843. The location would have been somewhere in the vicinity of the Iona Building and Brooklawn House on Crampton Avenue, Shelbourne Road.

Pl. 17—Sketch showing Beggar's Bush Mill in 1812, with the Dodder in the foreground. The mill stood on the site now occupied by houses in Lansdowne Road, opposite the Aviva Stadium.

Beggar's Bush

This mill stood on the southern side of Lansdowne Road, on the site now occupied by houses that face the Aviva Stadium. It is uncertain when the mill was established, though buildings are shown on that site on William Duncan's map of 1821. The 1843 Ordnance Survey map marks the building as a flour mill and by the 1850s it was referred to as Dodder Bank Mills and was occupied by Thomas Doyle, a maltster.[35] The 1864 Ordnance Survey map marks Dodder Bank Mills with a substantial millpond and it is labelled on the 1871 Ordnance Survey map as a malt manufactory. It appears to have closed shortly after that.

Dodder Bank Distillery

Haig's Dodder Bank Distillery at the corner of Newbridge Avenue and Herbert Road was located adjacent to the Dodder for its water-supply rather than its motive power. The site was the location of an earlier mill, described as a sawmill on Cullen's map of Ringsend and Irishtown prepared in 1706. The history of the distillery is examined below under 'Distilleries'.

WATERMILLS—PODDLE

Along the Poddle and the City Watercourse there were several mills and, as on the Dodder, the processes undertaken at the mills varied over time. The watercourse divides at Mount Argus, the Poddle or Liberty Watercourse continuing northward to enter the Liffey at Wellington Quay, while the City Watercourse ran north-westward to the City Basin off James's Street.

Ravensdale Mills/Kimmage Mills

The site of this mill is now the open space on the western side of Kimmage Road Lower, to the south of Ravensdale Park. The mill was noted on John Taylor's map of 1816 and was known as Tinker Mills. It went through various ownerships, including Patrick Regan, flour miller and baker in the 1840s and 1850s, and John Lennox in the 1860s, 1870s and 1880s. In the 1890s the mill was acquired by the Ravensdale Mills of Wellington Quay, which also opened premises at Duggan Place in Rathmines, and it became known as Ravensdale Mills. It remained in use until the 1920s.

Larkfield Mills

Larkfield Mill was on the site now occupied by the Supervalu shopping centre on Sundrive Road. There had been a mill on this site since the medieval period, known

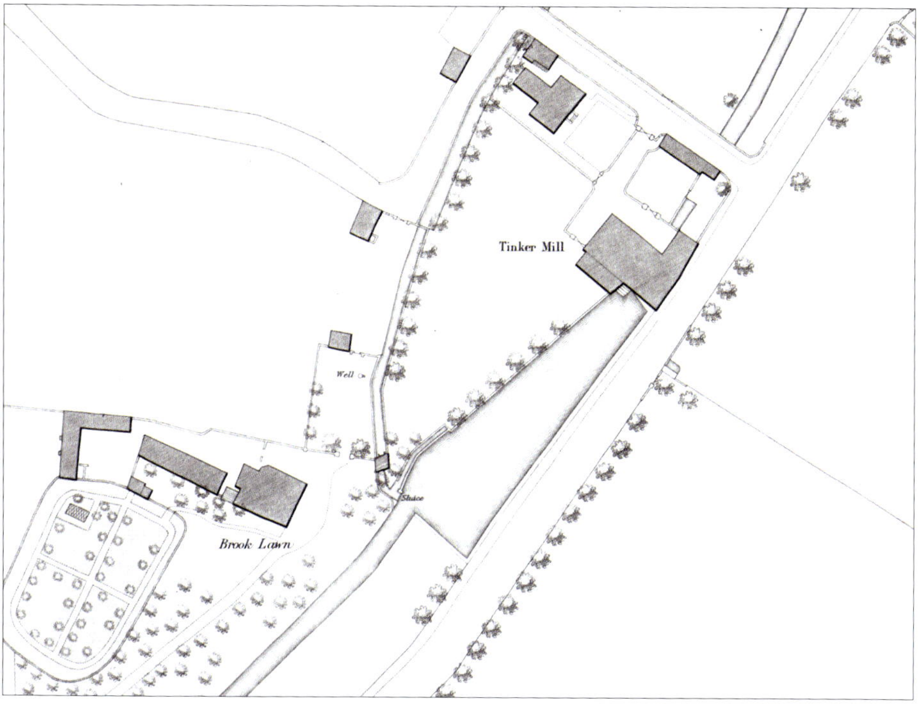

Pl. 18—Ordnance Survey map showing Kimmage Mills in 1876. The mill was on the site now laid out as open space on the western side of Kimmage Road Lower, to the south of Ravensdale Park.

as Mountdown Mills, and it was marked on Rocque's map of County Dublin, published in 1760. John Taylor's map of 1816 and William Duncan's map of 1821 label it 'Skin mill'. This mill, under a succession of proprietors, including Francis Tuite in the 1840s, was in use as a flour mill by that time. Later in the nineteenth century it was converted from using millstones to a roller mill, under the proprietorship of Herron, Connolly & Co. In the early twentieth century the mill was converted for the production of paint and colours.

Loader's Park Mills

The site of Loader's Park Mills is now occupied by the Mount Argus Mill apartments. A mill was shown at this location on Taylor's map of 1816, and it is shown as 'C. mill' on Rocque's map of 1760. This mill was leased by John Anderson in 1719, though it had previously been operated by Maurice Coffey.[36] It was converted into a paper mill in the late eighteenth century by George Cuppaige, who had developed a skill in weaving the wire screens used in the manufacture of paper. Cuppaige's son, William, lost the mill when he ran into financial difficulties and in 1836 it was leased to Joseph Martin.[37] In 1845 it was a paper mill run by Richard John Hicks, operated by water-power equal to 20hp; it could be used for a full day for six months each year, reduced to half a day for three months and a quarter of the time for the other three months.[38] Shortly after this Hicks leased the mill to Samuel Figgis, though he was bankrupted in the mid-1850s.[39] Around 1856 a high-pressure steam engine was installed along with a machine for processing straw into paper, improving the capabilities of the mill and allowing it to work all year round. The purchaser at this stage of what was now known as Loader's Park Paper Mills was William R. Stephens, partner in Courtney & Stephens.[40] In the 1870s it was converted for use as a flour mill, with William Ryan as proprietor; he installed a steam engine to supplement the water-power, and he had eight pairs of millstones. After a period of vacancy in the 1880s following a fire, the use of the mill was changed to oat-bruising and hay-cutting, with William Flanagan as proprietor.[41] It went out of use for milling in the 1920s and, after being used for a succession of non-industrial purposes, was demolished in the late twentieth century.

Harold's Cross Laundry

There was a mill at the Harold's Cross end of Mount Argus Road by the early nineteenth century, when Peter Murphy had flour mills there. In 1847 the mill had two

Pl. 19—Harold's Cross Laundry, from a view taken in 1896. The laundry had only opened recently, in a building that had previously been a flour mill. The site in Mount Argus Road is now occupied by Laurence Court apartments.

pairs of French burr stones, 4ft 8in. and 4ft 2in. in diameter, run by a water-wheel 14ft in diameter and 8ft wide, revolving six times a minute.[42] These mills were able to use water-power for eighteen hours a day during eight months of the year and for ten hours a day in the other four months. Later, the mill used water-power for three pairs of millstones and had auxiliary steam power available with a further pair of millstones. The mill was destroyed by fire in 1877 and was rebuilt with seven pairs of stones and with backup steam power, and it included a bakery in addition to the flour mill, run by Lewis Mulhall.[43] It closed in about 1890 and was converted into a laundry for the Harold's Cross Laundry Company (see below under 'Laundries').

Greenmount Spinning Manufactory

At the beginning of the nineteenth century James Greenham established a factory at Greenmount, Harold's Cross, in addition to one that he had at Roper's Rest in the Liberties and another at Celbridge. These concerns were spinning cotton and were producing 27 tons of cotton yarn a week that were then fed to local weavers.[44] Greenham's business ran into trouble in the depression that followed the end of the Napoleonic Wars in 1815 and he lost the mill to his creditors, Thomas, Jonathan and Joseph R. Pim, better known as Pim Brothers, who were successful Dublin merchants. The Pims refinanced Greenham rather than taking over the mill, but his business crashed again 1824–5 and the mill passed back to the Pim Brothers. It was used for spinning cotton and the Pims sold the cotton yarn to outworkers who wove calicoes, which the Pims bought from them for trading elsewhere.[45]

In 1834 the Pims decided to move into a new technology, installing power looms at the Greenmount mills. This improved efficiency, increasing output and also allowing for diversification into other textiles such as linen.[46] By 1837 the factory had 150 employees.[47] In 1845 the water-wheel was 22ft 6in. in diameter and 11ft broad, revolving 4½ times a minute. This produced 25hp for nine months of the year and 12hp in the remaining months, and it ran 5,000 mule spindles and 2,000 throstles.[48] The produce from the factory included tartan, velvets, silks and poplin, the latter being their most important product.[49]

In the 1850s the mill was expanded with the addition of new buildings of sufficient extent to increase the rateable valuation of the premises from £220 to £328, and this provided facilities for working with flax and producing linen goods. Water-power was still a significant contributor to the power of the mill and for nine months of the year it could produce 25hp, while in the three drier months of the year this fell to just 12hp.[50] At this stage the next generation of the Pim family was running the business and they now had a mill at Stratford on Slaney, a warehouse in Belfast

Pl. 20—Aerial view of the Greenmount Spinning Mill, taken in 1956. Many of the houses alongside the mill were built by the Pim family for workers in the mill. The site is now a business park at the end of Greenmount Avenue, Harold's Cross.

and offices in New York and London, and in the 1850s they built a substantial department store in South Great George's Street.[51] All this was in addition to their original core business as merchants, which they continued.

The Pims' control of the Greenmount Spinning Company continued into the fourth generation, but this came to an end in 1918 when the family sold the mill to a syndicate from Belfast.[52] Whatever the motives of that syndicate, their involvement did not last long and in 1921 one of their creditors, the Weaving Co. of Lambeg, Lisburn, sought to have the Greenmount Spinning Company wound up. The syndicate recognised that its involvement in the mill was no longer tenable and decided to put the company into voluntary liquidation.[53] The premises were immediately offered for sale, showing that by that time the mill had 488 plain and damask looms, a 350hp steam engine, a 100hp auxiliary engine and a 30hp water turbine.[54] In May 1922 it was announced that Cahill & Co., printers, had acquired the buildings at Greenmount, as their own works on Ormond Quay had been destroyed by fire.[55] As the printing business had no use for the machinery in the mill, this was offered for sale separately, and a list giving details of the steam engine, boilers, looms, winding machines and a host of other equipment was advertised in advance of an auction to take place in June 1922.[56] On the day of the auction the employees at the mill, totalling some 600 hands, entered the premises in protest at the closure.[57] The auction was postponed until October and then postponed again, and in November it was announced that the Boyne Weaving Company of Drogheda had purchased the premises, machinery and stock at Greenmount and would continue the work previously carried on at the mill.[58]

Under the name 'The Greenmount & Boyne Linen Co.' the production of fabrics continued at the Greenmount mill. It is unclear how many of the original employees were re-employed at this stage or whether there was a rationalisation. Fifty workers were laid off in 1936, and 200 workers went on strike in 1937, though it is not known whether that amounted to the entire workforce.[59] By 1948 there were 340 employees, operating 420 damask and plain looms, a bleachworks and other operations, and in addition the company was installing plant for spinning rayon.[60]

The business survived until 1965, when it closed with the loss of 150 jobs. The company cited the progressive reduction of tariffs pending entry into the European free trade area and the impending agreement resulting from Anglo-Irish free trade costs as contributing to the loss of viability of the firm, together with high costs and the difficulty in getting skilled operatives.[61] The machinery removed from the mill was brought to the company's mill at Drogheda and upgraded for continued use.[62]

The main mill building survives and the campus of the former Greenmount Spinning Mills continues in use for business purposes, occupied by a number of firms.

Greenmount Distillery

The story of the Greenmount Distillery is a short one—too short even to make it into the pages of Brian Townsend's *The lost distilleries of Ireland.* In the mid-1860s three cousins, Edward Alexander, William J. Perry and Robinson G. Perry, leased land from the Pim Brothers of Greenmount Spinning Works and erected the Greenmount Brewery, completed in 1868. The building was substantial, five storeys high, 30m long and 75m deep, but it had an extremely short existence and by 1873 it was being converted into a distillery, having been acquired by the Irish Whiskey Distillery Company.[63] The conversion works were completed in 1874, with E.H. Carson as architect, and cost about £10,000 over and above the £31,000 the company paid for the brewery.[64] In 1880, just six years later, the distillery was offered for sale by the High Court of Chancery.[65] The premises were acquired by Louis le Brocquy and opened as the Greenmount Oil Refinery, which continued to occupy the premises well into the twentieth century.[66]

Pl. 21—Advert for Greenmount Pale Ale, produced by the Greenmount Brewery, one of the shortest-lived breweries in Dublin, which lasted barely five years. It was based on Harold's Cross Road, on the site now occupied by Greenmount Office Park.

Rutland Mills

Rutland Mills were located on the site now occupied by the roundabout at the junction of Clogher Road and Rutland Avenue. This was a watermill that took its power from the flow of the City Watercourse. A mill was shown at this location on the Down Survey map of 1655 and it was listed in the Civil Survey, which noted 'at Dolphins Barne two verry faire Houses; a Mill in repaire and five thatched Houses'.[67] It was labelled as 'Mill' on Rocque's map of 1760, as 'Factory' on Taylor's map of 1816 and as 'Rutland Mills' on Duncan's map of 1821.

The mill was sold in 1832; at that time it derived its power from its water-wheel and also had a steam engine.[68] The new owner, Robert Guy, made axle-trees and was described as 'the only patent axletree maker in Ireland'.[69] The processes for fabricating the axles involved turning and forging rather than casting, and the mill had four forges and a workshop driven by a 15ft-diameter water-wheel with a breadth of 8ft. The wheel had 56 buckets and availed of a fall of water of 10ft 6in., providing 4hp, which was sufficient for turning the axle-trees. The mill worked for ten hours a day in winter and six hours a day in summer.[70]

The mill was subsequently operated by Charles O'Neill, a button-maker, described as 'almost the solitary representative of an industry that flourished in Ireland in a past age'.[71] By 1886, however, the button-making had gone and the mill was advertised to let, along with its water-supply and a powerful water-wheel.[72] There was no mention of the steam engine, which had been sold in 1879.[73] The premises were used for a time by a paint supplier, but had gone by the time the Ordnance Survey revised its maps of the area in 1907.

WATERMILLS—GRAND CANAL

The ideal canal is a level body of water that provides an uninterrupted route between two points. In reality canals usually run along land that slopes, and at intervals along the route there need to be locks that allow the canal to change levels and carry canal boats between one level and another. Canals also need to have running water to allow for some flow along the length, and also to compensate for the loss of water that results from the use of locks. Where the supply of water is plentiful, there is scope for a canal company to lease the use of water for the operation of mills; such mills are located at canal locks where there is a significant difference in levels, allowing for a sufficient head of water to turn a water-wheel. With a single lock the fall will be of the order of 2.5m, or 5m at a double lock.

There were two watermills on the Grand Canal within the south-east area, both on the main line. The fall along the circular line between Dolphin's Barn and the Liffey is relatively small and is accommodated at seven locks, all of them single, while the optimum location for a mill would be at a double lock to avail of the greater fall of water.

Mount Shannon Mills

Mount Shannon Mills were erected sometime after the opening of the Grand Canal in the late eighteenth century, and they are marked as 'Mills' on Taylor's map of 1816. The 1843 Ordnance Survey map marked the site as Mount Shannon Mills and at this time the mills were operated by James A. and Francis Journeaux.[74] In 1844 the mill had a breast-shot wheel, 16ft in diameter and 8ft wide with a fall of 11ft, revolving ten times a minute to generate 12hp. The mill operated day and night constantly throughout the year, 24 hours a day, six days a week, grinding logwood. Another mill-wheel at the mill had similar dimensions and drove four pairs of French burr millstones and one pair of Ballyhack stones for shelling wheat. This mill worked on average just three months each year for twenty hours a day, with two pairs of millstones working at a time.[75] From 1857 Francis Journeaux was advertising a kiln for drying wheat, stating that it could be seen at First Lock Mills.[76]

In 1866 Mount Shannon Mills were advertised to let, with both water-power and a new steam engine and with eight pairs of millstones; the mills remained in the family, however, and were occupied by James Journeaux as the Mountshannon dye, wool and flour mills.[77] This appears to have been in collaboration with R.V. Haines, who occupied the nearby Harcourt Mills, under the title the Harcourt & Rialto Mills & Mountshannon dye, wool and flour mills, and James Journeaux does not appear to have remained in the business for long.

In 1894 Mount Shannon Mills were occupied by Michael J. Cooney, who ran a business based on uses for peat moss litter. Initially this was advertised as a bedding for stables, but he was also involved with wood and dyes.[78] The business soon diversified, offering various products made from peat moss, including fire-lighters, disinfectant powder and granulated peat for horticulture, fruit-packing and fowl-runs.[79] Almost inevitably this highly flammable product led to the premises being destroyed by fire in 1906.[80] The company managed to stay in business, however, and continued with its trade in peat products, latterly as Umeras Peat Industries Ltd,[81] but it had gone by 1927 and the mill was vacant.[82] The 1936 Ordnance Survey map shows the site in use as a paint and varnish factory.

Harcourt Mills

Like Mount Shannon Mills, Harcourt Mills were built sometime between the late eighteenth and the early nineteenth century and they were marked on Taylor's map of 1816 as Harcourt Mill. The mill was located at the first lock, which was known as Harcourt Lock, as this was the scene for the laying of the first stone in the construction of the canal by Earl Harcourt in 1773.[83] This was a flour mill and was operated in the early nineteenth century by Luke Teeling until 1831, when it was sold by the Court of Exchequer, along with an iron foundry owned by Teeling in Thomas Street.[84]

For a time the mill was operated by Patrick Dowling as a flour mill, and in 1844 it had a breast-shot water-wheel 12ft in diameter and 10ft in breadth, all of metal except the bucket boards. This wheel was said to provide 36hp and there were three pairs of French burr millstones on the premises, though only two were worked at a time. At the time of that survey the mill had been idle for six months and was not in good order.[85] It was acquired by Patrick O'Toole, who operated as a miller and corn factor and had on his premises a kiln that was advertised for its efficient qualities in 1857. O'Toole was bankrupt by 1859, however, and the Harcourt Mills were acquired by Michael Dunne, who refurbished them and fitted modern machinery and burr stones for the grinding of wheat.[86]

The mills were taken over by Robert DuBedat, of a well-known Huguenot family, whose nephew Francis was to bring the family name into disrepute in 1890 when he reneged on a substantial portfolio of debts.[87] By 1877 R.V. Haines was occupying the mills as the Harcourt & Rialto Mills & Mountshannon dye, wool and flour mills.[88]

By 1884 the Dublin Portland Cement Company was in occupation at the first lock, and by 1891 Harcourt Mills had come into the possession of the Irish Portland Cement & Brick Company Ltd, at which time this company advertised the mill premises and its buildings to be sold by auction.[89] The property included more than just the mills, with lands on both sides of the canal in various locations that had been used by the company for the manufacture of Portland cement and bricks. The Harcourt & Rialto Mills were calculated to be capable of producing 4,000 tons of Portland cement per annum, and in addition to the water-power the machinery included a 230hp condensing engine, a compound condensing beam engine, a water-wheel 15ft in diameter and 8ft in width, four stone-crushers and seven pairs of millstones, along with kilns, drying sheds and other equipment.

Following the sale of the property, the Harcourt Mills came into the possession of the Dolphin's Barn Brick Works and the adjacent land was quarried for brick clay; in this form it was shown on the Ordnance Survey map of 1907.[90] The mill, however, remained vacant for a period, was in ruins by 1927 and was gone by the time the Ordnance Survey produced its 1936 map.[91]

DISCUSSION

From the above descriptions a pattern has emerged. Early in the eighteenth century there were mills for corn, paper and iron. By the end of the century most of the corn mills had gone, and not long afterwards the paper mills had followed. Both varieties returned, however—the corn mills or flour mills in the third quarter of the nineteenth century and Smurfit's paper mill in the twentieth century.

Textile mills made their appearance and disappearance in the first half of the nineteenth century. They first appeared within this area in the 1790s, and around 1820 several of the mills were engaged in some branch of the textile industry. By the early 1850s, however, they were all gone except the Greenmount Spinning Company. Their appearance was due to the rapid development of textile technology in the late eighteenth century, but factory production in Lancashire and Yorkshire and in the larger mills of Ireland such as Bessbrook and Portlaw would have undermined the viability of the small mills. The uneven nature of the water-supply would have been a particular disadvantage. A scheme for improving the water-supply to the Dodder mills was proposed in the 1840s, but it was not until the 1880s that the Bohernabreena Water Works incorporated a system for assisting the water-supply to the mills. By that time it was too late for many of the mills in this area.

The effect of mill closures on employment in the area must have been devastating, particularly in the late 1830s and early 1840s. The hat factory at Donnybrook closed with the loss of up to 200 jobs, the extensive woollen mills at Dartry closed and up to 300 jobs went at the calico works at Rathgar. At the same time the cotton and printing mills at Donnybrook closed, and these were said to have employed a great proportion of the population.

As mills were closing forever, late in the nineteenth century there came a boom in the laundry business, as this changed from a home-based industry to factory production. Most prominent in this locality was the Edmondson family, who had set up the Dublin Laundry at Milltown and the Dartry Dye Works nearby. A less positive feature of this industry was the Magdalene laundry at Donnybrook. Other mills came to prominence, including Johnston, Mooney & O'Brien with its extensive workforce, and other enterprises such as the peat products at Mount Shannon Mills.

As for the village of Milltown, the closure of the laundry in 1982 brought to an end the connection with mills which had given the village its name and which had lasted for at least 600 years.

5.

Light industry

Industrial processes are frequently referred to as either light industry or heavy industry. While the division between these categories is hazy, it is generally taken that light industry involves smaller-scale operations with less capital investment and its focus is on consumer goods for use by individuals. This includes food production, household goods and clothing. Very often light industry has a lesser impact on the environment, with fewer airborne and waterborne pollutants, and hence can be located nearer to residential areas.

Home-based industry

Originally most industries were home-based, whether spinning, weaving, dairying, butchery, shoemaking, pottery-making or brewing. Over time, many of these grew into larger concerns and moved into more specialised premises. The industrial revolution in the late eighteenth century and particularly in the early nineteenth century brought many of the workers into factories, with a few exceptions such as some food producers and finishers in the shoemaking and garment-making industries.

Dublin had a large number of home-based weavers in the eighteenth century and well into the nineteenth, though in diminishing numbers. It is difficult to put a figure on these home-based workers at any time, especially when trying to assign them to any particular area of the city. Early in the nineteenth century there were about 1,600 weavers in Dublin, but by 1816 this had decreased to about 300.[1] Generally, though not exclusively, most of the weavers were in the Liberties. Given that the looms would no longer survive on the premises, the only remaining element to indicate such activities would have been the houses, which often had large windows on the top floor to provide light to the looms. No houses of this type now survive in Dublin.

Lack of data makes it difficult to determine how many people were running industrial operations from home at any period. As the nineteenth century progressed, the decennial census returns offered greater detail as to the numbers involved in different forms of employment but without indicating how many of these were home-based. If those jobs that involved living on the premises are excluded, such as domestic servants, nuns, soldiers and police, there are few jobs listed where working at home is evident, other than boarding-house keepers and possibly hoteliers and innkeepers.[2]

SHOP-BASED AND SMALL-SCALE INDUSTRY

As with home-based industry, little information survives regarding shop-based industry in Dublin. Many retail shops were owner-occupied and the family lived over the shop, while many small industries had living accommodation for the owner's family on the premises. Quantifying this and providing information as to localities is very problematic, though.

The Dublin City Industrial Heritage Record has noted the existence of nineteen smithies within the south-east area; this represents only those that were shown on Ordnance Survey maps from the later nineteenth century onward, while those that had existed in earlier times are less visible in the historical record. Smithies were blacksmiths' forges that would have manufactured a variety of items from wrought iron, including tools, gates and balconettes, while many of them would also have acted as farriers, shoeing horses. Blacksmiths worked with wrought iron, while foundries worked with cast iron and whitesmiths with other metals such as tin.

BAKERIES

Baking was a home-based industry, and the first commercial bakeries were small-scale and shop-based. Both home-based and small-scale bakeries still survive, though the bulk of bread, cakes and biscuits are factory-made. The earliest larger bakeries were those based where there was community living, and there are records of bakeries in Castle Street, Christchurch Place and Patrick Street in the thirteenth and fourteenth centuries, probably serving Dublin Castle, Christ Church and St Patrick's. Not all medieval bakeries were based in communities; there is a record of the City Bakehouse in the twelfth century and of a bakery in Exchange Street Upper in the sixteenth.[3] In the seventeenth and eighteenth centuries the City Bakehouse was in Winetavern Street.[4]

In the late 1730s there were at least fourteen bakeries in Dublin city, of which at least eight were in the south-east area, at South Great George's Street, Exchequer Street, Bride's Alley, King Street South, Digges Street, Golden Lane and two in Dame Street.[5] A century later the number of bakers in the city had increased to about 120, of which more than 40 were in the south-east area.[6]

The bakery trade in Dublin began to change significantly in 1850, when Robert Johnston acquired a former cotton factory in Ballsbridge and fitted it out as a bakery and biscuit factory. As described above in the section on Dodder mills, this later became Johnston, Mooney & O'Brien and closed in 1989. Another large bakery was erected in the area in the 1860s when Patrick Boland expanded his business in Capel Street by acquiring a mill at Grand Canal Dock, and in the late 1860s he built a bakery on Grand Canal Street. The bakery was extended at various times and continued in production until the early 1980s.[7]

In 1851, shortly after Robert Johnston opened his bakery in Ballsbridge, two brothers from Waterford, William and Robert Jacob, acquired a site in Peter Row and developed a biscuit bakery there. It was destroyed by fire in 1880 but was back in business in the following year, after which the premises expanded almost continuously into the early years of the following century along the northern side of Bishop Street. Following a merger with Boland's Biscuits, the new company, Irish Biscuits Ltd, erected a new factory in Tallaght; this opened in 1975, following which operations at the original Jacob's site shut down in 1977.[8] Part of the factory remains at the corner of Bishop Street and Bride Street, reconstructed to house the National Archives of Ireland, while sections of the ground-floor façade survive at the eastern end of Bishop Street and on Peter Row.

The firm of R. & J. Fleming established its bakery business at No. 15 Baggot Street Upper in about 1900 and was later addressed at Fleming's Place, at the rear of Baggot Street. The firm closed in 1936, when the site and machinery were sold by auction.[9]

The Dublin Bread Company was established in the early 1890s with a bakery in Stephen Street, and R.N. Campbell moved his bakery from St Mary's Abbey to a site on the southern side of Ringsend Road next to Ringsend Bridge in about 1908.[10] Peter Kennedy acquired a bakery in the north city in the mid-nineteenth century and expanded the business to run six bakeries ultimately. In 1894 he opened a bakery in Patrick Street, in about 1920 he acquired the Ringsend Bakery from R.N. Campbell and shortly afterward he acquired the Dublin Bread Company, which by now had a second bakery in King Street South.[11] The Ringsend Bakery was destroyed by fire in 1947, while in the 1960s Kennedy's suffered from contraction in the bread trade, closing its King Street premises and the Patrick Street bakery.[12] The company went into liquidation in 1971, and the equipment in the Stephen Street confectionery division bakery was sold.[13]

BREWERIES

Brewing has a long history, though in early times it was mainly a domestic undertaking, with each family producing its own beer. The earliest known breweries in Dublin were associated with religious houses, as communities living together needed communal production of food and drink; hence the earliest brewhouse known in the south-east area was part of the building complex at Christ Church in the thirteenth century.[14]

It seems probable that there were breweries outside the home and outside the religious houses in the seventeenth century, if not earlier, though records of their existence are sparse. By the eighteenth century several breweries had emerged as businesses, though many of these may have left no trace in the historical record. A few are known, such as breweries in New Street South and in the Temple Bar area in the opening years of the century, another in King Street South in the 1720s and one in Bride Road in the 1740s.[15]

One significant brewery in the south-east area was Leeson's, founded by Hugh Leeson on the south side of St Stephen's Green in the later seventeenth century.[16] His son, Joseph Leeson, built this up into a substantial enterprise, and on his death in 1741 his son, also Joseph Leeson, used his inheritance to become involved in property and in parliament. He was subsequently elevated to the peerage as Earl of Miltown.[17] Joseph Leeson leased the brewery to the Sweetman family in 1741 and it was operated by the Sweetmans until the end of the century, mainly brewing porter.[18] In the 1790s they moved their operations to Francis Street and advertised the premises in St Stephen's Green to let.[19]After they relinquished the property it was no longer used as a brewery. The site was later occupied by Wesley College and then by an office development at Stokes Place.

In the latter half of the eighteenth century the number of breweries in the city increased substantially, and between the mid-eighteenth and mid-nineteenth centuries more than 150 breweries operated within the city boundaries, though not all at the same time.[20] By far the greater number of these were based in the Liberties area, though others were located throughout the rest of the city, with more than twenty in the south-east area. In the eighteenth century these included breweries at Aston Quay, Hawkins Street, Leeson Street and Dame Street.

By the early 1780s Christopher Sherlock had established a brewery on the southern side of King Street South, at the corner of Mercer Street. By the beginning of the nineteenth century the brewery was being run by John Connolly and Alex Summers. By 1828 John Connolly was in partnership with Francis Coleman, who had previously operated the Dock Brewery in Ringsend, but the brewery closed in about 1830.[21] Patrick Murray had a brewery on Ellis Quay, and he moved it in the early nineteenth century to Bishop Street. By the early 1820s it was operated by William Alley, though soon afterward Laurence Finn was in charge. It closed in about 1842.[22]

A number of the breweries in the south-east area were in the vicinity of Townsend Street. John Alley had established a brewery in Hawkins Street in the 1790s and shortly afterward moved to Townsend Street, on the western corner with Prince's Street, where his premises stretched back to Gloucester Street South. John Alley ran the brewery until the late 1820s, following which William Alley took over for a short period, while Eliza Alley and her son managed the brewery from the late 1830s until the early 1850s. In 1853 the machinery and equipment in the brewery were put up for auction, including a steam engine, two boilers and the tuns, vats and pumps. The brewery was subsequently sold through the Chancery Court.[23]

John Murphy opened a brewery on the northern side of Gloucester Street South, near the junction with Luke Street, at the beginning of the nineteenth century and it remained in business until about 1840.[24]

In 1800 Richard Pim acquired a site on City Quay, to the west of Prince's Street, and established a brewery, which survived bankruptcy in 1808. It was taken over by James Pim and then by his son Henry. In 1841 the business was merged to form Jameson, Pim & Co. and the brewery on City Quay was closed down.[25]

There were few breweries within the south-east area beyond the nineteenth-century city boundary. The brewery at Dartry run by Stoer & Sons is discussed above in the examination of the Dodder mills.

The number of breweries in Dublin declined during the nineteenth century while some became substantial operations. There were about ten in the south-east area in the early 1820s, just four in the late 1850s, and by the 1890s there were none other than the short-lived lager brewery at Dartry.

DISTILLERIES

Distilling has been practised in Ireland for many centuries and yet few records survive of the existence of individual distilleries. Government involvement in the distillery business didn't begin until 1608, when a royal patent became necessary for distilling; taxation began in 1661, while compulsory registration of stills was not required prior to 1761.[26] As a result, only two distilleries are known in the south-east area prior to the latter date, there being mentions of distilleries in Exchange Street Lower and in Townsend Street in the 1730s.[27] By contrast, in the last 40 years of the eighteenth century six distillers are known to have operated in the area, though three of these were in Dame Street and it is not clear whether or not they were successive owners of the same distillery.[28] The other three were in Fleet Street, Townsend Street and Bull Alley. Another five are known from the opening years of the nineteenth century, at Exchequer Street, Longford Street Great, South Great Georges Street, Sandymount and Grand Canal Street, while a fifth in Bull Alley was probably the same distillery as noted in 1786 but with a different owner.[29]

These distilleries were the last to be founded in the south-east area at that time. A change in the taxation on distilleries in 1779 led to a dramatic reduction in the number of legal distilleries in the country, and by 1822 the legitimate industry had been virtually wiped out to the extent that in 1824 only one distillery survived in the south-east area. A revision in the taxation system in 1823 stemmed the demise of the industry and allowed it to grow again, though for the most part it was the surviving distilleries that grew rather than new ones being established.[30] The industry was further compromised by the dramatic rise in the temperance movement from 1838.

Possibly the most important distillery in the south-east area of Dublin was one that was short-lived but of international significance. Aeneas Coffey served as a revenue officer in the operations against illicit stills but resigned in 1824 and began his own distillation operation. In 1828 he had a distillery in South King Street, on the brewery premises occupied by Connolly & Coleman's brewery, though this was short-term and its purpose may have been to experiment with and develop distillation equipment.[31] In 1830 he patented a new type of still that was more efficient than the old pot stills, producing a continuous product rather than in batches, using less fuel and producing a higher concentration of alcohol. The only drawback was that it was tasteless. While that discouraged Irish distillers from adopting the process, Scottish distillers had fewer reservations and adopted the system, which was also used for the production of industrial alcohol, as it still is.[32] In 1833 he opened the Dock Distillery in Grand Canal Street/Barrow Street, where he also manufactured his patent still. The business was closed by 1836, by which time Aeneas Coffey had moved to England.[33]

The largest distillery in the south-east area, and the last to close at this stage, was the Dodder Bank Distillery on a site that is now occupied by houses and apartments and lies partly under Herbert Road and Newbridge Avenue in Sandymount. Robert Haig established a distillery on the banks of the Dodder downstream from Ballsbridge in 1795 and it quickly became one of the largest distilleries in Dublin, with two substantial stills. In 1833 he installed a Coffey still and was the only distillery in

Pl. 22—Haig's Dodder Bank Distillery, *c.* 1795. The view also shows the works to enclose the Dodder within a narrower channel undertaken by William Vavasour from 1792.

Dublin to do so, other than Aeneas Coffey's own small operation in Barrow Street.[34] In common with other distilleries, Haig's Dodder Bank Distillery suffered from the success of the temperance movement, and it finally closed its doors in 1843. The machinery and equipment were auctioned in May of that year and included mash tuns, fermenting backs, six pairs of French burr millstones, a 24hp steam engine and a 15hp steam engine.[35]

Two other distilleries were established in Pearse Street in the late nineteenth and early twentieth centuries. In 1890 a new company, the Dublin City & Banagher Distillery Ltd, was formed in order to acquire the newly established Banagher Distillery in County Offaly and the Dublin City Distillery that was then being fitted out on the former sugar factory premises in Pearse Street. The distillery at Pearse Street was capable of producing six million litres of proof spirit a year but lasted only fifteen years before going into receivership in 1905. The premises were sold in 1908.[36] Shortly after this, E. & J. Burke established a distillery in Pearse Street, adjacent to Cumberland Street. It was still in existence during the Civil War, when it was hit by machine-gun fire, but was gone by 1925, when a postal sorting office was established on the site.[37]

COACHBUILDING

A substantial number of coachbuilding works have been recorded in Dublin over the years, particularly between the mid-eighteenth and early twentieth centuries. Two are known to have existed in the south-east area in the mid-seventeenth century, at Castle Street and Dame Street, while in the first half of the eighteenth century there were coachbuilders in South Great George's Street, Anglesea Street, Aungier Street, Exchequer Street, Gun Lane, St Andrew's Street and Grafton Street.[38]

Alderman Tom Kelly, in a number of articles written in 1909–10, described Dublin in about 1850, when, he noted, there was a concentration of coach-makers in the Kevin Street area. Amongst the firms that he noted were Magill's of Redmond's Hill, which employed 150; Guy's of St Stephen's Green, which employed 70 in its axle-making factory; Kilinger's in Westland Row, employing 30; Whittsit in Baggot Street with 35 employees; Atkin's in Baggot Street with fifteen men; Magill's in Mercer Street, with twenty men; Brown's in Pearse Street, with 40 employees; Hempenstall's in Camden Street, employing 25; and two workshops in Cuffe Lane, Foy's and Madden's. He listed only three coach manufacturers left in the south-east area at his time of writing: Colclough in Duke Street, Grady of Dawson Street, and Callow in Westland Row and Kevin Street. The trades employed in these firms were listed by Alderman Kelly as smiths, body-makers, carriage-makers, fitters, vicemen, wheelers, trimmers, painters, smiths' helpers, printers' helpers, trimmeresses, sawyers, spokemen, axe-makers, carriage lamp-makers, silver-platers, glass-makers and benders. In addition, hair, Moroccan leather, poplin, lace, tuft buttons and oilcloth were also made in Dublin for the coach trimmings.[39]

Alderman Kelly's list is a snapshot in time. Through the previous century, more than 200 coach-makers were listed in the administrative area of Dublin city, more than 70 of which were in the south-east area—though these numbers would include a significant degree of double counting, whereby the same coach factory is listed repeatedly throughout the period under the different names of successive proprietors.[40]

In the early years of the twentieth century motor cars became more common and horse-drawn coaches less so; many coachbuilders took on the manufacture of bicycles and cars, particularly the coachwork on cars, built onto a chassis and the engine bought in from elsewhere. In 1917 *Thom's Directory* listed eight 'carriage, cab, car and truck builders' in the south-east area. In the early 1920s this category was dropped from the listings, by which time 'motor engineers' had become a category of business listed in the directory. In 1927 Robert Callow in Westland Row was the only one of the former category now listed as a motor engineer, while the new category included 45 businesses in Dublin and its hinterland, of which 31 were in the south-east area, including Ashenhurst Williams and Crawford's, which would remain for many years.

ROPE-WALKS AND MARITIME INDUSTRY

Being a commercial port, Dublin had a significant number of maritime industries over time, including sailcloth-makers, block-makers, pump-borers, nail-makers and shipbuilders. Many other trades that were not specifically focused on manufacturing equipment for shipping would have included port-based activities, including coopers, sawyers, foundries and forges, not to mention the industries producing provisions.

The largest group of manufacturers supplying maritime equipment were the rope-makers, whose activities were generally highly visible on maps owing to the length of the rope-walks. Rope-making requires a rope-walk, which is a linear space somewhat longer than the length of rope being manufactured. Strands of fibre are attached to a number of hooks at one end of the walk. These hooks are on a frame known as a jack that can rotate the hooks; originally the jack was operated by hand, though the system was later mechanised. At the other end of the rope-walk the strands were attached to another hook that could rotate freely. The rope-maker held a conical block known as a top, in which were grooves for the strands to keep them apart. One operative turned the handle on the jack while the rope-maker with the top slowly walked along the rope-walk away from the hook at the end, while behind him the strands twisted into a rope.[41]

John Rocque's map of Dublin Bay, published in 1757, shows a rope-walk running southward from Sir John Rogerson's Quay, crossing Hanover Street East and reaching Pearse Street, extending over a distance of 320m. It is not certain when this rope-walk was laid out, but it was in existence by 1754 and lasted more than a century. It was still depicted on the Ordnance Survey map of 1889, though it was probably out of use by then. The street directories list Thomas Crosby & Son, patent rope manufacturers, at 29A and 33 Sir John Rogerson's Quay in 1879, while the 1880 edition indicates that the property was now occupied by T. & C. Martin, timber merchants and ship-owners. It is possible that they were manufacturing ropes, though this is not explicit in the directory entries. As noted below in the section on bridges, the length of this rope-walk necessitated the construction of a bridge to facilitate those who were travelling to Ringsend.

In the late eighteenth century and the beginning of the nineteenth there were rope-walks at Fleet Street, George's Quay, Burgh Quay and Townsend Street.[42] The large-scale Ordnance Survey maps published in the nineteenth century show a number of rope-walks. The 1847 map shows one about 130m long alongside the railway embankment between Cumberland Street and Sandwith Street, one to the east of Thorncastle Street in Ringsend, near the Liffey, that was about 70m long and which gave its name to the street, and another along the shoreline between Ringsend and Irishtown that was about 350m long. The 1864 edition of the map shows two rope-walks on the site at Thorncastle Street and two on the site between Ringsend and Irishtown, as well as one about 100m long along the southern side of Ringsend Road between South Lotts Road and Ringsend Bridge, with a long one about 400m long along the eastern side of South Lotts Road. Further south along the Dodder, another rope-walk was shown at Clonskeagh, while there was also one south of Kevin Street alongside the Cabbage Garden. In the 1880s the Ordnance Survey maps showed that the rope-walk alongside South Lotts Road was still in use, as was the one at the Cabbage Garden, though the others appear to have gone. There seem to have been no rope-walks left in the area by the end of the century.

LAUNDRIES AND DYEWORKS

Washing clothes was a domestic chore and, on a larger scale, hotels, hospitals and other institutions had to provide laundry facilities within their own premises prior to the mechanisation of the task. In the late eighteenth century, some religious and philanthropic bodies that provided accommodation for people in difficult circumstances realised that laundry was a task that was suited to unskilled labour. The first of these in Ireland was established in Leeson Street by Lady Arabella Denny in 1767. The name she gave to her facility was the Magdalen Asylum, and the name and system were later adopted by other religious and charitable institutions. In 1798 a charitable laundry was founded in Townsend Street, later moving to Donnybrook under the auspices of the Sisters of Charity, when its name was changed to the St Mary Magdalen Asylum. Lower-income families could not afford to have their clothes washed in commercial laundries and often had inadequate means of washing clothes and household linen until the advent of public wash-houses in the mid-nineteenth century. In 1884 Dublin Corporation commenced the construction of its first public wash-house in Tara Street, as part of Tara Street Baths, and this opened to the public in 1885.[43]

It was noted above in the description of the mill at Dartry that it was operated as a laundry by Thomas Bewley from the late 1840s through to the 1860s, and while this laundry had the availability of water-power it is not clear what use would have been made of it. The mechanisation of laundries did not commence until the 1860s,

Pl. 23—Tara Street Baths. The baths were a very useful facility for those who lived in houses with poor sanitation, and they also provided facilities for washing clothes.

and despite the number of institutional laundries the lists of trades in *Thom's Directory* did not include laundries before the 1860s, when the listing was headed 'Laundry keepers'. In 1868 this list included Joseph Beggs at Dodder Bank in Donnybrook, M. Hague in Aungier Street and Mrs Waller in Donnybrook. The latter would refer to the Sisters of Charity in The Crescent.

It was in the new century that the number of laundries in the south-east area increased dramatically. The various editions of *Thom's Directory* list five laundries in the area at the beginning of the twentieth century, including the Dublin Laundry in Milltown, the Harold's Cross Laundry, Brookvale Laundry in Donnybrook, the Hygienic Family Laundry in William Street South and the City and District Laundry in Waterloo Lane. Despite the disappearance of the latter three by 1917, the directory lists ten laundries in the area in that year, being the maximum number reached before a reduction to seven by 1921. The three short-lived laundries were the National Laundry in William Street South, the Mespil Laundry and the Pembroke Laundry, both in Mespil Road. The remaining seven were the laundries that lasted through to the second half of the twentieth century. The lists in the directories do not always represent the full picture, as the Magdalene Laundry in Donnybrook is not included, and neither is a laundry at Rutland Hall in Crumlin.

The first of these long-term laundries in the south-east area was the Dublin Laundry, which was established on the banks of the Dodder in Milltown in 1888. In 1894 the company acquired the Dartry mill on the Dodder and fitted it out as the Dartry Dye Works, carrying out dyeing and dry-cleaning.[44] The Dublin Laundry closed in 1982.[45] The site was developed for apartments, though the laundry chimney survives alongside the Luas bridge and the tail-race arch may be seen at the side of the Dodder. The office building of the Dartry Dye Works survives in Dartry Road, bearing the date 1895.

The Harold's Cross Laundry occupied an existing mill site on Mount Argus Road from 1894 and remained in business until its closure in 1968 with the loss of 75 jobs.[46] The site has been redeveloped to provide apartments. Jean Kelso, an employee in the Harold's Cross Laundry, left to establish her own business. She opened the Kelso Laundry on Rathmines Road in 1914 and it was run as a family concern until 1993, when it became Jeeves-Kelso, but it closed in 1994 with the loss of 60 jobs.[47] The building has been demolished, though the façade survives at 103–105 Rathmines Road Lower.

The Court Laundry was established in 1903 at the corner of Harcourt Street and Hatch Street, and the archway that gave access to the laundry survives as a coffee-shop on the Harcourt Street frontage. The laundry was demolished in 1971.[48] The Kenilworth Laundry was established in the opening years of the twentieth century on a site to the west of Harold's Cross Road. It was acquired by the Court Laundry in the 1930s and closed down.

The Terenure Laundry was advertising for staff in 1902 and describing itself as 'The newest laundry in Dublin' in 1904.[49] It lasted 70 years, closing in 1974, following which the site was acquired by Sunday Newspapers for conversion to a printing works.[50]

As noted above, the Magdalene Laundry in Donnybrook had been founded in Townsend Street in the 1790s. It moved to Donnybrook in 1837 and in 1992 it was sold to a private company, which continued to run the laundry until 2006.[51] The laundry building and chimney survive on the site.

The Swastika Laundry opened in Shelbourne Road, Ballsbridge, in 1912, advertising itself as 'the greatest laundry enterprise ever started in Ireland'. The name and its accompanying logo were stated to be 'called after the world-famous "Good Luck" Charm and signifies "Goodness" and "excellence"'.[52] As a result of the reuse of the swastika by a political party elsewhere in Europe, in 1939 the company was renamed 'Swastika Laundry (1912) Ltd'. The laundry remained in use into the opening years of the 21st century with its name changed to Spring Grove Services, and the development of the site for offices commenced in 2004.[53] The imposing red-brick chimney with its tapering octagonal shaft and broad corbelled capping remains as a memory of the site, within the courtyard of the Oval, Shelbourne Road, though without its insignia and the word 'Swastika' in white lettering.

ASTRONOMICAL WORKS

Thomas Grubb established a factory to manufacture machine tools and telescopes in about 1830 on the southern side of Canal Street, between Ontario Terrace and the rear of houses at 1–4 Ranelagh Road. He quickly became internationally renowned, providing a reflector to Armagh Observatory in 1835. He later produced the largest refracting telescope in the world for the Vienna Observatory, a 48in. reflector for the Melbourne Observatory and many others. The firm moved to a site at the rear of 57 Rathmines Road in the 1860s and continued to produce telescopes, mirrors and other optical and scientific instruments. In 1870 Thomas Grubb retired and his son Howard Grubb took on the running of the business, which included inventing the periscope for the first submarine. During the First World War the works provided most of the periscopes for the Royal Navy's submarines and many gun sights. This made it a potential target for terrorist attack and the company relocated to England. The memory of the works survives in the name Observatory Lane in Rathmines.[54]

OTHER INDUSTRIES

Some industries in the city were either unique or few in number and there were many small-scale industries scattered throughout Dublin, too many to mention in this work. Beyond the canal the majority of industries were to be found along the rivers, as described above, or in the Ringsend area. The Dublin City Industrial Heritage Record (DCIHR) lists many factories and other industries in the area. Amongst those in Ringsend at various periods in addition to those mentioned above were four bottle factories, three saltworks and a sal-ammoniac factory. On Pearse Street is the IDA business park, with its iron-framed, stone-faced tower building constructed in 1862 as a sugar factory, which closed in the late 1880s.[55] Its subsequent uses are discussed above under distilleries and in Chapter 6 under ironworks.

The DCIHR lists several printing works dotted around the inner-city area, including Alexander Thom in Dame Lane, Dollard's on Wellington Quay, Browne & Nolan in Fenian Street and two newspaper printers, the *Dublin Express* and *Evening Mail* in Parliament Street and the *Irish Press* on Burgh Quay.

As a result of the trade war with Britain from the early 1930s, a number of factories were set up in Ireland to manufacture goods for import substitution or to undertake partial manufacturing of goods from British factories. Amongst the latter were G.A. Brittain Ltd, on Ringsend Road, which imported parts of Morris and Reilly cars and assembled them for the Irish market; the company also had a sales and service station at Rathmines Road. McCairn's Motors Ltd assembled Vauxhall, Bedford and Chevrolet cars at their works in Tara Street.[56] Other companies that set up a base in Dublin in the 1930s included Kodak, whose art-deco premises in Rathmines Road, at the corner of Blackberry Lane, remains extant, though no longer occupied by Kodak.

6.
Heavy industry

Heavy industries are usually more capital-intensive than light industries, involving the use of heavy plant and machinery. As noted above in discussing light industry, heavy industry is often more polluting than light industry and this was certainly the case in the past. As a result, it was usually sited downwind of the populated areas and this could be enforced through acts of parliament, banning the burning of bricks near the city or the establishment of new glassworks. In Dublin the prevailing wind is westerly, which encouraged polluting industries to locate in the Ringsend area, which also had the advantage of proximity to the port.

Glass

While glass-making is an ancient craft, the earliest indication of a glassworks in Dublin does not appear until 1673, when a 'Glass house' was depicted on Bernard de Gomme's map, located to the east of the city on a site close to the present-day junction of Westland Row with Pearse Street. At the beginning of the eighteenth century there is a reference to bottle-manufacturing in Townsend Street, though the location is uncertain.[1] There are a number of references to glass-making in the Glasshouse in Fleet Street during that century, in 1738, 1753 and 1786.[2]

In 1783–4 the parliament in Dublin passed 'An Act to prevent the pernicious Practice of erecting Glass Houses within the City of Dublin, or a certain Distance thereof'.[3] This noted the existence of several glasshouses, or glassworks, in the city, 'by means whereof the inhabitants of the said city have been and are grievously annoyed, the health of many has been much injured, and the lives of several weakly persons lost'. This act banned the building of glassworks within 800 yards beyond the north wall and circular road, or nearer than Ringsend, or within three quarters of a mile of the circular road elsewhere. Chimneys of glasshouses had to be at least 50ft high.

In the 1790s a glasshouse was established at Ringsend, possibly as a result of the legislation, and the Ringsend Crown Glass Manufactory sold 'window glass of a large size and good colour'.[4]

Pl. 24—A view of Ringsend in the early nineteenth century. The smoking tower to left of centre is a glasshouse, or glassworks, and to the left of it is the arch of Ringsend Bridge. The identity of the tower structure to the right is uncertain. It looks like a glasshouse, but there is no record of one in that position. It may have been a misinterpretation of the tower of St Matthew's Church, Irishtown.

This legislation did not affect existing glasshouses, and Pigot's directory in 1824 listed James Donovan as a flint-glass manufacturer with premises fronting onto George's Quay and Poolbeg Street, though listing his factory as located at Ringsend. It seems probable that he was not making glass at his George's Quay–Poolbeg Street premises. Wilson's 1822 directory gives the Ringsend address as Richard Street.[5] Pigot's directory also lists Thomas Hodgens & Co. as having a glassworks at Ringsend.[6]

The Dublin Almanac and General Register of Ireland for 1834 lists a number of glass manufacturers around the city, including at 15 Dawson Street, 61 Grafton Street and 31 Westmoreland Street, but it is likely that these addresses were the retail outlets rather than that any glass-manufacturing was taking place on the premises.[7]

The 1847 street directory lists two glassworks at Ringsend, E.S. Irwin on Fitzwilliam Street and the National Glass Company at Fitzwilliam Quay. This glasshouse was marked on Thomas Campbell's map of Dublin in 1811, which showed that it was located at the southern end of Fitzwilliam Quay. It later became the Irish Glass

Bottle Company and remained on the site until the early 1970s, when it relocated to a larger site at Pigeon House Road.[8] Another bottle factory was established on the northern side of Ringsend Road by the King family in the early 1870s, and this became part of the Irish Glass Bottle Company. It remained on that site until the late twentieth century.[9]

Another glass bottle company, the Hibernian Glass Bottle Works, was located at the northern end of Thorncastle Street in Ringsend by May 1892, but less than two years later it faced bankruptcy.[10] The works survived this setback as well as an explosion in 1898 that killed one of its employees, and it remained on the site until the late 1920s.[11]

IRON

Ironworking was probably taking place in Dublin from an early period, and excavations have found evidence for an iron furnace in Werburgh Street in the eleventh century.[12] Evidence for a foundry in the city does not appear until the eighteenth century, when Edward Constable and Abraham Nickson had one at the eastern end of Sir John Rogerson's Quay in 1731.[13] Subsequently John Pounden and Walter Onge established a foundry in Luke Street in 1754, and in the following year a Mr Constable had a foundry in Bride Street.[14]

Coal and iron were needed in large quantities for foundries and a location near the port was preferable, though many foundries elsewhere in the city did not have that advantage. Apart from foundries, which produced cast iron, there were iron-

Pl. 25—The Hammersmith Iron Works, on Pembroke Road, Ballsbridge. The site is now occupied by Hume House. The works was run by Richard Turner, who produced the Curvilinear Range in the Botanic Gardens and the Palm House at Kew.

Pl. 26—Aerial view of the Hammersmith Iron Works, at that time occupied by G. & T. Crampton, building contractors, who had extensive workshops on the site. Workers' housing may be seen at the rear, off Shelbourne Road.

works for processing wrought iron, and these could avail of water-power to operate hammers, being in effect mechanised forges or smithies. In 1800 a paper mill in Clonskeagh was converted into an iron mill and later became a spade mill, a form of forge specialising in producing various types of spades; this works is described in more detail in the section on watermills.

In the later nineteenth century Stephens & Co. had the Vulcan Iron Works in Windmill Lane.[15] However, two iron companies dominated the trade in the south-east area in the nineteenth century: the Ringsend Iron Foundry and the Hammersmith Iron Works.

In the early 1780s James Clarke had a business as a whitesmith and crane-maker on Aston Quay, and in the mid-1790s he and his son took on additional premises on City Quay, presumably as a base for manufacturing. In about 1813 the Clarkes acquired a property on Fitzwilliam Quay in Ringsend, where they operated a foundry while still maintaining the property on Aston Quay.[16] In the early 1830s Joseph Clarke was operating the foundry with a partnership as Courtney, Kenny, Clarke at

Pl. 27—Frontage of the Hammersmith Iron Works on Pembroke Road when G. & T. Crampton, building contractors, had their headquarters and workshops on the former ironworks site.

the Ringsend Iron Works. In the mid-1840s the business was taken over by Frederick Barrington, trading as the Ringsend Iron Company and later as the Ringsend Foundry.[17] This business continued until 1886, when the premises were sold to the Mining Company of Ireland for use as a leadworks (discussed below).[18] The site has been partly developed for apartments, while the rest is in use for car body repairs.

Following the failure of the Dublin City Distillery in Pearse Street and Grand Canal Quay in 1905, the site was occupied by the Hammond Lane Foundry until the early 1980s, when the property was acquired by the Industrial Development Authority and redeveloped as business units, with the eight-storey building retained.[19]

The ironworks with the highest profile in Dublin and the widest dissemination of its works was the Hammersmith Iron Works on Pembroke Road, Ballsbridge, established in 1834 by Richard Turner. Turner's uncle, also Richard, had been an ironmonger based at 4 St Stephen's Green North, and the younger Richard appears to have worked with him and inherited his ironworks.[20] By the early 1830s Richard Turner had produced his first curvilinear conservatory, and in 1834 he moved his business to Ballsbridge.[21] The Hammersmith Iron Works were extensive, occupying more than 40m of frontage on Pembroke Road (not including Richard Turner's house, adjacent to the works, and where he had his own curvilinear glasshouse). From this works Turner produced a substantial corpus of work, including the Curvilinear Range at the Botanic Gardens at Glasnevin and the Palm House at Kew. In the 1870s, following his retirement, his son William Turner relocated the works to North King Street.[22] The Hammersmith Iron Works site had a brief existence as a skating rink before being acquired by G. & T. Crampton as its headquarters in 1891.[23]

SHIPBUILDING

Shipbuilding is known to have been carried on in the Dublin area over a very long period. There can be no doubt that some kind of craft, however small, would have been built in the area in prehistory, while analysis of the timbers of a ship found in Denmark indicated that it had been built somewhere in the Dublin area in the eleventh century.[24] The earliest evidence for shipbuilding that can be positively located within the south-east area relates to the seventeenth century in the area around Townsend Street, which was the shoreline prior to later land reclamation.[25]

In 1708 lighters were built for the Ballast Office by James Adair, Nathaniel Dyer and Francis Drake; while the location of their yard is not known, it may have been at George's Quay, as some years later an 80-ton brigantine was built by the firm of Adair & Smith at that location.[26] Of the other yards, perhaps the most significant was that of Cardiff & Kehoe on City Quay, and in 1790 they launched a ship of 550 tons, which was the largest ship built in Ireland in the eighteenth century.[27] By way of illustration, ships using Dublin port around this time were generally around 100–300 tons, with some larger ships occasionally calling.

Ships built in the eighteenth and early nineteenth centuries were generally of wood, using oak, elm and other timbers. The first iron boats built in the city came relatively early, when William Mallet built an iron passage boat for the Grand Canal Company, not on the Liffey but at the Grand Canal Harbour at Portobello.[28] The Grand Canal Company ordered several iron boats over the next few years, including one built at Ringsend by John Marshall in 1830 and another vessel built two years later at Ringsend by Courtney Clarke at the Ringsend Iron Works.

In essence, the three locations in the south-east area where shipbuilding took place were along the quays from George's Quay to Sir John Rogerson's Quay, within the Grand Canal Dock and in the Dodder estuary at Ringsend, though in the nineteenth and twentieth centuries shipbuilding was discontinued on the quays.

John Clements built lifeboats for the Ballast Office in 1801, and Anthony Hill, also at Ringsend, built the hull of the city's first steam dredger in 1814.[29] This was a very early use of steam, as the first crossing between Britain and Ireland by a steamship did not occur until the following year. Over the years a number of shipbuilders, shipwrights and boat-builders were based at Thorncastle Street, Ringsend, where their premises backed onto the Dodder, and each had a slipway into the river. The Clements family were represented into the middle of the nineteenth century, by which time there were about six families involved in the trade. The last were the Murphys, who were boat-builders from the mid-nineteenth century and operated as shipwrights well into the twentieth.[30]

The largest shipbuilder in the south-east area in the nineteenth century was the Dublin Dockyard Company, which operated from Grand Canal Dock. Frederick Barrington had taken over the Ringsend Iron Works on Fitzwilliam Quay in the 1840s, and in 1851 he and Wight Pike approached the Grand Canal Company with a proposal to take on the running of Grand Canal Dock with its graving docks on behalf of a consortium. This was approved and shipbuilding was carried on for nearly twenty years, though struggling financially in the latter years. In 1870 the company

Pl. 28—The middle dry dock at Grand Canal Dock. In this photograph the dock is flooded, and boats may enter or leave. To carry out work on a boat, lock gates would be closed at the entrance and water drained out of the dock into the adjacent Dodder, leaving the boat dry and capable of having maintenance or repairs carried out.

attempted to surrender its lease, but the Grand Canal Company refused to accept the surrender, and the Dublin Dockyard Company struggled on until the lease expired in 1881.[31]

Frederick Barrington's first contracts were to build two iron passenger boats for the Grand Canal Company, and these were delivered in 1852. They were not commercially successful, however, given that there was competition from the railways, and the canal company ceased operating passenger boats. Barrington also built steam towing barges for the canal company, but the speed that they could attain while towing was disappointing.[32]

Following the closure of Barrington's yard, the graving docks at Grand Canal Dock were used for routine repairs and maintenance over the next 30 years until 1913, when the Ringsend Dockyard Company was founded and entered into a lease with the canal company for the dry docks. This operation closed in 1963.[33] The Ringsend Dockyard Company's main business was general ship repairs; smaller vessels were brought into the dry docks, while some work was carried out on larger vessels while they were tied up at the Liffey quays. In 1918 a company called Dublin Shipbuilders was formed and, while its main operations were on the northern side of the river, it incorporated the Ringsend Dockyard Company.[34]

Economies of scale and competition from shipyards elsewhere gradually brought the operation of significant shipyards in Dublin to an end in the mid-twentieth century. Little evidence survives to show where these yards were, other than the dry docks at Grand Canal Dock.

RAILWAY WORKS

When the Dublin & Kingstown Railway was constructed in 1833–4, a site was needed for servicing locomotives. The location selected was at the point where the railway reached ground level, to the west of Serpentine Avenue.[35] This works was only in use for a very short period, and as early as 1837, when the Ordnance Survey produced the draft of its first map of the area, the building was labelled as 'Old Engine Ho.'. By the time the map was published in 1843 the building had been deleted, though the label remained.

In 1836 the Dublin & Kingstown Railway Company acquired the distillery formerly occupied by Aeneas Coffey at Barrow Street and converted it into a workshop to serve the railway. The company built railway coaches on this site and, from 1839, also serviced the locomotives and built many of the locomotives used on the line. By the mid-1850s the works included a foundry, a boiler shop, a smithy, an en-

Pl. 29—The Dublin & Kingstown Railway's works at Barrow Street, where they built and maintained rolling stock and locomotives. The works operated from the 1830s until the 1920s and the site is now occupied by Grand Canal Plaza.

gine room, a punching and sawing shop, a copper shop, a fitting shop and a pattern room. The works remained in use until the mid-1920s.[36]

LEADWORKS

As noted above, the Mining Company of Ireland acquired the former Ringsend Foundry in Fitzwilliam Street in 1886. This company had been mining lead in the Glendalough area and elsewhere since the 1820s and had its leadworks at Ballycorus, south of Dublin, as well as operating other mines for copper and coal. The company was struggling by 1886, however, and the move to Ringsend came at a time of falling productivity in all of its mines. The directors began winding the company down in 1889 and disposing of its property. The Ringsend leadworks were sold in 1891 to James Williams and Robert Woods, who were best known for their jam and confectionery company but who also owned Strachan Brothers, lead manufacturers. A new company was formed, entitled the Mining Company of Ireland & Strachan Brothers Ltd, and this company remained on the site at Ringsend until the early 1990s, when it relocated to Clondalkin.[37]

Industrial housing

The earliest housing directly related to industrial enterprises would have been the miller's accommodation at a watermill, and it is probable that many of the larger mills had living quarters of some kind for the workers. Dock Mills, at Grand Canal Basin, had workers' houses in the 1820s.[38] Griffith's Valuation, carried out in the Dublin area in the late 1840s and early 1850s, listed a number of houses in the vicinity of mills where the lessor of the houses was the mill owner, implying that they were workers' houses. Examples include the mill at Milltown that was later to become the Dublin Laundry, where Griffith's Valuation listed seventeen houses in the ownership of the proprietor of the mills. Nearby at Dartry the presence of a small lane with houses opening onto it, adjacent to the mill, strongly suggests that the houses were for mill workers, and this is confirmed by the valuation, which lists the property as 'Cotton factory, houses and land'. Similarly, at Donnybrook, John Duffy, who ran the calico printworks, was listed as owning five houses in the vicinity. On the Poddle, Samuel Figgis, who operated the paper mill at Harold's Cross, had five houses associated with the mill; Francis Tuite lived in the miller's house at the Larkfield Mills and had two other houses occupied by tenants; and Patrick Regan lived in a house adjoining his mill at Kimmage, with no other houses. Nearby, Madden & Company, who operated the limestone quarries, had four workers' houses.

The largest number of workers' houses owned by any manufacturing company in the south-east area were the houses associated with the Greenmount Spinning Company in Harold's Cross. By the mid-nineteenth century the Pim family, owners of the company, had 35 houses in the vicinity. By the end of the century this had increased to 73, some of which belonged to the company and some to the Pim family, while one member of the family, Frederic Pim, built twenty houses in Greenmount Lane in 1889.[39] One group of houses, including eleven in Limekiln Lane and another eleven backing onto them in Greenmount Lane, were built in 1864 with segmental roofs based on Belfast trusses and mineralised felt. This was a form of construction found in a number of places where Quaker businessmen had factories with workers' houses, including some at Clara associated with the jute factory and a substantial part of the town of Portlaw, associated with the Malcolmsons' cotton factory.

In Ballsbridge in 1834 Richard Turner established his Hammersmith Iron Works, at the rear of which he provided fourteen houses for his employees, opening onto Shelbourne Road.[40] By the 1870s this number had increased to 26 houses, with the name Turner's Cottages.[41]

Once the tram companies were established in the city, they began to provide housing for their workers. Within the south-east area the Dublin United Tramways Company built fourteen single-storey cottages at what is now Simmonscourt Terrace, adjacent to the tram depot that is now Donnybrook Garage for buses. The company built 26 single-storey cottages and two two-storey houses at Tramway Terrace, off Highfield Road (now Highfield Grove), and these would have served the Dartry depot, while other cottages built by the company were in two groups near the Terenure tram depots, including twenty single-storey houses and four two-storey houses at Tramway Terrace (now Cormac Terrace), off Rathfarnham Road, and seven single-storey and two two-storey houses at Tramway Ville (now Rathmore Villas), off Terenure Road North. At Gilford Road fourteen single-storey and four two-storey houses were built in 1894 adjacent to the tram depot.

7.
Transport

Dublin was founded on the banks of the Liffey as two distinct settlements: the land-based Gaelic *Áth Cliath*, located where a road crossed the river, and the maritime Viking *Dubh Linn*, where the waterway met the land. This duality of transportation has been at the heart of the city ever since, as the meeting point between land-based goods and water-based port. Throughout its history Dublin has been primarily a commercial port, and even today almost half of the total trade in and out of the Republic of Ireland travels through Dublin city and its port.[1]

Over the centuries there has been much change. The initial land-based travel on the roadways has been expanded enormously and has been augmented with travel by rail and canal, while the water-based travel has seen the river contract and the port expand, with substantial areas originally covered by water now part of the dry land of the city.

Roads

The land-based element of the early city of Dublin grew up because of the presence of the last crossing of the Liffey before it reached the sea—the *Áth Cliath* or hurdle ford. This crossing facilitated what was probably a long-distance route from Tara. The road that emerged from this crossing on the southern bank then crossed another long-distance route, the *Slige Mhór*, which ran east–west across the country.[2]

The early street network of the medieval city and its vicinity survives more or less intact, though with some streets widened and straightened. The longer routes leading to the city have been added to over the years and mapping evidence provides the best picture of how this network has evolved.

John Speed's map of the city, produced in 1610, shows little beyond the medieval city, and the only routes within the south-east area that connect to the hinterland are Patrick Street–Clanbrassil Street, another southbound road along Bride Street and the eastbound route along Baggot Street. For clarity, the present-day street names are used rather than the historic names.

Bernard de Gomme's map, dated 1673, shows a wider area around the city, and

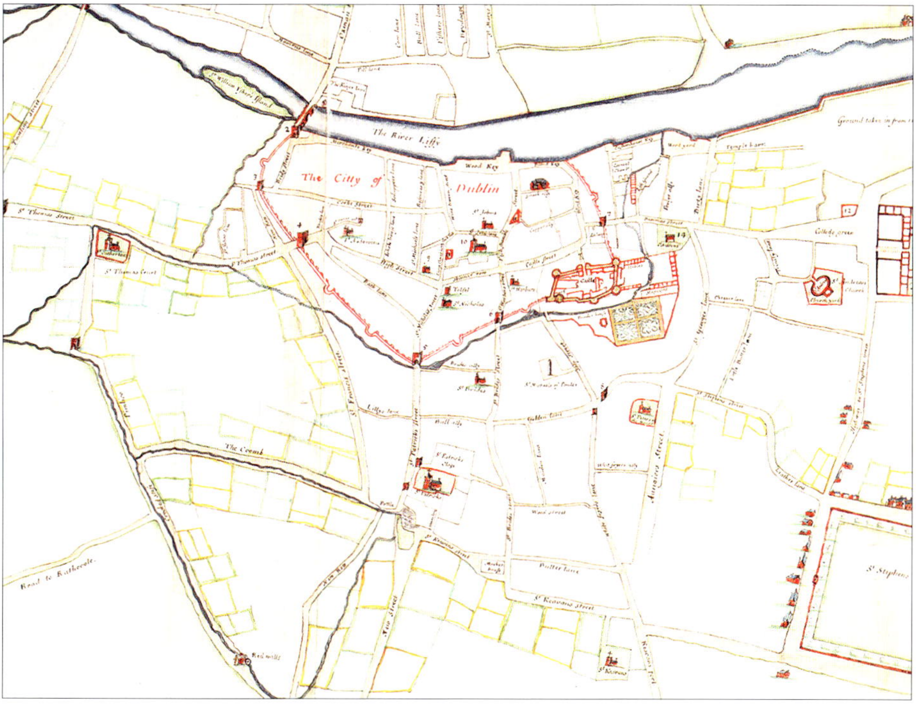

Pl. 30—Bernard de Gomme's map of Dublin city, 1673, showing the various routes leading out of the city.

six routes within the south-east area leading to and from the city are more clearly shown: 'Road to Rathcoole', which led to Crumlin Road; Patrick Street–Clanbrassil Street; Ship Street–Whitefriar Street–Camden Street; Cuffe Street–St Stephen's Green–Leeson Street; Stephen Street–St Stephen's Green–Baggot Street; and Dame Street–College Green–Townsend Street–Sandwith Street–Grand Canal Street. Some variations on these routes were also available, such as Nassau Street–Fenian Street to link with the coastal route via Grand Canal Street. At that time significant suburbs were growing beyond the medieval core of the city, notably at Aungier Street and St Stephen's Green. In addition to those routes, the map also showed a path across the strand to Ringsend, which would only have been available at low tide.

Many of the maps produced over the following two centuries depicted the city itself without information about the roads leading out of it. John Rocque's large-scale map of 1756, while superb for many purposes, does not show the hinterland of the city, though his map of Dublin Bay shows the route across the strand to Ringsend as 'Foot road to Ringsend'. The version of the 1756 map produced by Bernard Scalé in 1773 has an additional area added on to the eastern side of the map, and this indicates that the route over the strand to Ringsend was now on dry land, running from along Hanover Street East and Misery Hill.

To alleviate Dublin's growing traffic problems, an act of parliament was passed in 1763 for the purpose of building a ring-road, followed by a second act in 1775. When the project had not progressed significantly, a third act was passed in 1778, though owing to objections from Dublin Corporation it would not be a full circuit, as the act did not permit a bridge to link across the Liffey on the eastern side.[3] The result was the construction of the circular roads and these were to be turnpike roads, which discouraged development along their length in the eighteenth century.[4] Adelaide Road, Mespil Road and Haddington Road were built as part of the circular road, and there was a turnpike gate (no trace of which survives) on South Circular Road immediately to the west of the Heytesbury Street junction.

A major player in the development of the road network in Dublin from the mid-eighteenth to the mid-nineteenth century was the Wide Streets Commission. Within the south-east area the commissioners were responsible for several very significant new roads, including Westmoreland Street, D'Olier Street and Pearse Street, as well as for widening and straightening others, such as Christchurch Place, Dame Street, College Green and Nassau Street.[5]

Many of the other streets in the south-east area were laid out by private developers, at gradually greater distances from the medieval city. These included Aungier Street and others nearby developed in the seventeenth century, followed by the gradual eastward progression from there, through Harcourt Street, Drury Street, South William Street, Clarendon Street, Dawson Street, Molesworth Street and Kildare Street and others in the vicinity, while from the mid-eighteenth century the Fitzwilliams developed their substantial estate with new streets such as Merrion and Fitzwilliam Squares.

As the southern suburbs expanded from the early nineteenth century, some of the suburban routes began to develop, including Rathgar Road, Templeogue Road, Terenure Road–Kimmage Road and Northumberland Road.

Road surfaces

By the eighteenth century road surfaces were generally of broken stone beaten into the ground to form a hard-wearing surface. Very little information survives to indicate whether any of the city's streets were cobbled, but cobbles may have been used in the principal streets. Some cobbles were certainly used in backstreets; during works in recent years to Swan Yard, off Harry Street, some trace of cobbles could be seen. Swan Yard was laid out in 1774.[6]

Towards the end of the eighteenth century the technology of road-building improved significantly, as the materials were better understood and the advent of springing on wheeled vehicles helped to reduce the wear.

The streets of Dublin were maintained by each of the parishes until 1774, when an act of parliament established the Paving Board to centralise the tasks.[7] Within cities, footways were separated from the carriageways, at least in the principal streets. In Dublin the paving was of granite flagstones laid on compacted gravel on which was a bed of sand, and with kerbstones of harder granite.[8] These granite flagstones survive in some streets and are protected as an objective in the city's development plan. In those cases where the houses had coal-cellars beneath the footway, cast-iron coal-hole covers are frequently to be found.

From the mid-nineteenth century new types of road surfaces were introduced to the city, including paving setts. Initially the setts were imported from Wales but pressure from various sources encouraged the opening of quarries in Ireland.[9] The stone used for setts needed to be extremely hard to withstand the traffic of steel-shod wagon wheels carrying heavy loads. Experiments with local granite in the 1850s in Grafton Street and elsewhere suggested that this was not a good material for the heavy wear that would occur.[10] Other stones such as basalt, diorite, dolerite and andesite proved to be tougher and were used more widely.[11] Faced with evidence that there was diorite suitable for use as paving setts, Charles Stewart Parnell opened a quarry on his estate in Wicklow to supply the market.[12]

Wooden setts were also used at this period, though how widely they were used in the city is uncertain. Some wood was impregnated with creosote as a preservative and various species of timber were utilised.[13] One of the advantages of timber was that it reduced the noise of traffic passing over it, as compared with stone setts, and so it was used outside hospitals and churches, one example being Peter Street at the Adelaide Hospital, which was paved in 1886.[14]

Asphalt was also introduced to the city's streets in the mid-nineteenth century. In the late 1860s the Limmer Company was engaged to pave Grafton Street with asphalt, though work had to stop for a while owing to obstruction to trade.[15] In 1872 the setts were lifted in Henry Street and asphalt was laid by the Irish subsidiary of the Swiss Val de Travers company.[16]

Concrete began to be used for footpaths in the 1880s and the townships of Drumcondra, Blackrock and Kingstown began to provide footways in this material, though Dublin Corporation does not appear to have gone down this route until the twentieth century.[17]

The Dublin City Development Plan includes policies to protect streets where historic paving survives, including many streets with stone setts in the Temple Bar area and around Hanover Quay and Grand Canal Dock. A number of streets with surviving granite kerbing or flagstones are also scheduled for protection.

Fords

Prior to the nineteenth century many smaller rivers were crossed by fords rather than bridges. As the history of Dublin shows, the city was founded at a ford over the River Liffey, and this would have been a common form of river-crossing. Travellers would have to wait until low tide to cross, but in a time of slower travel this was not an issue.

Evidence for the existence of fords is scanty, though the locations were usually close to where a bridge would later be built. The first-edition Ordnance Survey map of the Dublin area marks only one ford in the Dublin south-east area and that is over the Dodder at the back of Anglesea Road on what would have been a private pathway. Dundrum Road crossed the Dodder via a ford until about 1820, when Milltown Bridge was built, and the alignment of the road to the ford was still distinguishable more than 40 years later on the first Ordnance Survey 1:2,500 map. The ford was located about 100m downstream from the bridge and there is no trace of it remaining today. A ford that pre-dated Rathfarnham Bridge is discussed in the description of that bridge.

BRIDGES

The bridges associated with railways and canals are considered under those headings; this section looks at the other bridges within the area, which are predominantly, but not exclusively, those that cross the rivers. The bridges over the Liffey have been covered in detail in the book *Bridges of Dublin*[18] and hence are not examined in any detail here, though they are mentioned briefly, given their importance in the area.

Liffey bridges

There are eleven Liffey bridges within the south-east area—though eleven half-bridges might be more correct, as only the southern half of each bridge lies within the area. Of these, three are footbridges, one is a railway bridge, one is for restricted use by pedestrians and public transport, and the remainder are road bridges. None are particularly old, the earliest being O'Donovan Rossa Bridge at Winetavern Street, built in the second decade of the nineteenth century, while three of them—Samuel Beckett Bridge, Seán O'Casey Bridge and Rosie Hackett Bridge—were built in the present century.

Pl. 31—The construction of the original Butt Bridge in 1879. This was a swivel bridge, and the swivel deck may be seen in the centre left in the photograph. This bridge was replaced by the present Butt Bridge in the early 1930s.

Pl. 32—The Samuel Beckett Bridge under construction. A large part of the bridge was constructed in Rotterdam and was floated over to Dublin on a barge in 2007.

Dodder bridges

The Dodder is the second-largest river in the south-east area and there are no less than eighteen bridges over it within the area, though two of those are railway bridges and are considered elsewhere. Of the remainder, many are relatively modern concrete bridges, including Orwell Road and the two graceful concrete pedestrian bridges at Dodder Park Lower and Orwell Gardens.

The earliest of these bridges is the Packhorse Bridge at Milltown and the lack of earlier bridges is probably due to the Dodder's notorious flash-floods. Many of the bridges have been damaged or destroyed in floods, and it was not until the advent of single-arch bridges on the river that they became less likely to be broken down. Packhorse Bridge is of unknown date but was probably built in the seventeenth century. It seems to have been a private bridge, probably built by millers to ensure access to and from their mills for corn, flour and other raw materials and products. The bridge was never on any main road; it would have provided a means of crossing during floods and may have been a toll bridge.[19]

The second-oldest surviving bridge is Classon's Bridge at Lower Churchtown Road. This was also a private bridge, built in 1760 by John Classon, probably to get access to his quarries on the southern bank, as Lower Churchtown Road was not in existence until long after the bridge was built. Classon's Bridge is a three-span bridge of limestone and was widened with concrete in 1928.[20]

Pl. 33—Classon's Bridge prior to its widening in 1928. The bridge is still extant, though heavily altered by the addition of a cantilevered concrete deck. In the background is the nine-arched bridge on the former Harcourt Street railway line, and behind it is the Dublin Laundry.

Pl. 34—Rathfarnham Bridge, built on the site of an early ford; this bridge was widened in the 1950s and renamed in honour of Patrick and Willie Pearse.

The Down Survey maps, compiled in the 1650s, are inconsistent in their coverage of roads and bridges, though they show clearly that there were bridges at Rathfarnham, Milltown (Packhorse) and Clonskeagh, the Packhorse Bridge at Milltown being the only one of these to survive today. John Rocque's 1760 map also showed Classon's Bridge and bridges at Donnybrook, Ballsbridge, Lansdowne Road and Ringsend, of which only Classon's Bridge now survives.

There is a reference to a wooden bridge crossing the Dodder at Rathfarnham in the fourteenth century, while in the seventeenth century Gerard Boate referred to a wooden bridge which had been carried away by floods several times. Evidence for a ford was discovered beneath the bridge in 1912 when drainage works were being carried out; this consisted of substantial stone blocks into which deep grooves had been cut by wheeled vehicles, though the date of this crossing is unknown. Floods carried away three bridges between 1728 and 1765 and finally this repeating problem was solved by the construction of the present single-span bridge in the latter year. The bridge was widened in 1953 with a concrete arch that was faced with stone to match the original.[21]

Many of today's masonry bridges on the Dodder were built over a short period of 30 years or so at the beginning of the nineteenth century. There was a wooden

Pl. 35—The old bridge at Donnybrook, sketched by Francis Place in the 1690s. This bridge was replaced on a revised alignment in 1832.

bridge near the site of the present bridge at Herbert Road–Lansdowne Road, while the present bridge was built in the mid-nineteenth century. Clonskeagh Bridge (1807), Ringsend Bridge (1812) and Donnybrook Bridge (1831–2) were built by the grand jury to the designs of John Semple, and it seems logical that he also designed the present Milltown Bridge (1820).[22] A major flood on the Dodder in November 1834 damaged the new Donnybrook Bridge and carried away the timber centring for the reconstruction of Ball's Bridge along with the temporary wooden bridge at Ball's Bridge; these timbers were swept downstream and destroyed the new stone railway bridge at Lansdowne Road.[23] Ball's Bridge was later widened to accommodate tram traffic in the opening years of the twentieth century.

The old Orwell Bridge was very similar in style to Milltown Bridge but was not built until 1863, when it replaced a wooden bridge.[24] It was demolished in 1972 and replaced with a concrete bridge.[25]

London Bridge was built as a wooden bridge in the 1790s by William Vavasour and replaced with a masonry bridge to the designs of Richard Frith in 1856–7.[26] A steel bridge crosses the Dodder at the rear of the former Darty Dye Works and was built in the early twentieth century to facilitate that company, probably owing to the

Pl. 36—London Bridge, built in the 1790s by William Vavasour as part of his works to enclose the Dodder into a narrower channel.

need for access to grazing land on the opposite bank for the horses used for deliveries.

The only iron bridge across the Dodder within the south-east area is the footbridge at Beaver Row. A bridge was shown at this location on Duncan's 1821 map and was indicated as a wooden bridge on the first Ordnance Survey map. It is uncertain when the iron bridge replaced the old wooden bridge, but it has been beautifully restored recently. The name Beaver Row refers to the use of beaver fur for making felt for hats, and the bridge provided access for workers in Wright's Donnybrook Hat Factory on the western bank from their homes on the other side of the river in Beaver Row.

Ringsend Bridge

Ringsend was a spit, projecting out into Dublin Bay alongside the Dodder estuary. Access to the village was either by boat or via a route along the spit, roughly where Serpentine Avenue and Tritonville Road now run, or else over the tidal flats at low tide, on the line of Hanover Street East and Misery Hill. Bernard de Gomme's map of Dublin, dated 1673, shows a route across the tidal flats, though it is unclear whether this was just a proposal; the fact that it was on the same alignment as the later route suggests that it may have been in existence. By the mid-eighteenth century Sir John Rogerson had built his wall along the Liffey margin and along the Dodder, now South Lotts Road, and John Rocque's 1757 map of Dublin Bay shows a footpath to Ringsend leading across the flats, with a flight of steps at the end to enable travellers to climb to the Dodder wall. Beyond that point a road led to Ringsend, crossing the Dodder on a bridge of five arches, built in 1727.

Building that bridge cannot have been easy. Rogerson's wall left a 200m gap to be crossed, which would have been under water at high tide and mud at low tide, with difficulty in providing an adequate foundation. The Dodder is subject to flash-floods, which have always tested bridges along the river; as a result, and owing to the lack of adequate foundation, any bridge at this location would be liable to scour undermining the piers and abutments, leading to collapse.

The bridge lasted 60 years before being destroyed by a flood in 1787. The breach was spanned by timber beams on a temporary basis until a new bridge was built in 1789, though this was also destroyed in a flood in 1802.

Following this destruction, temporary repairs were undertaken while arrangements were made for a new bridge. Things did not move rapidly, however, and by 1807 the media were showing exasperation at the delay, particularly as this was the principal route for those travelling to the Pigeon House Harbour for the packet-boats to Holyhead.[27] Furthermore, a number of people had fallen to their deaths from the temporary bridge.[28] Later that year the grand jury voted the money for the construction of the bridge and the old bridge was taken down, a temporary bridge being provided slightly downstream at the personal expense of the landowner.[29]

Work came to a halt less than two years later, however, and it transpired that the treasurer had absconded with the £7,555 that had been allocated for the bridge.[30] The bridge was finally completed in 1812.[31]

The architect and engineer for the bridge was John Semple, and he adopted a novel design, aimed at ensuring that the bridge would never collapse through being undermined by flood waters. Given that the bridge had to be built on muds, he opted for a full ellipse rather than a normal elliptical arch, which would only include the top half of the ellipse. This spread the weight of the bridge over a much wider area to increase its stability. He used a single span to maximise the area for water to flow through and minimise the obstruction to flow. The margins of the arch are chamfered, which adds to the beauty of the bridge and makes good engineering sense, as it helps to smooth the flow of water through the arch, reducing drag and therefore increasing the stability of the bridge.[32]

Pl. 37—Ringsend Bridge at low tide, when the elliptical span of the bridge may be seen to turn back to continue as a full ellipse beneath the river bed.

Ringsend Bridge is a beautiful essay in stone, but it is also an innovative example of bridge engineering, as is testified by its survival over more than two centuries in contrast to its predecessors.

Poddle bridges

The Poddle is a much smaller river than the Dodder and the bridges are likely to have been relatively simple. Where a bridge is to be widened, it would be more financially viable to remove a very small bridge than a larger one, and as a result few early bridges survive on the Poddle within the south-east area. It is possible that some part of a bridge may survive beneath widened roads such as Sundrive Road or Terenure Road West, but no obvious signs of historic bridges were identified for this volume.

Other bridges

There have been many bridges in the Dublin south-east area over the centuries other than the ones listed above along the Liffey, the Dodder and the Poddle. There are other watercourses that are now below ground, such as the Stein, that would have had bridges at various points, and it is possible that some of these may still exist beneath the road surfaces and are now part of the underground culverts. Other bridges would have been found along mill-races and some may survive, though the width of mill-races is narrow and technically such crossings would be classified as culverts rather than bridges. The most prominent bridge crossing a road is the one that connects Christ Church to the former Synod Hall, now Dublinia. This bridge was built to the designs of George Edward Street in 1875 and is a graceful Gothic arch.[33]

One intriguing hidden bridge never involved water or railways. Travelling eastward along Hanover Street East toward Cardiff's Lane, the road narrows just after Lime Street and rises up briefly before sloping down again. This rise in the road seems illogical, as this is all land reclaimed from the estuary and there should be no hills. Examination of John Rocque's map of Dublin Bay, published in 1757, shows the reason for the rise. The old footpath to Ringsend crossed a rope-walk, where ropes were stretched out during their manufacture. As this was incompatible with the use of the footpath, a bridge was built over the rope-walk to facilitate pedestrians going to Ringsend. The ropeworks was still indicated on the Ordnance Survey's large-scale map of 1889, and it is possible that the bridge is still present below the street surface.

DUBLIN PORT

The port of Dublin has been one of the most important elements in the economy of the city since medieval times. Although the various writings on the history of the city say much about the importance of the parliament in the eighteenth century and the effects of its loss at the start of the nineteenth, the reality was that Dublin's economy was primarily based more on commerce than on politics. The port remains critically important to the city and the country and today handles almost half of the trade in the Republic.[34]

Between the seventeenth century and the mid-twentieth century the port gradually moved downstream, and even before that the quays were gradually moved out into the river onto reclaimed land in a succession of revetments, followed by a stone wall.[35] As a result, the vast majority of port activity in Dublin over the centuries has been conducted on reclaimed land. Land reclamation is discussed elsewhere in this volume, though reference is made in this section to some aspects of the increased land area. Industries based in the port, such as transportation, gas, electricity and other manufacturing, are also discussed elsewhere; this section concentrates on the activities of the various port authorities, the facilities that they provided and the surviving historic features related to the port.

The port was originally the responsibility of Dublin Corporation as the local authority for the city. The city's charter gave it jurisdiction over the waters adjacent to the city, and from this it followed that any land reclaimed from the river or the bay, where it adjoined the city, fell under the control of the city authorities. In 1707 the city assembly was made aware that within a few years the Liffey and the port of Dublin would be choked up unless a Ballast Office was established to cleanse the river and the channel to the port and to regulate the taking up and deposition of ballast.[36] Later that same year an act of parliament established the Ballast Office, under the auspices of Dublin Corporation, in view of the fact that the River Liffey 'is become extremely shallow, and well-nigh choked from the bridge, commonly called Arrans-Bridge, to the bar of the said port … which mischiefs have been principally occasioned by the licentious and irregular taking up of ballast, and breaking the banks of the channel, for want of proper laws …'.[37]

In 1786 parliament passed 'An Act for promoting the Trade of Dublin, by rendering its Port and Harbour more commodious' and this took the care of the port out of the hands of Dublin Corporation, establishing an independent body to take over responsibility.[38] This body was to be known as the Corporation for Preserving and Improving the Port of Dublin, though in practice it was generally referred to as the Ballast Board or the Ballast Office. In 1967 that body was replaced by the Dublin Port and Docks Board, which was in turn replaced by the Dublin Port Company in 1997.

The South Wall

In January 1714–15 the Ballast Office reported to the city assembly that if piles, kishes and other materials were erected to the south of the river channel this would raise the south bank of the channel high enough to provide shelter for ships lying in the harbour.[39] It is clear from this that the inner bay, to the east of Ringsend, was being used as an anchorage, and it was here that ships were unloading onto smaller boats, including lighters and wherries, so as not to have to sail further up the river. This is certainly what was happening by the middle of the century and is clearly shown on John Rocque's map of Dublin Bay, published in 1757. The map shows many ships in the river and in the channel to the north of what was to become the South Wall and downstream from the future site of the Pigeon House Harbour, and quite a few of the ships in the channel are depicted with anchor chains visible. One is obviously a permanent feature, as it is labelled 'Quarantine Sloop', while another area is marked as 'The Paquet Moorings'. The packet-boats carried the mail, while passage boats carried passengers. These boats anchored at this location and passengers were carried to the city by boatmen who were hired by the passengers, much like taking a taxi from a station or airport today.

At its meeting in April 1715 the city assembly received a report from the Ballast Office with the costings for the proposed works and gave permission for work to proceed.[40] The proposal at this stage was to erect a barrier consisting of timber piles driven into the sands, supplemented by kishes, which were large containers of basketwork which would be filled with stones and sunk. The materials to be used consisted of 200 tons of oak timber 6–9in. square and 10–15ft long, 1,200 straight oak poles 4–6in. in diameter and 10–14ft long, and 1,000 kishes.

Work got under way in 1716, starting in relatively shallow water somewhere to the east of the future Pigeon House and working in both directions. A pile-driver was obtained from the Netherlands, along with its crew, and this worked on the project until the Ballast Office was able to fabricate a copy, thereby dispensing with the cost of the Dutch boat and crew. By 1721 the piles had been completed in the shallower water and, instead of piles, the work then involved the use of timber frames the size of modern-day shipping containers prefabricated at Ringsend, floated to the site, loaded with stones and sunk to the bottom.[41]

John de Courcy suggested, from the available evidence, that the early part of the work consisted of three rows of piles braced together and sheeted along the two outer rows with woven wattle hurdles to form a casing 3m wide that was then filled with shingle and stones to a height of about 1.5m above high-tide level.[42] By 1731 this structure had been completed, running between the future sites of Pigeon House Harbour and Poolbeg Lighthouse, and in this form it was depicted on John Rocque's maps of Dublin Bay (1757) and County Dublin (1760), both of which show a lightship moored off the end of the piles.

Connecting from this line of piles to the nearest point of land at Ringsend was more problematic, as the water was deeper along that stretch. It became clear, however, that some form of barrier would be necessary along the 2.4km gap between the western end of the piles and the end of the spit at Ringsend. At its meeting on 22 April 1748, the city assembly approved a proposal from the Ballast Office to build a double wall of stone between the piles and Ringsend Point.[43] In April 1759 the Ballast Office reported that the construction of the wall was almost complete.[44]

In the meantime, however, the piles were proving to be difficult to keep in repair—by this time the cost of repairs was amounting to more than 10% of the total cost of operating the port.[45] The Ballast Office decided that the best solution to this

Pl. 38—The anchorage in the Liffey channel as seen on John Rocque's map of Dublin Bay, 1757. The South Wall is shown in the area between Ringsend and the Pigeon House, though it was not quite complete at that time. Further to the east the map shows the piles where the wall was to be continued to Poolbeg.

would be to continue the stone wall eastward to replace the timber-based piles with the more durable material and, once again, the city assembly gave its permission.[46] Work proceeded but was not completed until the mid-1790s.

The wall is not straight owing to the initial plan's having been for just the piles, which did not align on Ringsend point. The final version is dog-legged and bends slightly again towards the east; in this form it measures some 5.3km in length and for many years it was the longest sea wall in the world. Almost half of it is now buried under reclaimed land between Ringsend and the Pigeon House, beneath Pigeon House Road, while about another 700m lies within the lands of Poolbeg power station, leaving just 2km available for public use. To ensure its long-term survival, it is carefully monitored by the Dublin Port Company for any unusual movement that might suggest damage.

Poolbeg Lighthouse

As has been noted, the Ballast Office established a lightship at the end of the piles to warn ships of the existence of this potential navigation hazard. Rocque's 1757 map

Pl. 39—Poolbeg Lighthouse in its original form, seen in an engraving published in 1801. The Half-Moon Battery is seen at right, though in reality the battery is much further from the lighthouse.

of Dublin Bay shows the lightship with a light suspended from each end of a beam hoisted high on the mast.

Knowing the potential dangers posed by the piles, the Ballast Office considered a more permanent arrangement than a lightship. In July 1762 they reported to the city assembly that they had begun the foundations for the eastern end of the wall, adding that this 'may also serve for a foundation for a light house, if hereafter it should be thought proper to build one'.[47] There appears to be no further mention of a lighthouse until April 1766, when the Ballast Office reported that they had 'made all the progress in our power in raising the new light house'.[48] Construction was completed in 1767 and first shone its light at the end of September. The light was powered by candles, in contrast to the norm, which was to have coal braziers providing the illumination.[49] In October the city assembly resolved to present the architect, John Smith, with a piece of plate to the value of twenty guineas 'for his great ingenuity in planning, and his indefatigable zeal and assiduity in carrying into execution, that masterly work of the lighthouse, so justly and universally admired'.[50]

In 1786 the new Ballast Board decided to experiment with using oil and patent lamps in the lighthouse, and they asked the masters of the packet-ships to provide feedback on the quality of the new system. The feedback was very positive and the switch-over to oil lamps was made permanent, this being one of the first lighthouses in these islands to be so lit.[51] The lighthouse was built with a gallery and is shown in this form in several paintings and engravings from the eighteenth and early nineteenth centuries. In 1813, however, the gallery was removed and the lighthouse raised. It was completely rebuilt in 1820.[52] In 1869 experiments were undertaken at Poolbeg in the use of gas for lighting lighthouses, and a gas plant was installed at Poolbeg in 1888 for this purpose.[53] The lighthouse was converted to electric operation in 1964, when three diesel generators were installed.[54] Having been one of the first lit by candle power and then by oil and gas power and finally by electricity, the Poolbeg Lighthouse became the last to be manned and it was automated in 1964.[55]

Pigeon House Harbour

As has been noted, passenger ships and mail packet-boats arriving in the port anchored in the area to the north of the piles, and passengers were brought upriver to the city by boatmen. From 1759, when the South Wall was completed as far as the present Pigeon House site, passengers had the alternative to be delivered to the South Wall and walk from there or take an outside car. In view of the number of passengers landing on the wall, the Ballast Office erected a building, referred to as a blockhouse, to accommodate a watchman and his family, and the terms of employment permitted the watchman to provide refreshments to passengers. The first watchman employed was John Pidgeon and the blockhouse became known as Pidgeon's House.[56]

As the construction of the eastern section of the South Wall progressed westward to join the section coming from Ringsend, the Ballast Board decided to provide better facilities for the packet-boats and passenger boats by providing a harbour at the point where the two sections of wall met. Contracts for the construction of the harbour were awarded in 1792, and the harbour was completed in the following year.[57] Now that the use of the South Wall by passengers had been formalised, a similar approach was taken to the provision of facilities and in 1793 it was decided to erect a hotel at the harbour. An architectural competition was held for the design of the hotel and the premium was awarded to Robert Pool.[58]

The construction of the Pigeon House fort is discussed in the section relating to military installations; while the harbour was closed to commercial traffic, this did not affect its use by the mail packets, which continued until 1818.

The ongoing problem of packet-boats obtaining access to Dublin port across the sand bar in the bay was not resolved by the construction of Pigeon House Harbour, as it lay inside the bar. With Ireland's incorporation into the United Kingdom in 1801, the need for improved communications between the administration in Dublin and the government in London became an urgent matter, and this was exacerbated by the political unrest in the country, including the 1798 Rising and Emmet's abortive rebellion in 1803. The Commissioners for Inland Navigation had been given responsibility for improving navigation in Dublin and they sponsored a number of reports from experts in the field, including an eminent nautical engineer, Sir Thomas Hyde Page. His report contained a number of recommendations in relation to various parts of Dublin Bay, one of which related to the packet-boats; his conclusion was that 'no situation would … be so proper as Howth, as the station for the packets'.[59] This set in train the decision to build a harbour for the packet-boats at Howth, that location having the advantages of a shorter distance to Holyhead and of being outside the bar and also outside the dangers of Dublin Bay. The harbour at Howth was finally ready for packet-boats in 1818 and the service transferred there from the Pigeon House on 1 July in that year.[60]

In the 1890s Dublin Corporation commenced work on the Dublin Main Drainage Scheme, as is described in the section relating to drainage. To facilitate these works, the corporation acquired Pigeon House Harbour from the War Office to provide a site for a treatment and outfall works.[61] A significant part of the harbour was infilled to provide space for settling ponds, though part of it remains as open water.

Pl. 40—Sir John Rogerson's Quay in its original form, as depicted in James Malton's print, 1795. This view shows the Marine School, with shipbuilding taking place to the left.

The piers are extant and the hotel, having served as the officers' quarters when the barracks was in operation, became used as offices. The use of the harbour for electricity generation is discussed under that heading.

QUAYS AND QUAY FURNITURE

The present quay walls westward from the East Link Bridge were built in the mid-nineteenth century, and earlier views of the river, such as Malton's engraving of the Marine School on Sir John Rogerson's Quay, show a very different river margin. Construction of the present quay walls commenced in the early 1860s, and the Dublin Port and Docks Board undertook to rebuild 300m of the wall along Sir John Rogerson's Quay in 1868. This brought the river margin further out into the river to allow foreign-going ships to berth in deeper water.[62]

Pl. 41—Sir John Rogerson's Quay in the 1980s, showing the quayside cranes and the broad track on which they moved, with bollards and mooring chains; the surface is paved with stone setts.

It follows from this that the port furniture along the quays is also of no earlier a date than the mid-nineteenth century. The quays have been refurbished in recent years with new paving, though many examples of this furniture have been retained, including mooring hooks, granite bollards and flights of steps leading down to the river. The larger-scale Ordnance Survey maps show the bollards along the quays, marked MP (for mooring post) on some of the maps. The maps also depict cranes, which can be seen in historic photographs of the quays, particularly of Sir John Rogerson's Quay. Maps also show a plethora of slipways leading into the Dodder from the rear of Thorncastle Street in Ringsend.

From the later nineteenth century, the larger-scale maps also show the railway lines on the quays, with the routes of the lines into adjacent properties. These were private tracks that facilitated the unloading of bulk goods, particularly coal, into premises such as coal-yards and gasworks.

GRAND CANAL

The scheme to construct the Grand Canal was preceded by a number of proposals in the early eighteenth century for a canal connecting Dublin with the Shannon. The project got under way in the mid-1750s, and in 1756 work commenced on the canal at Harcourt Lock, Dolphin's Barn. After some years the scheme had moved westwards, but not eastwards towards the city. A new company was formed in the early 1770s to take over the project and it is unclear how much had been constructed at the Dublin end by then. John Rocque's large-scale map of the city of 1756 shows nothing of the canal, while his smaller-scale map of County Dublin of 1760 shows the canal reaching the canal basin at James's Street, with a spur descending to the Liffey. This anticipated the actual construction, however, as the basin shown on the map was not in the right location, while the spur to the Liffey was never built. Rocque's successor, Bernard Scalé, showed the canal on his map of 1773, but without any basin at all. The canal may have been under construction in the Kilmainham area at the time. In 1780 Pool and Cash showed exactly the same 'line of the new canal' on their map of Dublin, with a dashed line indicating the intended line to the terminus at Grand Canal Harbour, James's Street. In fact, the canal opened to Dublin in 1779, though not necessarily all the way to James's Street. The engineer for the canal from the time when the project was taken over by the new company in 1770 was William Jessop.

After ten years the company began to think of connecting the canal to the Liffey. The original scheme, shown on Rocque's map of 1760, had been to connect from the James's Street area to Old Kilmainham. The more ambitious proposal was to connect a new line around the southern perimeter of the city, outside the built-up area, to bring the canal to Ringsend, and this was suggested by William Chapman, engineer. This plan was adopted and began on site in 1790, the same year that the Royal Canal began at Phibsborough. The new spur ran off the original line at Goldenbridge, later to be the site of Suir Road and its bridge. The first bridge along the route is Griffith Bridge, immediately adjoining the canal junction and bearing the date 1791.

The route ran from there to Harberton Bridge, continuing on to Camac Bridge at Dolphin's Barn, just beyond which was a small harbour, with a pair of canal docks a little further to the east. These were shown in detail on the Ordnance Survey 5ft map of 1847. Both of the features have now disappeared.

The canal continued beyond Dolphin's Barn, turning a little more to the east as it came to Clanbrassil Street and crossed the road to Harold's Cross. Continuing eastwards, it turned slightly north of due east as it ran towards Richmond Street and the road to Rathmines. Here a number of water features were associated with the canal. In the urban space known today as Portobello Harbour there was a canal harbour more extensive than that at Dolphin's Barn. Campbell's map of 1811 shows the harbour and indicates that it was on an area embanked up from the surrounding land. To the west of the harbour, the large rectangle is the city basin, which was a reservoir to contain water from the canal that fed into the city's water-supply. To the west of that again, not yet laid out at the time of Campbell's map, was Portobello Gardens, which included an ornamental pond, again fed from the canal. All of these features have now gone. Barge traffic on the canal ceased in 1959; the closure of Portobello Harbour was announced in 1960, and it was filled in soon afterward.[63] Associated with the harbour was a canal hotel, and this building survives as Portobello House, rising prominently above the canal lock and La Touche Bridge.

The circular line of the Grand Canal opened to the Liffey with great pomp and ceremony in 1796, after the completion of the substantial Grand Canal Docks at Ringsend, for which see below. The canal suffered greatly from competition from the railways but managed to remain open until the 1950s. In the 1970s it was planned to close it, backfill it, run a sewer down the line and build a road on top. The public outcry was sufficient to save the canal, which now remains as a public amenity and is once again navigable.

The construction of the Grand Canal brought a significant change in both the topography and the development of the area. As the canal needed to run along level ground, punctuated by locks to change its level, it was necessary to construct em-

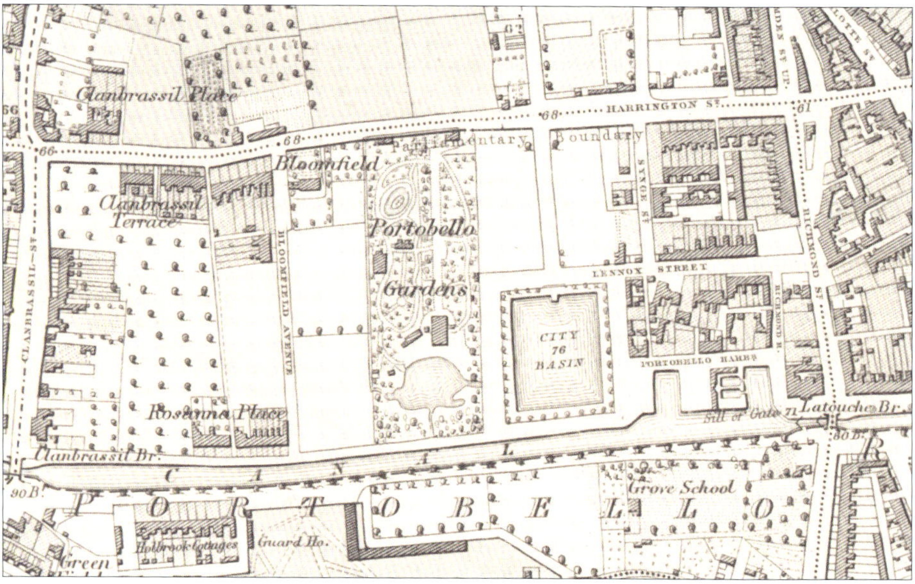

Pl. 42—The reservoir at Portobello, labelled 'City Basin', as seen on the Ordnance Survey map of 1843 on the site now occupied by Martin Street and Warren Street. The canal harbour at Portobello may also be seen, and the Portobello Gardens, now the site of Victoria Street.

bankments in places. At various points of approach to the canal it is evident that the roads rise up before they reach the rise for the bridge; this is noticeable at Charlemont Street, for instance, and at the steps that lead down from Grand Parade to Dartmouth Square. The change in levels is more evident on the southern side of the canal along the stretch from Portobello to Grand Canal Street.

The changes in the development of the area were brought about by the barrier to movement created by the canal, with some roads, such as Leeson Street, being diverted onto a new alignment at the canal crossing, the road having previously run along Sussex Road. Northumberland Street had been laid out in the late eighteenth century to connect Charlemont Street with Sussex Road, though the few buildings that had been erected along its length were at either end. The new canal cut through this route, most of which was abandoned; at the western end all that remains is a slight change in the angle of Charlemont Place, while at the eastern end a short stretch of Northumberland Street survives as the link between Leeson Street Upper and Sussex Road. The influence on the streets that were constructed after the route of the canal was fixed is more evident, as the area between the existing streets and houses and the canal was gradually infilled. The extent to which the layout was influenced by the canal must not be overstated, however, as the canal itself was planned

Pl. 43—Fasces railings at Wilton Terrace. These railings ran alongside the canal between Baggot Street and Leeson Street. Many were removed for safety reasons when the cycle path was provided.

to run along the fringe of the built-up area, and the South Circular Road had been constructed some years before, thereby defining the route of Adelaide Road and Harcourt Road. The turn in Adelaide Road just before it reaches Leeson Street marks the point at which the South Circular Road had to be diverted and was cut off from the next section on its eastbound route, which ran down Mespil Road and Haddington Road to Beggar's Bush.

One feature of Wilton Terrace was the set of railings that stretched from Leeson Street Bridge almost to Baggot Street, consisting of fasces acting as posts with supporting chains running from one post to the next. These were of cast concrete, with cast-iron spearhead finials. The railings were unique to this stretch of the canal, appearing only along Wilton Terrace and not on the Mespil Road side nor elsewhere along the canal. It is rarely easy to determine the date of a feature such as this, though examination of the available evidence suggests that these railings were erected in about 1840 but were subsequently altered. Most of them were removed during the construction of a cycle lane along the canal because of the potential danger posed by their spiked finials, while a group remains at the north-western side of Leeson Street Bridge.

Wilton Terrace was laid out for the Pembroke Estate in about 1830, with a triangular park focused on a cast-iron fountain fed by water from the canal; this fountain was still operative until recent years.

The route of a canal is designed to run along level ground as far as possible, but inevitably it involves changes in levels. It is essential that a canal has a water-supply at its highest point; canal water is not still but flows downstream all the time, and the operation of canal locks depends on a supply of water to flow into the lock to raise the level or out of it to lower the level. Within the south-east area there are two locks on the original line of the canal. The locks were numbered, commencing at the Grand Canal Harbour at James's Street, so the two locks within this area were the 1st Lock, adjacent to the Suir Road Bridge, and the 2nd Lock, by the Luas stop at Goldenbridge. The 1st Lock is a double lock, meaning that there are three pairs of lock gates and two lock chambers, so that boats have to ascend or descend twice. The 2nd Lock is a single lock with two pairs of gates and one lock chamber.

Along the circular line of the Grand Canal there are seven locks, all of them single locks. These are located at Portobello, Charlemont, Leeson Street Bridge, Wilton Place, Huband Bridge, Baggot Street Bridge and Maquay Bridge at Grand Canal Street. Associated with each of the locks are bollards, allowing the canal boats to tie up while waiting to go through a lock.

Grand Canal bridges

Each of the bridges on the Grand Canal that is within or partly within the south-east area is briefly described here, except for the bridge carrying the DART railway over the canal, which is considered in the section covering the railway.

SUIR ROAD BRIDGE

Suir Road Bridge is on the main line of the Grand Canal, close to the junction with the canal's circular route. It was built in 1938 and is of mass concrete, crossing the canal with a graceful shallow segmental arch.

ANN DEVLIN BRIDGE

Ann Devlin Bridge carries the Red Line Luas over the canal, to the north of which it runs along the former line of the canal to James's Street. The bridge is of white concrete, crossing the canal in a very shallow arch, its sides fluted and curving round into the soffit. It is named for Ann Devlin, Robert Emmet's housekeeper and protector, and it was opened in 2004.

GRIFFITH BRIDGE

Griffith Bridge is one of the original bridges on this part of the canal and bears the date 1791. It was named in honour of Richard Griffith, one of the directors of the canal company. It is faced with squared limestone, with granite copings, plat band and arch ring, and it crosses the canal and towpath with an elliptical arch.

HARBERTON BRIDGE

The original bridge was named in honour of Viscount Harberton, one of the directors of the canal company, though the Ordnance Survey maps call it Herberton Bridge. It was replaced in the 1930s by a concrete bridge.

CAMAC BRIDGE

Camac Bridge, also known as Dolphin's Barn Bridge, was built in 1791 and named in honour of Turner Camac, one of the directors of the canal company.[64] The original bridge has an elliptical arch with a granite arch ring, and it has been widened twice, both times with a mass concrete arch that matches the original geometry. The western face is a replica of the original face of the bridge, though in a modern interpretation.

PARNELL BRIDGE

Parnell Bridge carries Donore Avenue over the canal. It was built in 1791 and named in honour of John Parnell, a director of the company. The original bridge has an elliptical arch with a granite arch ring, and it was widened with a mass concrete arch, the original eastern face of the bridge being re-erected on the new bridge while the eastern arch ring is a mass concrete replica of the original.

EMMET BRIDGE

The original Clanbrassil Bridge at Harold's Cross was replaced in 1938 with a mass concrete bridge that replicates the elliptical geometry of the original, to which is added concrete balustrades. The new bridge was named in honour of Robert Emmet, who was captured at Harold's Cross after his attempted rebellion.

LA TOUCHE BRIDGE

The original La Touche Bridge, commonly known as Portobello Bridge, was built in 1791 and crosses the canal with a shallow segmental arch. It was named in honour of banker William D. La Touche, one of the directors of the canal company. It was widened on both sides with cast-iron balustrades by Ross, Stephens & Walpole of Dublin in the late 1920s,[65] and was refurbished by Dublin City Council in 2004.

CHARLEMONT BRIDGE

The original Charlemont Bridge was replaced with a mass concrete bridge in the late 1930s.[66]

SIMON PERRY BRIDGE

The Luas bridge over the Grand Canal was opened in 2004 and named in the following year in honour of Professor Simon H. Perry, Professor of Engineering at Trinity College Dublin. The bridge crosses the canal, Grand Parade and Charlemont Place with three spans of steel beams supported on concrete piers and with cantilevered staircases.

EUSTACE BRIDGE

Eustace Bridge, commonly known as Leeson Street Bridge, is faced with granite ashlar and crosses the canal with a shallow segmental arch. It was built in 1791 and named in honour of Colonel Charles Eustace, one of the directors of the canal company.

MACARTNEY BRIDGE

Macartney Bridge, or Baggot Street Bridge, crosses the canal and towpath with an elliptical arch. The bridge and its parapets are faced with granite ashlar. This is one of the original canal bridges, built in 1791 and named in honour of John Macartney, one of the most active of the canal company's directors at the time.[67]

HUBAND BRIDGE

Huband Bridge is one of the most picturesque bridges on the Dublin section of the canal and is frequently the subject of artworks and photographs. It was built in 1791 and named for Joseph Huband, who paid for the ornamentation of the bridge, which is more elaborate than other bridges on the canal.[68] The bridge crosses the canal with a shallow segmental arch. It is faced with granite ashlar and has cast-iron balusters.

MCKENNY BRIDGE

The original McKenny Bridge crosses the canal at Lower Mount Street with a shallow segmental arch. It has been widened on both sides by concrete beam bridges, though these have parapets of granite ashlar. The bridge was originally named Conyngham Bridge and was renamed in about 1810 in honour of Thomas McKenny, who joined the board of the canal company at that time and became one of the major figures in running the company.[69]

MAQUAY BRIDGE

Maquay Bridge on Grand Canal Street was named in honour of George Maquay, a director of the canal company.[70] It has since been replaced with a concrete beam bridge.

MCMAHON BRIDGE

The original bridge carrying Pearse Street–Ringsend Road over the Grand Canal Dock was a double drawbridge, with tall piers carrying a counterbalance structure to assist its opening. That bridge lasted until 1856, when the Sandymount Committee for the Removal of the Old Drawbridge informed its subscribers that it had entered into a contract with Frederick Barrington of the Ringsend Iron Works for the replacement of the bridge.[71] The new swivel bridge was completed in 1857 and named Victoria Bridge.

In 1898 the Dublin United Tramways Company proposed a number of new tram routes in and around the city, including the extension of the route on Pearse Street across Victoria Bridge, though the Grand Canal Company was opposed to the route unless the bridge was rebuilt. Reconstruction was carried out in 1900, when a new, more robust swivel bridge was built, consisting of three bowed iron plate girders flanking and separating two narrow roadways. The mechanism for opening it was a hand-operated windlass.[72] As traffic on the bridge increased, there came calls to re-

Pl. 44—The original double drawbridge on the road crossing Grand Canal Dock and separating the two sections of the dock, as seen in a view taken in the 1840s. This was the first of five bridges at this location and was replaced in 1856.

Pl. 45—Swivel bridge at Grand Canal Dock, built in 1900 and replaced in 1960. The Alliance & Consumers Gas Company gasworks is in the background.

place it, but a disagreement over the responsibility for maintenance and replacement between Dublin Corporation, the Grand Canal Company and CIÉ led to arbitration, followed by court action that ended in the Supreme Court.[73] The condition of the bridge was so poor at that stage that a speed limit of five miles per hour was introduced for heavy vehicles, though it was more than a decade before reconstruction was planned and the new bridge was not completed until 1963.[74]

The new bridge was named McMahon Bridge in honour of the chief of staff of the National Army in 1922 and it lasted until 2007, when it was replaced by the present bridge, which is the first fixed bridge at this location.[75]

GRAND CANAL DOCK

While the circular route of the canal was under construction, the works were inspected by the engineer, William Jessop, in 1790; amongst his suggestions was that floating docks and graving docks would be needed at the point where the canal met the Liffey. It is worth noting that there were no floating docks in Dublin port at that time, though the original Custom House dock was built in 1792–7, contemporaneously with the Grand Canal Dock. The canal company took up the suggestion and in 1791 it successfully sought a grant from parliament for the project. Work commenced under the direction of William Chapman and was completed in 1796, and the docks were opened in April of that year. The opening ceremony was con-

Pl. 46—The opening of Grand Canal Dock in 1796, as depicted in a painting by William Ashford. Contemporary reports claimed that 150,000 people attended the official opening ceremony.

ducted by the lord lieutenant, the Earl of Camden, and the first vessel to enter the dock was the viceregal yacht *Dorset*.[76]

In its original form the Grand Canal Dock was L-shaped, with a northern section running more or less east–west and measuring a little over 500m by 115m, and a southern section at right angles measuring about 600m by 100m. The canal entered in the centre of the southern end of the dock and the exit to the Liffey is at the eastern end of the northern arm. The quay walls were constructed with calp limestone blocks.

Connection to the Liffey was via three locks. Camden Lock is the widest of the three, measuring about 12m in width and located at the eastern side of the entrance. Buckingham Lock, in the centre, is about 8m wide, while Westmoreland Lock is about 5m wide and is a double lock. This system would minimise the amount of water lost to the Liffey when a boat passed through the locks, as a small boat exiting to the Liffey, such as a canal barge, would not result in the loss of the same quantity of water as a large boat. The locks were constructed of granite ashlar, this being finer stonework than would have been possible with the quality of calp used in the rest of the dock.

It will be recalled that the entire area covered by the Grand Canal Dock is on land that was reclaimed from the estuary as a result of Sir John Rogerson's construction of the walls along the southern side of the Liffey and the western side of the Dodder in the early eighteenth century. The construction of the dock required that this fill be removed and deposited elsewhere. The simplest solution was to deposit it on the ground surrounding the dock, thereby raising the ground level and resulting not only in the disposal of the fill but also in reducing the depth needed for the excavation. This may be seen in the rise in Pearse Street as it approaches the dock. It is seen also in the spot heights marked on the Ordnance Survey's 1:2,500 map of 1907, where the level of the quay at Grand Canal Quay is given as 24ft above sea level, while 150m away, at the junction with Macken Street, the level is down to 16ft. A lesser drop is seen along Forbes Street, where Sir John Rogerson's Quay is 4ft lower than the canal quay at the other end of the street. While there are slight variations in the level of Rogerson's reclaimed land, it is clear that the quays at the Grand Canal Dock are at a higher level than the surroundings.

Recent works at the Grand Canal Dock have resulted in the resurfacing of much of the quaysides and the loss of original features such as mooring posts. The new granite kerbs have small steel bollards bolted to them, though some earlier bollards survive at the three locks.

In addition to the need for a floating dock, William Jessop had pointed to the need for graving docks in Dublin, and the Grand Canal Company decided to provide this facility. As part of the project designed by William Chapman, three graving docks were built at the eastern end of the northern arm of the dock. As with the entrance locks, these docks were of different sizes to accommodate different craft. The smallest, at the north, measures approximately 34m by 15m at the top, the middle one is about 52m by 17m, and the southern one about 80m by 15m. As the docks were stepped, the dimensions at the bottom are significantly smaller. These dry docks were unusual in that they didn't require pumps. To fill them, sluices were opened at the canal dock end and water flowed in by gravity to the same level as the water in the dock; to empty them, sluices at the opposite end were opened and the water flowed by gravity into the Dodder.[77]

In 1850 a proposal was put to the Grand Canal Company for a lease of the Grand Canal Dock and its graving docks for the purpose of shipbuilding. As the company had struggled to keep the dock on a sound financial footing, this proposal was accepted and the Dublin Dockyard Company took over the medium-sized and large graving docks, remaining in occupation until the expiration of the lease in 1881.[78] A subsequent lease to the Ringsend Dockyard Company in 1915 was followed by a lease of the large dry dock to Heiton's as a coal-yard. The other two dry docks were filled in by the Gas Company. At present the two northern graving docks are open.

The Grand Canal Dock was an ambitious enterprise that never fulfilled the expectations of the canal company. The development of docks on the northern side of the Liffey provided competition for its use, the advent of paddle-steamers with their wide paddle-boxes precluded its use by that type of craft and the advent of the railways hit the revenues of the canals in general. Today the Grand Canal Dock has received a new lease of life with pleasure craft, while its environs have been largely redeveloped with new uses.

RAILWAYS AND THEIR BRIDGES

Introduction

The concept of railways is an old one; the early examples were boards placed on the ground to assist moving wagons over rough ground, such as in mines and quarries. Iron was first used for this purpose in the 1760s, though in the form of plates rather than rails, these being broad and flat.

In the early nineteenth century a number of railways were built in Britain and Germany; these were either used for a single purpose, as in a mine, or were open for public use. Those that could be used by the public were similar to canals in that users of the facility paid a toll to the company that owned the railway. Examples of railways for a single purpose in Ireland were those built to carry the stone to build Howth Harbour in 1810 and Dún Laoghaire Harbour in 1816–17. Perhaps the best-known railway for public use was the Stockton & Darlington Railway, built in northern England in 1825, as this was the first one on which steam locomotives were used, though horses also used it, and it was open for public use.

The first railway in the form that we understand railways today was the Liverpool & Manchester Railway, which opened between those cities in 1830. This line was built for steam haulage only, and the trains were owned and run by the railway company rather than by general carriers.

Dublin & Kingstown Railway

As early as 1825 a scheme was presented to parliament for the construction of a railway between Dublin and Dún Laoghaire, then called Kingstown. Although that failed to get support, a subsequent petition succeeded, and the necessary act of parliament was passed in September 1831.[79]

The design was prepared by Alexander Nimmo, though following his untimely death in 1832 the company engaged Charles Vignoles, an engineer from Wexford. Tenders were invited for the construction and the contract was awarded to Carlow-born contractor William Dargan. Work commenced in April 1833 and the first stone was laid in the retaining wall at Westland Row on the 24th of that month.[80]

It is all too easy to take the DART line between Pearse Station and Old Dunleary for granted, but it represented a significant engineering feat in its day. The city terminus at Westland Row is high above the street, with the railway accessed at first-floor level in the station. Beyond the station building the line was raised on a viaduct comprised of two substantial retaining walls approximately 18m apart and rising above the level of the track. These walls continue all the way to Lansdowne Road, gradually descending to ground level and narrowing to approximately 12m beyond Barrow Street. Not only was the construction of these walls a major task but also the space between them had to be filled to track level, requiring a substantial volume of fill.

Within the section between Westland Row and Lansdowne Road the railway crossed nine roads, and each required a bridge. Owing to the alignment of the nine roads and the curvature of the railway viaduct, the majority of these bridges crossed the street at an angle, requiring more complex engineering than with a bridge that crosses at right angles. Bridges crossing at an angle are known as skew bridges; where the angle is significant, they require an elaborate form of construction known as rifle

Pl. 47—The original Westland Row railway station, built in the 1830s and depicted in this view in the 1840s. This façade was removed in the 1890s to facilitate the construction of the Loop Line railway.

vaulting, where the stonework beneath the arch twists like a corkscrew. The most notable example on this stretch of railway is the bridge at Grand Canal Quay. Here the construction is complicated not only by the angle between the railway and the road but also by the very low height of the bridge above the street. As noted above, the deposition of spoil from the construction of the Grand Canal Dock raised the ground level. The space is so tight that the track is almost resting on the masonry of the arch, and in order to ensure that the bridge was strong enough to carry the weight of trains the stonework beneath the arch was constructed with beautifully cut granite blocks laid in a helical arrangement.

The bridge at Grand Canal Quay is actually three-arched, and originally the arches crossed Grand Canal Quay, the quayside and part of the Grand Canal Dock. All three have similar low, broad segmental arches, though the central arch is now within a former maltings and is part of a restaurant, with the arch concealed beneath decorative cladding.

Beyond the triple bridge at Grand Canal Quay the railway had to cross the Grand Canal Dock, and this necessitated building a causeway across the dock. There is a pedestrian archway through this causeway at the quay on the eastern side of the dock.

At the time of the construction of this railway the Wide Streets Commissioners acted as a form of planning authority in the city. Proposals for new streets had to be approved by the commissioners and they also had a say in the design of bridges that crossed streets. To ensure pedestrian safety, the commissioners required that the bridges at Sandwith Street, Erne Street and Macken Street should have pedestrian arches, separate to the arch carrying wheeled traffic.

Another bridge built within the city area carried the railway over the River Dodder at Lansdowne Road. This bridge was of stone with three elliptical arches but

Pl. 48—A train approaching Sydney Parade Station in the mid-twentieth century. The station closed in 1960 and reopened in 1972. The signal cabin was closed and the gates replaced in 1985 owing to the re-signalling programme as part of the DART upgrade, though the signal cabin survives.

was destroyed in a flood shortly before the railway was to open and had to be replaced on a temporary measure by a wooden bridge. The present steel bridge was erected in 1934 and remodelled in the 1980s.[81]

Beyond Lansdowne Road the railway ran over level ground, on an embankment slightly above the level of the adjacent fields, until it reached Merrion Gates. From there to Blackrock the railway was constructed on an embankment across the open sea and was protected from the waves by a wall.

This substantial project was more or less completed in an incredible fifteen months. The line could not be opened at that time, however, as it was necessary for the fill between the retaining walls to settle sufficiently to carry the weight of locomotives, and the first trip along its length, carrying the directors in July 1834, was hauled by a horse. The line finally opened to traffic in December 1834, twenty months after work had commenced.

At the time when the line opened to traffic, Westland Row was the only station on the line within the city. In the following year the company opened stations at Serpentine Avenue, Sandymount, Sydney Parade and Merrion, though the station at Serpentine Avenue closed almost immediately.[82] The other stations were closed at various times and then reopened, and Merrion Station closed permanently in 1934. In 1870 a station was opened at Lansdowne Road, and it has remained open ever since.

To the south of the railway viaduct at Barrow Street, the Dublin & Kingstown Railway Company built a works for the manufacture of railway carriages and locomotives. For a short period there had been a small works adjacent to the line near Serpentine Avenue for the maintenance of the locomotives, but that site was not suitable for expansion to the size required in the long term. The land was acquired in 1836 and the works opened in the following year to build railway coaches, with the construction of locomotives commencing shortly afterward.[83]

The station at Westland Row was widened in 1877 to facilitate sidings for the increased traffic on the railway, and in the 1890s the original frontage of the station was replaced to allow for the construction of the Loop Line railway.[84]

Harcourt Street Railway

Following the opening of the railway from Dublin to Dún Laoghaire in 1834, three further lines opened in the 1840s, connecting to Cork, Galway and Drogheda, with their termini at Kingsbridge (now Heuston), Broadstone and Amiens Street (now Connolly) stations respectively. With the north, west and south catered for, it was expected that the rest of the country would be served from branches leading off those lines. The Wicklow and Wexford area would be covered by an extension to the Dublin & Kingstown Railway, which had already extended to the present Dún Laoghaire station in 1837 and to Dalkey in 1844.

A new route entered the picture, however. From a complex network of negotiations and company formations starting in 1844 two companies emerged: the Waterford, Wexford, Wicklow & Dublin Railway and the Dublin, Dundrum & Enniskerry Railway. Their proposals eventually resulted in the construction of a railway between Harcourt Road in Dublin and Bray, opening in 1854, when it joined with the Dublin & Kingstown Railway just north of Bray. This new railway became the Dublin & Wicklow Railway, and its terminus was transferred to Harcourt Street when that sta-

Pl. 49—Bridge on Harcourt Street railway at Harcourt Road. This railway line closed in 1958, and the bridge was dismantled not long after.

tion was completed in 1859. The line was later extended to Wicklow, Wexford and Waterford.[85]

The line was elevated at both the original terminus at Harcourt Road and the eventual one at Harcourt Street, necessitating the construction of bridges over each of the streets that were crossed and over the Grand Canal, with viaducts between the bridges. As with the Dublin & Kingstown Railway, the viaducts were constructed with two substantial retaining walls of rubble limestone, between which was fill to bring the track bed up to the required level. To the south of Ranelagh the track gradually descended to ground level, which it reached to the south of Dunville Avenue.

Unlike the Dublin & Kingstown Railway, the bridges within the city on the Harcourt Street line were mainly of iron rather than masonry arches. This was partly because arched bridges take up more space than beam bridges, which would have restricted the width beneath the bridge at locations such as Harcourt Road, while also restricting the height. In the twenty years since the construction of the earlier railway the technology of building iron railway bridges had improved, facilitating the use of beam bridges rather than arches.

The Harcourt Street Railway had six iron bridges within the present city area, crossing Harcourt Road, the Grand Canal, Dartmouth Road, Northbrook Road, Ranelagh and Charleston Road, and there was also a subway at Dunville Avenue. Each of these was a lattice girder bridge of wrought iron, supported on abutments of limestone on either side. These bridges were replaced in the 1890s by plate girder bridges.[86]

In addition to the iron bridges there were two masonry arch bridges within the city, one providing the entrance to the convent at Ranelagh and the other, the well-known Nine Arches Bridge, spanning the deep valley of the Dodder at Milltown. This bridge, built with local limestone, is elegant in proportion and is almost identical to the Cherrywood Viaduct further along the same railway, though the latter is built with granite. Both bridges have holes in the masonry in some of the piers: these were drilled in the early 1940s by the Defence Forces as a precaution in case the bridges needed to be blown up to obstruct an invading army during the Second World War.

Later in the nineteenth century, as the suburbs expanded, a footbridge was provided across the railway at Cowper Road. Footbridges were not normally provided at railway stations in the early days and passengers crossed over the track, just as they do now on the Luas. From the 1880s iron footbridges began to be provided and one such example was constructed at Milltown Station.

When the Harcourt Street Railway first opened, the only station within the present Dublin city area was at Harcourt Road. This was closed in favour of Harcourt Street Station in 1859 and in the following year a station was opened at Milltown. A further station was opened in 1896, named Rathmines and Ranelagh Station, and this was located immediately to the south of Dunville Avenue, where the Beechwood Luas stop is today.[87]

The Harcourt Street railway closed in December 1958, at which time passenger numbers outside peak times were extremely low. Soon after the closure, the rails were lifted and the iron bridge decks removed, leaving only the abutments. After some initial proposals to convert the line into a road, the route was mothballed and was protected in successive development plans to facilitate future reopening. This finally occurred in 2004 when the Luas Green Line opened, utilising the former Harcourt Street line to the south of the Grand Canal.

Harcourt Street Station survives today, though the extensive sidings, locomotive sheds, goods stores, signal-box, water tank and so forth have gone. The principal survivors to the south of the canal are the viaduct between its two retaining walls, the abutments of the bridges at Dartmouth Road, Northbrook Road, Ranelagh and Charleston Road, and the two masonry arch bridges. Nothing survives of the original Milltown Station or Rathmines and Ranelagh Station, while the track bed has been regraded to lower it in the vicinity of Dunville Avenue, which is now crossed at grade.

Loop Line railway

The Loop Line is the popular name for the City of Dublin Junction Railway. With five stations built around the city serving five locations around the country, passengers and goods were obliged to find their own way between one station and another when passing through the city to another destination. Moves to provide access between these stations and also to Dublin port began in the mid-nineteenth century, but it was not until the 1880s that any initiative was put forward to link the railway at Westland Row with the lines to the north of the Liffey. As there were already links between Kingsbridge (Heuston) Station, Broadstone Station and Amiens Street (Connolly) Station, a link between Westland Row and Amiens Street would give access to those other lines and to the port. This was particularly important, as the Dublin & Kingstown Railway connected to the mail-boats at Kingstown (Dún Laoghaire), which was the principal route for the mails between Ireland and Britain.

An act of parliament was passed in 1884 to authorise the construction of the link railway, passing above the streets in a broad curve and crossing the Liffey adjacent to Butt Bridge. The construction of the bridge was divided into three contracts, one for the Liffey bridge and the others for the two sections north and south of the river. Work was completed on the link between Westland Row and Amiens Street late in 1890, though legal problems arose with the other link, which was to connect to the Midland Great Western Railway line at Newcomen Bridge, and it did not open for another year.[88]

While the Loop Line is elevated, it was not built on solid viaducts like those of the Dublin & Kingstown Railway and the Harcourt Street Railway. Instead, the line runs on a series of brick arches with a mix of red brick, yellow brick, calp limestone rubble and a small amount of dressed limestone. This allows for the continuation of use of the land beneath the arches.

Five bridges were built on the Loop Line to the south of the Liffey, crossing West-

Pl. 50—Arches on the Loop Line railway at Tara Street Station. The majority of the Loop Line is elevated on arches of brick and stone, while the bridges are of iron.

land Row, Pearse Street, Shaw Street, Townsend Street and Luke Street/Poolbeg Street. The widest span is the bridge over Pearse Street and that is a lattice girder bridge, while the others are plate girder bridges. The bridge at Westland Row has decorative fretted cast-iron plates, as it was a requirement of the act of parliament that it be decorated. The act also laid down strict conditions for the nature of the bridge across the Liffey, requiring that it be decorative and that it did not obstruct river navigation. The bridge crosses the river in three spans of lattice girders, supported in the river by cast-iron caissons filled with concrete and at the southern end by a brick pier.[89]

There is just one station on the Loop Line, at Tara Street. The station platforms are part-cantilevered from the viaduct and part-supported on plate girders.

TRAMS AND TRAM DEPOTS

The origin of the use of rails on which to run vehicles is described in the section on railways. Suffice it to say that rails provide a smoother ride than normal road surfaces.

Pl. 51—Horse-drawn trams in College Green in the days before electrification. One single-deck tram is seen and three double-deckers. The single-decker is a Drumcondra tram, while the one in the distance is arriving from Donnybrook.

In the nineteenth century this was a significant factor, as road surfaces were not as smooth as they are today, with the result that a horse could pull a significantly heavier load along rails than it could on a normal road surface.

Omnibuses were first introduced onto the streets of Dublin in 1848, running on regular routes and carrying many more passengers than the private hire vehicles.[90] While these have left no trace on the Dublin landscape, the vehicles themselves were easily adapted to serve as the city's first trams.

While the vehicles would be relatively straightforward, the provision of rails was less so, as this involved carrying out significant works to the public streets. Acts of parliament had been passed in 1860 and 1861 to allow for the construction of tramways in Ireland, though this was aimed more at rural trams as alternatives to railways. There was already a tramway in existence at Fintona in County Tyrone, though this was not on the public road. The Tramways (Ireland) Act of 1867 provided powers more amenable to urban trams and attempts were made to establish trams in the city. These were not successful, mainly because the rail that was used included a section standing above the street surface at great inconvenience to road-users.[91] It is possible that a section of this tramway was laid down on Aston Quay on an experimental basis but was quickly removed.[92]

In 1871 the Dublin Tramways Company was incorporated, and it obtained an act of parliament in that year to enable it to construct a number of tram routes, the first being between College Green and Rathgar. Over the next two years the company opened five more routes and extended the original route to run between O'Connell Street and Terenure. The areas served by this company were predominantly in wealthy suburbs and the fares, aimed at the more opulent passenger, reflected this. Uncomfortable with this approach, one of the directors of the company, William Barrington, resigned in 1873 and established the North Dublin Street Tramways Company. This served the areas being developed at the time to the north of the Liffey and with one line running to Inchicore. A third company, the Dublin Central Tramways Company, was founded in 1878 and by the following year had opened four routes running to the south suburbs, including one travelling as far as Rathfarnham. In 1881 the three companies decided to pool their resources, and the result was their amalgamation into the Dublin United Tramways Company.[93]

It is remarkable to consider what had been achieved in such a short time. The three companies had opened routes with a total of 32 route miles within eight years, though in reality this was closer to six years, as the first two companies had their routes completed by 1876 and the third only started in 1878. The work involved getting the necessary permissions from the local authorities (Dublin Corporation and six separate townships) and constructing the lines—laying the track, usually double track, along with points, and laying the stone setts around the track.

These were not the only tram companies in Dublin. The Dublin Southern Districts Tramways Company was formed in 1878, with an act of parliament authorising it to construct a line between Kingstown and Dalkey and another between Haddington Road and Blackrock. This company had its base at Shelbourne Road[94] and in 1896 it amalgamated with the Dublin United Tramways Company as a new company, the Dublin United Tramways Company (1896) Ltd, though they technically remained as separate legal entities until 1905.[95]

For the longer distances horse traction was impractical, but steam offered an alternative. In 1888 the Dublin & Blessington Steam Tramway began a service between Terenure and Blessington, requiring a horse-drawn connection to the city, as Dublin Corporation would not let steam trams travel within the city. Terenure was selected as the terminus, as it was already the terminus for the horse trams connecting to the city.[96]

Other tramways experimented with steam traction as a means of overcoming the limitations of speed and distance of the horse-drawn trams. Gradient had also been

Pl. 52—The Dublin & Blessington Steam Tram, which consisted of a double-ended steam locomotive pulling a double-decker tram.

a problem, and the tram companies kept horses, known as trace horses, at the steeper hills, such as the hump-backed canal bridges, to supplement the hauling power of the usual single horse. In July 1877 a steam engine was brought on a trial run from Donnybrook tram depot to Morehampton Road and back with great success, and four years later a similar trial, also successful, took place between Ballsbridge and Blackrock.[97] In both cases the reports said that the ride was smooth and that the engine emitted no smoke or steam. The report of the Donnybrook trial stated that the tram was brought to a halt from eight miles per hour within its own length. Nevertheless, as long as Dublin Corporation was unwilling to allow steam trams within the city their future was limited.

The world's first electric tramway opened at the Giant's Causeway in 1883, and another electric tramway opened between Bessbrook and Newry in 1885. The Dublin United Tramways Company opted at that time to convert to electric running once the technology improved, and they decided to go ahead in 1894.[98] They were not the first company to electrify, however. The Southern Districts Tramways Company had acquired the tramway between Blackrock and Kingstown, giving it control over the route between Haddington Road and Dalkey, and in 1892 the company commenced its conversion to electric traction. This involved the construction of a

Pl. 53—An exterior view of the tram power station at Shelbourne Road, Ballsbridge, viewed from across the Dodder. There was also a tram depot at the site, not all of the buildings being part of the power station.

Pl. 54—The steam engines and generators in the tram power station at Ballsbridge. The power station was short-lived, operating between 1896 and 1899; the site was later used as a tram depot and was subsequently occupied by Ballsbridge Motors.

generating station at Shelbourne Road and substations at Blackrock and Dalkey, the erection of poles and cabling along the route and re-laying of the track. The electrified line opened in 1896.[99]

The Southern District Tramway Company had the advantage that no part of its line ran within what were then the boundaries of the city and hence Dublin Corporation had no say in its electrification. The city had opposed electrification but once the Southern District Tramway Company was amalgamated with the Dublin United Tramways Company (DUTC) the prospects for electrification within the city improved. Even so, its electrification programme began outside the city limits with a line between Lansdowne Road and Kenilworth Square, following which a generating station was built at Clontarf and electric trams began running between Clontarf and the city boundary at Annesley Bridge in 1897. The city authorities were eventually won over, and in March 1898 the first electric tram arrived at Nelson's Pillar from Clontarf.[100] This was achieved through an agreement signed in May 1897 between the tramways company and Dublin Corporation, following which the DUTC erected a power station at Ringsend Road, backing onto Grand Canal Dock, thereby facilitating the supply of water for the boilers and the delivery of coal. The new power

Pl. 55—One of the final tram types to run in Dublin, known as the Luxury car, is seen at Terenure Road East; the cables are slung on armatures extending from poles on the northern side of the road and braced with an elaborate series of wrought-iron swirls.

station was commissioned in August 1899 and once it was fully operational the power stations at Shelbourne Road and Clontarf were decommissioned.[101] The power station on Ringsend Road served the tramways until 1931, when the company decided to avail of the cheaper electricity available from the Shannon Scheme. A transformer station was built alongside the old power station to step down the power from the grid and the power station was decommissioned.[102]

The advent of buses and the private motor car brought about the end of Dublin's tramway system, though it is argued that its demise was not inevitable. The trams ran at eight miles per hour in the middle of the road within the city, increasing up to fifteen miles per hour in the less urban areas. The routes were inflexible, whereas bus routes could be varied to cater for new development. The system began to be run down towards closure in the 1930s but gained a reprieve owing to the Second World War and its attendant fuel shortages. One by one the routes were closed down, until the last tram ran from Dublin to Blackrock in July 1949, leaving a gap of more than 50 years before the Luas trams were introduced onto the city streets.

The former tram power station in Ringsend Road survived until the early 1970s after a period as a bus garage and then a motor assembly plant, while the transformer station was taken over by the Bovril company. The two tall chimneys, 68m high, that served the power station were demolished in the 1930s.[103]

Of all the entries in the Dublin City Industrial Heritage Record the most common is 'Tramway', reflecting the large number of streets along which the tramlines ran. The DCIHR entries for each street indicate when trams began to use that track and when the line closed, but almost nothing remains visible of this extensive network and the best information on its extent may be seen on the large-scale Ordnance Survey maps of the early twentieth century. Much of the track has been lifted but some may still remain beneath the modern road surfaces. In recent years wear of the surface has revealed rails still existing beneath the road at Leeson Street, Ringsend Road and Gilford Road.

Along some routes cables providing power for the trams were supported by wires strung between the electric lighting poles, though for the most part the tram companies erected their own poles. These supported the power cables in two ways: either with wires running across the street between the poles, with the power cables slung beneath them, or with armatures projecting over the street from the poles, sometimes with the pole in the middle of the street with armatures running in both directions. Those in the centre of the street could represent traffic hazards and were sometimes replaced with poles at the side, though Dublin Corporation occasionally insisted on centrally placed poles. Most of the poles disappeared from the streets soon after the closure of the tram routes, but notable survivals are to be found along Chapelizod Road between Islandbridge and Chapelizod; these supported the cables for the Dublin & Lucan Electric Railway, which replaced the steam tram after its closure in 1900. Some tram poles survive as lampposts.[104]

Tram depots

The most visible remnants of Dublin's earlier tram system are the surviving tram depots. Originally most of the depots housed the horse-drawn trams and had stabling for the horses. Later electric trams were taller and larger; they needed bigger sheds but didn't need stabling, and the depots were modified accordingly. Many of the depots were retained in use as bus depots after the disappearance of the trams and survive in this way today. Others were converted for other uses, while some have disappeared. There were more than twenty tram depots in the wider Dublin area, some of which were small outliers at the end of the line. Of these, fifteen were in the area now included in Dublin City, nine of which were in the south-east area.[105]

BALLSBRIDGE

The Ballsbridge depot was built in 1878 on Shelbourne Road for the Dublin Southern District Tramways Company to service its route between Haddington Road and Blackrock. It was absorbed into the DUTC and in 1910 had accommodation for 40

Pl. 56—Interior of the tram depot at Ballsbridge, showing the kind of work carried out. Two tram bodies have been raised off their bogies to facilitate maintenance. An inspection pit is seen in the foreground.

tram cars. After the closure of the tram routes the depot was demolished and it is now the site of a motor showroom, with only the wall of one of the sheds surviving.

CLONSKEAGH

Built in 1879 for the Dublin Central Tramways Company to facilitate its service between College Green and Clonskeagh, this depot accommodated 23 cars in 1910. It survives on Clonskeagh Road, now in commercial use.

DARTRY

A new tram service commenced in 1905, branching off the Rathmines to Terenure line to finish at Dartry Road. A new depot was opened at Dartry at this time, with more substantial sheds than the earlier depots in view of the increase in size of the trams. It survives in commercial use.

DONNYBROOK

The tram service to Donnybrook commenced in 1873, with its depot beside a disused quarry at the junction of Stillorgan Road with Beaver Row. This depot housed 24 cars in 1910. The original sheds were demolished in the 1950s when the new Donnybrook Garage was built.

RATHFARNHAM ROAD

The Dublin Central Tramways Company built a depot at Rathfarnham Road in Terenure which had space for seven cars in 1910, though the depot was closed by then. It was subsequently demolished and houses at Cormac Terrace built on the site.

RINGSEND

The Dublin United Tramways Company built its own power station at Ringsend Road in the 1890s and subsequently used the adjacent land as a maintenance yard and depot. The power station became redundant following the implementation of the Shannon Scheme in 1930, though the tram depot continued in use. In 1941 the trams were relocated to Donnybrook and the depot became a bus depot, remaining in that use today.

SANDYMOUNT

The tram to Sandymount was one of the first to open in 1872 with horse-drawn trams. The height of the trams was limited by the low bridge at Bath Avenue and this route remained horse-drawn as a result. The sheds survive at Gilford Road, with traces of the track leading in from the street. The buildings are now in commercial use.

Templeogue Road

The Dublin & Blessington Steam Tramway had a depot at Terenure, on the eastern side of Templeogue Road, adjacent to the Dublin Central Tramways depot on Rathfarnham Road. The depot was demolished and a cinema built on the site in 1938.

Terenure

The depot at Terenure Road East was built for the Dublin Tramways Company in 1872 to house its horse-drawn service and it was electrified in 1899, necessitating the addition of some larger buildings. In 1910 the depot accommodated 48 tram cars. The site and the surviving buildings are now in commercial use.

Buses and coaches

The era of public transport in Dublin began in the late eighteenth century, particularly with mail coaches, which were introduced in the 1780s and carried both mails and passengers. In this context, public transport is taken to include conveyances that are shared by people not known to each other, as opposed to private vehicles such as the hire of horse-drawn cars or cabs as ancestors of taxis. By the end of the eighteenth century there were numerous mail coach routes operating from Dublin; those for destinations in the southern half of the country were based in Dawson Street, each of these carrying four passengers inside and one or two on top. There were also nine stagecoach routes, which were similar but didn't carry mails; they, with the northern mail coaches, were based in the north of the city.[106] By 1812 the number of coaches had increased, as had the number of termini. Two were based in Dawson Street, at No. 12 and at the Hibernian Hotel in No. 40, while a third was based in Harry Street; other coaches commenced in the north city.[107] By 1818 there were more than twenty coach routes operating from Dublin and the termini included Nos 12, 16 and 46 Dawson Street and 14 Harry Street. All of these ran on trunk routes, however, and the nearest to a local route was the coach to Blackrock and Dunleary, which ran seven times a day in each direction from 133 Baggot Street Lower.[108]

A new type of vehicle, the caravan, began to operate from Dublin at the beginning of the nineteenth century. This was a more basic vehicle, having only two wheels, and it was covered rather than fully enclosed; it had springs and could carry up to eight passengers.[109] These were also on trunk routes rather than local.

Pl. 57—An omnibus taking on passengers in College Street before departing for Kingstown (now Dún Laoghaire) in about 1870. This conveyance could carry about twenty passengers and was hauled by two horses.

The concept of public transport within cities began in Nantes in 1823, when a system of vehicles began operating in the city under the title 'omnibus' (meaning 'for all' in Latin). A similar system was proposed for Dublin in 1834, but the city's jarveys objected, claiming that they were not permitted under the city's carriage laws. It was not until 1848 that the Police Act of that year legitimised the concept and horse buses began to run in the city; by 1850 an omnibus route known as 'Favourite' operated between Terenure, Rathmines, Rathgar and the city.[110] By the late 1860s several routes ran in the city, including several omnibuses a day to Clonskeagh, every ten minutes to Rathmines from Nelson's Pillar and a route to the Royal Hotel in Terenure.[111]

Trams eventually replaced omnibuses in the city, but only for 30 years or so. Soon after the start of the new century no new tram track was being laid, and buses started to operate in the city to cover areas not served by trams. Buses were run by private operators, and some began to run in competition with trams, as a result of which the Dublin United Tramways Company (DUTC) began investing in its own fleet of buses. In the 1930s private operators were put out of business by legislation and the DUTC had a monopoly. With the closure of the tram network between 1938 and

1949 buses became the principal form of public transport within the city.[112]

With the disappearance of the trams many of the tram depots were closed, some being given over to use by buses, and a new bus station was opened on Ringsend Road in 1941 adjacent to the tram power station. At Donnybrook a bus garage was erected in 1937 at the rear of the tram depot and opening onto Beaver Row. In the late 1940s it was decided to close the tram depot and demolish it and to redevelop the site as a bus garage. The new garage was designed by Michael Scott and Jim Brennan, with the structural elements designed by Ove Arup. It was completed in 1951.[113]

Airports

In the 1930s the idea of establishing an airport for Dublin gained traction and a number of potential sites were put forward. Dublin Corporation favoured a former RAF airfield at Collinstown to the north of the city, but a paper published in 1935 argued that the most favourable site would be on a section of land to be reclaimed from the sea at Merrion.[114] The Port of Dublin Authority agreed with this proposal

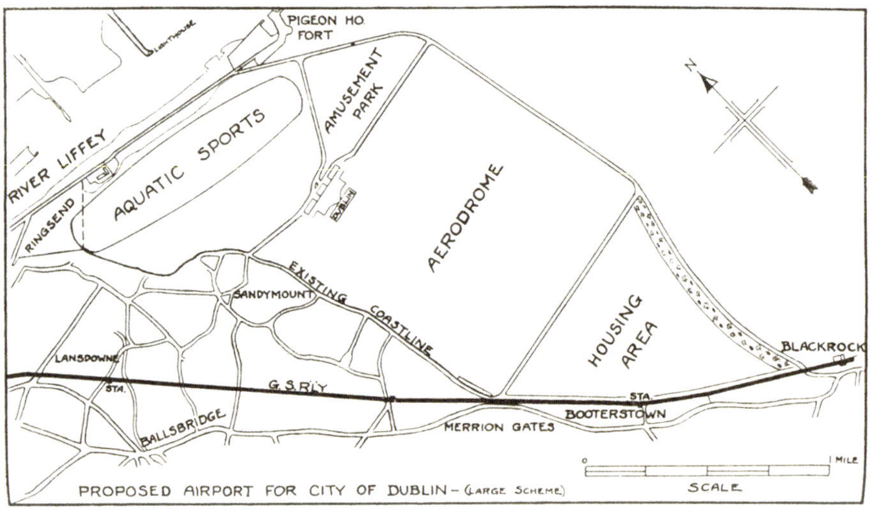

Pl. 58—Site put forward in 1935 for an airport on land to be reclaimed at Merrion. The northern element with the sports ground and park went ahead in the 1960s, while the rest of the proposal was never implemented.

and resolved to seek government funding to implement the plan.[115] As is now clear, however, this proposal did not progress and the site at Collinstown was to become the present Dublin Airport.

STREET FURNITURE

There is a wealth of street furniture in Dublin city, most of which dates from the 21st century or the latter part of the twentieth. This includes street signs, lampposts, telecom boxes, traffic lights and their control boxes, statues and memorials. A significant amount of historic street furniture survives in the Dublin south-east area, the most obvious elements being the historic street lamps, which are found both in the city centre and in the Victorian suburbs. Less obvious are a small number of surviving milestones and some boundary stones that are similar in scale to the milestones. Other elements include some cast-iron cabinets designed to contain electrical equipment and some sewer vent pipes. Some types of street furniture that are of heritage interest are discussed elsewhere in this volume, including street lights, tram cable poles and letter-boxes. Four categories remain and are discussed below: milestones, boundary markers, street name-plates and coal-hole covers.

MILESTONES

Milestones along roadsides are generally of stone, as the name implies, and may have a cast-iron plate bearing the information, though most do not. In some parts of Ireland the milestones are of cast iron, but not in the Dublin area. In the Irish context, most milestones date from the mid-eighteenth century to the mid-nineteenth and they are usually found along trunk roads. On any particular road the milestones tend to be of the same design, differing only in the distances recorded.

Most milestones have disappeared, some relatively recently, and it is not always easy to determine whether there was one at any particular location. In the Dublin area, pre-Ordnance Survey maps such as those of John Rocque (1760), Taylor and Skinner (1783), John Taylor (1816) and William Duncan (1821) record distances along roads. Comparison of these maps, however, suggests that these were distances from the city and not necessarily the locations of milestones, as each map tends to mark a distance in a slightly different location. When the Ordnance Survey produced its maps at the scale of 1:2,500 these marked the locations of milestones—though not reliably, as some stones that are still extant were not marked.

Prior to 1826 the standard length in Ireland was the Irish mile, which measured roughly 2,000m, and in that year the statute mile became the official measure, being approximately 1,600m. After that date new milestones were placed at the shorter distance, though no attempt was made to systematically replace the earlier series. The earliest stones recorded the distance from Dublin Castle, while in the later eighteenth century the distance was from the GPO in College Green. From 1818 the distance was measured from the GPO in O'Connell Street.

Few milestones survive in the south-east area of Dublin, and it is not certain how many were erected within the area originally. One prismatic granite milestone is placed against the front of a shop on Pembroke Road, near the junction with Shelbourne Road, and this records the distances to Dublin and Kingstown, indicating that it post-dates the change of name to Kingstown. As it uses statute miles, it would be no earlier than 1826 and may have been erected in that year, when a mail service was opened between Kingstown and Liverpool, or in 1832, when the Holyhead mail-boats transferred to Kingstown. Another milestone in that series was located on Merrion Road just to the east of the junction with Ailesbury Road, though that disappeared in about 1974.[116]

Pl. 59—Milestone at Walkinstown. This was on the road to Blessington and records a distance to that location of fifteen statute miles.

A milestone on the northern side of Terenure Road East is a rectangular granite stone set into the front boundary wall of a house, with a cast-iron plate recording the distance of three miles from the GPO. This distance is in statute miles, so it was placed there no earlier than 1826. On Orwell Road, close to the junction with Zion Road, is another milestone set into a boundary wall. This one has a triangular top and a flat front face into which is cut the text 'From G.P.O. 3' in similar style to the cast-iron plaque in Terenure Road East. This stone has been partly buried in the concrete footway and presumably the word 'miles' is below the surface. The next milestone on from

Terenure Road East is to be found a few metres outside the Dublin city boundary on Templeogue Road and bears a cast-iron plaque. This stone is on the road to Blessington and Baltinglass, and another stone back towards the city just north of the Walkinstown roundabout records the distances of two miles to Dublin and fifteen miles to Blessington, these being statute miles. This is an older style of milestone, of granite and triangular in plan with angled faces, though the use of statute miles suggests a date after 1826. Other milestones that still existed a century ago have now disappeared, such as one on Crumlin Road near the junction with Cooley Road.

BOUNDARY MARKERS

Three types of boundary markers are to be found in the south-east area, each consisting of a cut-granite stone with a metal plaque attached, though the plaque is sometimes missing. The first group are markers that define the boundaries of wards; these are flat-fronted with a rounded top and have, or had, a rectangular cast-iron plaque bearing the name of the ward. Examples are seen along the quays, such as two against the quay wall opposite Fishamble Street.

Pl. 60—Rathmines township boundary marker on the Dodder at Rathgar. These boundary markers are found at various locations around the margins of the township, and they include the date of the foundation of the township in 1847.

The second are the markers that define the boundaries of Rathmines township. These are also flat-fronted with a rounded top and the cast-iron plaque is circular, bearing the legend 'Township of Rathmines' around the perimeter and the date 1847 in the centre. An example may be seen in Morehampton Road, close to its junction with Leeson Street Upper.

The third group are to be found in the medieval city and are of smooth-surfaced granite with a rounded top and with the upper part of the front face sloping back. The circular bronze plaque carries a diagram without words. Dublin city declared 1988 to be its millennium year and these stones were erected as part of that commemoration. The diagram represents the medieval city walls, towers and gates, and the markers were placed at points where the line of the walls crossed streets. Each plaque has a stud to indicate its location on the diagram. Examples may be found at either side of Essex Gate and in various other streets.

STREET NAME-PLATES

Streets were named from an early period, the name sometimes purely stating where the road led to; sometimes they were named for the developer or for a significant

Pl. 61—Street name-plates at Ram Alley and Skinner Row as seen in James Malton's view of the Tholsel, taken in the 1790s at the site that is now the corner of Christchurch Place and Nicholas Street.

Pl. 62—Street name-plate for Warrington Place. The relevance of the date is uncertain, as Warrington Place was laid out in 1791 and was known by that name at least as early as 1792.

feature such as a church, cathedral or monastery. Some names were recorded in documents, such as St Kevin's Street in the thirteenth century, while Exchange Street was known as Scarlett Lane at that time.[117] In 1775 legislation was passed requiring that streets in the city be clearly labelled with the street name, while each building was given a number.[118] The resultant street name-plates may be seen in some of the engravings by James Malton, executed in the early 1790s, examples being Ram Alley and Skinner Row in his view of the Tholsel, and Cross Poddle in his view of St Patrick's Cathedral.

Enforcement of this requirement was a function of the Commissioners for Paving, Cleansing and Lighting of the Streets of Dublin, otherwise known as the Paving Commissioners. Another State-sponsored body at that time were the Commissioners for Making Wide and Convenient Streets in the City of Dublin, commonly known as the Wide Streets Commissioners. A number of name-plaques survive in the city giving the names of streets that were laid out by the commissioners in the late eighteenth and early nineteenth centuries, or which were approved by them and laid out or improved by others.

A puzzling feature of some of these name-plaques is that the dates do not accord with the year in which the street was laid out or when it was named. Examples are

Hatch Street, which is given the date 1810 on the name-plaque although the street was laid out in 1791. The name-plaques for Lower Mount Street and Warrington Place both carry the date 1814, though the former was named in a deed in 1780 and the latter was laid out in 1791 and appears under that name in a deed dated 1792. Molesworth Place has the date 1831 on its name-plaque, though the street or lane is seen on Rocque's map of 1756; in this case it may be when the name was given, as it is labelled on Scalé's map of 1773 as Stable Lane and may have gone under that description until 1831.[119]

COAL-HOLE COVERS

At the time when the houses in Georgian Dublin were being built, coal was the most common fuel used to heat the houses and cook the food. Even the simplest Georgian town house, with three storeys over basement, would have at least eight hearths, and there might be more in a return. Many of the Georgian town houses in Dublin were

Pl. 63—Typical eighteenth-century coal-hole cover, set in a granite flagstone and with a drainage channel cut around the coal-hole and leading water away towards the gutter.

set back slightly from the street behind a small basement area, while beyond that area there were cellars beneath the street. The easiest way to deliver coal to the cellars was through a circular hole in the pavement, which was covered over with a cast-iron lid or cover at all times, except during deliveries. These are generally referred to as coal-hole covers, though James Joyce called them cellarflaps in *Ulysses*.[120]

Dublin's coal-hole covers vary in style. Many of the early examples have decorative patterns cast into the upper surface and a variety of these may be seen in the streets. Others have very simple patterns, such as concentric circles, while some of the later ones have the name of the foundry cast into the surface. The latter type would generally be replacements, as the foundry would not have existed at the time the house was built. Each cover was set into the centre of a granite paving stone, usually a smaller stone than the average, and in most cases a circular channel was cut around the hole, with a channel running from it towards the gutter; these channels were designed to prevent rainwater from running down into the coal-cellar.

Many coal-hole covers have disappeared; often the footway has been repaved and the coal-holes covered over. In other instances, such as on the northern side of Merrion Square, the footway has been repaved but many of the original coal-hole covers have been retained, set in their granite paving stones with the hole cut out of the centre.

8.
Communication

Post

The postal service in Ireland had its tentative beginnings in the sixteenth century and was put on a more permanent footing in the seventeenth. The earliest reference to a post office in Dublin relates to one in Cork Hill, probably at Cork House, which was on a site at the rear of City Hall.[1] In the 1680s a post office was established in Fishamble Street and in about 1709 it moved to Sycamore Alley, now Sycamore Street.[2] It subsequently moved to Dame Street, where it is marked in a yard on the northern side of that street on Rocque's map of 1756. The yard is shown, though not named, on Brooking's map of 1728.

The General Post Office moved from Dame Street to College Green in 1771, and in 1784 it became independent of the Post Office in London.[3] As the quantity of mail being handled increased in subsequent years, adjacent properties in Suffolk Street were acquired and the Post Office expanded, moving to purpose-built premises in O'Connell Street in 1818. The College Green site was subsequently developed as a shopping arcade and hotel, then as a bank, retaining its connection through from College Green to Suffolk Street until recent years.

The General Post Office handled general post, which was carried between towns and not locally. Various attempts were made to establish local postal services, and a system was finally established in 1765.[4] Under this system, letters left into the Post Office would be delivered within the city at the price of one penny. The system did not prove popular and in 1773 it was revised, now based on a number of receiving houses around the city in shops, coffee-houses, booksellers and so forth.[5] Of the eighteen receiving houses appointed, eight were within the south-east area, at grocery shops in Bride Street, Cuffe Street, Clare Street, George's Quay and Ship Street, at a milliner's shop in South Anne Street, a bookseller's in Castle Street and a coffee-house in the Custom House.[6] These receiving houses were not listed as such in the Dublin directories for some years after this, suggesting that there may have been no change; however, when listing began in the 1798 directory only twelve were listed in the city, including four in the south-east area at Royal Exchange, Essex Street,

Pl. 64—The General Post Office in College Green. It gradually expanded by taking on adjacent properties, extending from College Green to Suffolk Street. Subsequent occupiers of the site had access from both sides until the present century.

South Great George's Street and Merrion Street, with a further two outside the then city boundary at Milltown and Ringsend.[7] By 1804 the number had fallen to ten, with only three in the south-east area at Essex Street, Merrion Street and Ringsend.[8]

The number of receiving houses continued to fall and by 1809 there were no receiving houses in the city, as the owners of the premises were not paid for the work involved and opted out of the system.[9] In 1810 the system was revised and by 1812 there were no less than 54 receiving houses within the city and another 30 in the environs.[10] This included nineteen within the city in the south-east area and another ten in the environs. In 1831 the Irish Post Office was subsumed into the London Post Office, following which significant changes took place, including a reduction

Pl. 65—Rathmines post office, built in 1932–4 to the designs of William H.H. Cooke, incorporated a telephone exchange and a delivery office.

in the number of receiving houses. By 1837 there were 37 remaining in the city, including seventeen in the south-east area, while the adoption of the uniform penny post throughout the United Kingdom in 1840 brought an end to the original penny post system.[11]

In parallel with the penny post a twopenny post was established, catering for areas at a greater distance from the city, and this included about 140 locations, a number of which were in the south-east area at such places as Bath Avenue, Charlemont Street, Crumlin, Donnybrook, Harold's Cross, Kimmage, Milltown, Rathmines and Sandymount.[12] This system was also brought to an end with the introduction of the new postal system in 1840.

The general post remained separate to the penny and twopenny post until 1840, though the three services were run from the same headquarters and under the same control. The movement of general post via mail coaches, with a number of termini around the city, continued through this period and is described in more detail in the section on buses and coaches. In addition, the mails to and from other countries were brought through Pigeon House Harbour from the late eighteenth century until 1818, and this is discussed under the heading of Pigeon House Harbour.

In the late 1830s proposals for the reform of the Post Office were put forward by Rowland Hill and Robert Wallace, and this led to the introduction, amongst other things, of a penny post system whereby any letter could be sent any distance within the United Kingdom for a penny, not just within a city.[13]

The concept of sub-post offices in local areas originated in the receiving offices for the penny post and remained in place after the reforms of 1840; they retained the name 'receiving office' and were operated by subcontractors who were generally grocers, coffee-houses and the like.[14] In 1847 there were 38 such offices within the city and fourteen in the environs, of which seventeen and seven respectively were within the south-east area. Ten years later the number within the city was similar, at 39, while those in the environs had increased to 59, those in the south-eastern area amounting to eighteen and nine respectively.[15] In the twentieth century the Ordnance Survey noted the locations of these sub-post offices on its medium- and large-scale maps, sometimes written in full, as seen at Donnybrook on the 1907 edition, while at other times in the abbreviation 'P.O.', as noted at Harold's Cross on the same edition.

The Post Office built some of its own post offices, these being the larger offices, originally serving as the district sorting office initially and sometimes with a telephone exchange. These included Rathmines Road Lower in 1883, Ballsbridge post office on Shelbourne Road in 1891, Rathmines Road Upper, with a telephone exchange, in 1932–4 and Andrew Street in 1947.[16] A sorting office was provided in a converted distillery in Pearse Street in 1925.[17]

Letter-boxes

The most prominent features of the postal system have been the letter-boxes, and in particular the pillar letter-boxes. Letter-boxes were first introduced into the Channel Islands, England and Ireland by the novelist Anthony Trollope, who worked as a surveyor for the Post Office. The first letter-boxes erected in Dublin arrived in 1857, and among the first eight were pillar-boxes in Palace Street, St Stephen's Green and Clanbrassil Street; some premises, such as the Commercial Buildings in Dame Street, had their own letter-boxes.[18]

After ten years the number of pillar-boxes in the city had increased to 50, of which 24 were in the south-east area, while in the suburbs there were 25 pillar and wall letter-boxes, of which thirteen were in the south-east area.[19] The Ordnance Survey's maps that were produced in the 1860s show the locations of these letter-boxes, and it is notable that almost none of those sites have letter-boxes at them today; a small number of pillar-boxes of later date occupy the same sites, as at Palace Street, Sandymount Road, the eastern end of Leeson Street Upper and Palmerston Park at the junction with Dartry Road.

The first pillar-boxes were large rectangular boxes, and the only one known to survive is now in the National Museum of Ireland, Collins Barracks. These were superseded by a cylindrical box with a hexagonal cap, though not many of these were erected in Ireland and they are now represented by a single example at Cork railway station. The third design was a hexagonal pillar of a type known as a Penfold box, after its designer. These were erected from 1866, though none survive in Dublin other than one in the GPO Museum.[20]

The cylindrical pillar-box was introduced in 1879 and it has remained in the streets ever since, with subtle modifications such as the size of the aperture, the design of the cap and, most obviously, the cipher. The royal cipher, VR for Victoria Regina, had appeared on the Penfold boxes but was missing from the early cylindrical pillar-boxes between 1879 and 1887, as a result of which they have become known as anonymous boxes.[21] From 1888 to 1901 the pillar-boxes carried the VR cipher; this was replaced with EviiR when Edward VII came to the throne in 1901 and GR when George VI succeeded him in 1911. Examples of anonymous boxes may be seen in several places in the south-east area, including Mount Street Upper at the junction with Fitzwilliam Street, Belgrave Square East and Ely Place. Another that was on Harold's Cross Road near Mount Tallant Terrace has been moved from this location. A variation on the anonymous box has a raised circle on the top of the cap; these are not common, and the function of this feature is not known. An example may be seen on Clanbrassil Street, just south of the junction with South Circular Road.

Quite a number of pillar-boxes bearing the VR cipher survive, and there are examples on Fitzwilliam Square South and East, Pembroke Street Lower, Palmerston Road and Zion Road. An example on the eastern side of St Stephen's Green has its aperture closed up and is out of use. Pillar-boxes bearing the EviiR cipher are also plentiful, and examples are on Burgh Quay, Leeson Street Lower and Kenilworth Square North. The GR cipher may be seen on pillar-boxes in Burlington Road and Harcourt Street.

Wall letter-boxes were initially used outside the city, where volumes of mail would be lower, and they were introduced soon after pillar letter-boxes. As noted above, seven wall letter-boxes were provided in the city initially, three of which were in the south-east area, at Westland Row, Harcourt Road and the Commercial Buildings in Dame Street. This had increased to 24 in the suburbs by 1868. Probably the oldest letter-box in use in the city is a wall box dating from 1861 at the junction of Strand Road and John's Road in Sandymount.[22] Unlike most of the letter-boxes that were made in England or Scotland, the Sandymount wall box was made in Cork and carries the maker's name, H. & C. Smith, Cork. Other wall boxes with the VR cipher

Pl. 66—Wall letter-box at the junction of Strand Road and St John's Road, Sandymount. This is one of the earliest letter-boxes in the city, dating from1861.

Pl. 67—Pillar letter-box in Dame Street, at the junction with Palace Street. This was the first letter-box in the state to be painted green following independence in 1922.

include one at Herbert Road in Ballsbridge, while another on Merrion Road near Merrion Gates has gone.

Independence brought change in many forms, and letter-boxes were one of the most prominent symbols of the new state. The first letter-boxes were green throughout the United Kingdom, and it was not until 1874 that red was adopted as the colour—not for political reasons but to make it easier for the public to see them.[23] In February 1922 the postmaster general made the decision that all letter-boxes should be painted emerald green, with 'An Post' in Gaelic characters in yellow over the doors.[24] The first letter-box to be painted green was the one at the corner of Dame Street and Palace Street, which was painted in time for St Patrick's Day in 1922.[25]

Deciding on the logo to be cast onto the doors of letter-boxes in place of the cipher took longer than the choice of colour and painted logo. In 1928 the decision was finally made that the letters 'SÉ', representing 'Saorstát Éireann', should be used, surrounded by an interlaced circle topped by a harp. This symbol was only used on wall letter-boxes and not on pillar-boxes. With the change of name of the state to Éire, the SÉ cipher was replaced in 1939 with the simple P⁊T logo, which remained in place until the establishment of An Post in 1984.[26] An example of a wall letter-box with the P⁊T logo may be seen on Crumlin Road outside Loreto College. The style of pillar-box has also varied over time, and examples of all these variations may be seen throughout the area.

TELEGRAPH

Systems for sending messages by electric telegraph were devised independently by Samuel Morse and William Cooke in the 1830s, but it was not until the mid-1840s that the commercial potential of the systems was reflected in the establishment of companies to exploit the ideas and invest in the necessary infrastructure. The concept then took off rapidly. With the development of underwater cables, it became necessary to have a single compatible system worldwide and Morse's system was adopted.[27] The first undersea cable between Ireland and Britain was laid in 1852, and the Martello tower at Howth was selected as the receiving station, being at the nearest point to Holyhead. The first cable was unsuccessful and it was not until the following year that the system became truly operational.[28] The most obvious route for the telegraph wires was alongside railway lines; when the Telegraph Act was passed in 1868, it gave responsibility for the telegraph to the Post Office but recognised that the railways would act as agents.[29] The Grand Canal Company also had an agreement for the running of telegraph lines, while outside the city the lines also ran along public roads. The Central Telegraph Office of the Post Office was located at No. 29 College Green, at the corner of Church Lane, while there were other staff based at railway stations.[30] The premises in College Green continued in use as a telegraph office until the early 1950s, though a significant telegraph office was also housed in the GPO in O'Connell Street.[31]

In its initial form, telegraphs involved the staff in the receiving office listening to the dots and dashes transmitted over the wires in Morse code and writing down the message. As the system developed, new technology allowed the messages to be printed out onto paper tape, and a message received in this way was pasted onto a telegram form and delivered by a telegram messenger to the recipient's address. A service allied to telegraph was telex, which was like a combination of telegram and telephone; subscribers had a printer in their office and messages were sent directly. This system was introduced into Ireland in 1956 with 24 subscribers, increasing to 733 subscribers nationwide by 1969.[32]

With the advent of telephones—and, almost a century later, the internet and mobile phones—the use of telegrams declined significantly, and no trace of this extensive communications network survives in the south-east area.

Telephone

The telephone was invented by Alexander Graham Bell in 1876; a rival system was devised by Thomas Edison in 1879, though the companies established by Bell and Edison amalgamated as the United Telephone Company. In January 1878, less than two years after Bell's invention, a telephone line was installed to connect Maguire's Hardware in Dawson Street with the Gresham Hotel.[33] The Post Office claimed that the telephone was a form of telegraph as defined in the 1869 Telegraph Act and thus should come under its control, though in practice the provision of a telephone system was licensed to the United Telephone Company, which opened the first telephone exchange in Ireland in the Commercial Buildings in Dame Street in 1880. The system was transferred to the Telephone Company of Ireland in 1882 and to the National Telephone Company in 1893.[34]

The National Telephone Company constructed the first purpose-built telephone exchange in Crown Alley in Temple Bar to the designs of Thomas Manly Deane, and this opened in 1900. By this time the company was only handling local services, with trunk lines managed by the Post Office, and in 1912 the entire telephone system was taken over by the Post Office.

Subsequent telephone exchanges were established in other locations, including the post office in Rathmines, which was built in 1932–4 to the designs of Howard Cooke, and Andrew Street, built in 1947 to the designs of Sydney Maskell and John Fox.[35] In 1925 the introduction of automatic telephone exchanges commenced with the fitting up of an exchange in Ship Street with this new technology, while another in Terenure was built in 1937, the year that Rathmines was also automated.[36] In 1969 a new telephone exchange building was built in Dame Court, with 35 new trunk switchboards; as radio and microwaves began to be used for telephone transmission, this building became an important hub for this purpose, with a substantial antenna mast on the roof.[37]

One of the most prominent features of the telephone system in Dublin streets in the twentieth century was the telephone kiosk. The first one in Dublin was installed in College Green in May 1925.[38] This was soon followed by others, including in

Pl. 68—Telephone box of the original design, introduced in the mid-1920s. This example was located in Dawson Street for a period to commemorate the introduction of telephone boxes.

Dawson Street, where a telephone kiosk of the original design was located for a period to commemorate the former existence of these facilities. Telephone kiosks have virtually disappeared from our streets today.

Mobile phones became a possibility in the 1970s, and the Irish telephone service, Telecom Éireann, launched its mobile phone system, Eircell, in 1985, based on car phones with a high cost.[39] The system evolved rapidly and in 1993 the first GSM service was launched, based on the European standard Global Systems for Mobile Communications, and voicemail and text messaging followed in 1995. Other companies entered the market in 1996, when Esat Digifone was launched, followed in 2001 by Meteor.[40] In its early days the mobile phone network was based on a series of telecommunications masts up to 30m high, or located at a height on buildings, each mast forming a cell within which a mobile device would connect to the mast. This allowed for connection of mobile devices over a distance. As the number of devices increased, however, the distances to be covered decreased significantly and the number of antennae grew substantially. Paradoxically, the greater the number of antennae the less visible they are, as they are now mainly mounted directly on buildings rather than raised above them, and they are frequently painted to blend in with the building on which they are mounted. A discerning eye can spot them mounted on buildings throughout the city.

RADIO AND TELEVISION

Ireland's role in the development of radio is little known but nonetheless extremely important. Guglielmo Marconi, the Irish-Italian pioneer of radio, failed to interest the Italian government in his invention and travelled to England, where he met with promotors, many of them Irish, resulting in the formation of the Wireless Telegraph & Signals Company, with substantial Irish investment. After failing to get British government support despite extensive successful demonstrations of radio, Marconi moved to Ireland in 1898 and here he carried out significant further developments of the technology, backed by Irish entrepreneurs.[41]

Dublin's first national radio broadcasts were based in other parts of the city from the inception of 2RN, later rebranded as Radio Éireann. In 1960 the Broadcasting Act authorised the establishment of a television service to be known as Telefís Éireann. The site selected as the base for the television studios was a house in large grounds, known as Montrose, at Donnybrook, and this was acquired from UCD as part of a land swap for property owned by the Department of Posts and Telegraphs on the opposite side of the road. Scott Tallon Walker were selected as architects and the service commenced broadcasting on New Year's Eve 1961. The radio and television services were subsequently amalgamated under the name Radio Telefís Éireann, and the radio studios were gradually relocated to Montrose in the early 1970s; a second radio station, 2FM, was launched in 1973.[42]

9.
Utilities

This section looks at water-supply, drainage, gas and electricity. It also includes street lighting as a separate category to gas and electricity and this is a significant topic in view of the high visibility of historic lamp standards in the streetscape. Other utilities such as telephone and telegraph have been described above in the section on communications.

STREET LIGHTING

Street lighting was virtually non-existent in Dublin until the seventeenth century, except where a private citizen chose to display a lamp on his premises to light the area to the front. In 1616 the city authorities passed a law requiring every fifth house throughout the city and suburbs to display a lantern and candlelight from six o'clock until nine o'clock every dark night during the winter.[1]

In 1697 a merchant by the name of Michael Cole proposed to the city authorities that he should be given the task of providing lighting in the city. His intention was to provide lamps on both sides of the streets, eight houses apart, while in lanes and alleys there would be a light every six houses. He would provide the tallow for the lights and the staff needed to keep them lit. He further proposed to extend lighting-up time to midnight rather than nine o'clock. His fee would be to collect three shillings from each house in a street each year and two shillings from each house in a lane or alley, and he calculated that this was a cheaper price than the householders would pay to provide lighting themselves. This proposal would require an act of parliament, and he undertook to pay the cost. The city assembly granted his request and the act of parliament was duly passed.[2]

That act expired twenty years later and the Dublin parliament renewed it, permitting the city authorities to make similar arrangements as they had with Michael Cole for lighting the streets between 1 September and 31 March, though lighting-up time was now to run from an hour after sunset to two o'clock in the morning, except on moonlit nights.[3]

During the late eighteenth century whale oil came into use for illumination and

Pl. 69—Detail of James Malton's view of Grafton Street, showing street lamps fixed to the fronts of buildings and extending out over the footway.

street lights were erected to accommodate oil-lamps. Like the candles, these were lit and maintained by lamplighters. From 1759 the responsibility for providing public lighting in the streets of Dublin city lay with the parishes. These were the parishes of the Church of Ireland, which, being the established church at that time, also had civic functions.

In 1784 the Paving Board was given the responsibility for lighting Dublin's streets; they hired contractors to maintain the lights and ensure that they were lit during the hours of darkness. At this time there were almost 10,000 lamps in the city.[4]

In addition to this, some houses in the city provided lamps near the front door, some in lanterns set into the fanlight, others with wrought-iron brackets set onto the railings at the front of the house. Examples of lamps in fanlights may be seen at Nos 41, 69 and 76 Merrion Square, 29 Fitzwilliam Square and 4 Pembroke Street Upper, and a lamp bracket is to be found on the railings at the front of 38 Merrion Square. At 42 St Stephen's Green a wrought-iron arch spanning the approach to the front door would have carried a light, while a few doors up at No. 51 granite piers carry cast-iron lamp poles with white glass lamp globes. The wrought-iron work of two lamps also survives on the gate piers at the entrance to Mountpleasant Square.

James Malton's views of Dublin, executed between 1792 and around 1798, are an excellent source of information regarding the lamps in the city at this time.[5] The views exhibit a very high standard of draughtsmanship and a minute level of detail and appear to record the scenes with a high degree of accuracy. Seven of them depict street scenes within the south-east area of the city, another has a view from the river that is too distant to make out the lighting and five are on private land without street scenes. Amongst the seven street scenes, the only lamp standards on the public road are six located outside the entrances to the Parliament House in College Green, while there are another ten lamps distributed along the railings at the front of the parliament, and more are seen within the grounds of the building. In other views the lamps that occur the most frequently are those mounted on buildings or on railings at the front of buildings, implying that they were provided by the buildings' owners rather than by the Paving Board; these include at least fourteen along the railings at the front of Trinity College, eleven visible on the balustrade and railings at the Royal Exchange (now City Hall), and others at the entrances to Powerscourt Town House, the Provost's House and the Tholsel. The only lights that appear to be public street lighting are mounted at a high level on buildings and project over the pavement on brackets. These are seen at the entrance to Ram Alley from Skinner Row, at the corner of Nicholas Street and High Street, and at the corner of William Street South with Coppinger Row. Three very long brackets, possibly more than 2m in length, project from the front of the buildings in Grafton Street to the north of the corner with Suffolk Street. An additional view, of Capel Street, shows Essex Bridge, which is partly within the south-east area; eighteen lamps are shown on the balustrades of the bridge, with brackets projecting the lamps out over the pavement.

Malton's views of Dublin show that lamp standards were not the norm in the city at the end of the eighteenth century, implying that they may have become more usual with the introduction of gas lighting, probably owing to the need to connect them to gas mains beneath the street. Other artists showed similar gas lamps on brackets, such as the view of College Green by Brocas in 1828. Half a century after Malton, the Ordnance Survey's large-scale maps of the city show street lamps as very small circles. These are very close together to the front of the Bank of Ireland in College Green, almost appearing on the map as bollards, though mid-nineteenth-century photographs confirm that these were lamp standards. The maps show that lights were located at the kerb line and were often at street junctions, such as the junctions between Dame Street and Fownes Street, Temple Lane and Eustace Street. However, the maps also show lights at building frontages, suggesting that some bracketed lamps attached to buildings still remained, and these may be seen along the narrower streets such as Fownes Street, Temple Lane and Eustace Street.

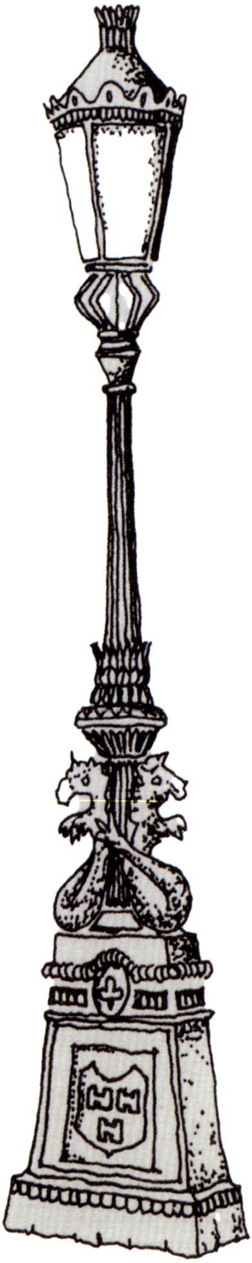

Pl. 70—Sketch by Derry O'Connell of a gas lamp adjacent to the statue of Henry Grattan in College Green. The lamp is now lit by electricity.

The Alliance and Consumers Gas Company contracted to supply gas lamps in Rathmines in 1847, and 152 lamps had been erected by 1852. To improve the supply, a 12in. gas main was laid from Portobello Bridge to Terenure in 1872.[6] Dublin city had 3,750 gas lamps in 1884, maintained on a daily basis by 23 full-time gaslighters.[7] By 1886 there were 5,940 public gas lamps in the city. The number of gas lamps continued to increase until 1903, when there were 7,001 lamps supplied by the Alliance and Dublin Consumers Gas Company in the city. Thereafter there was a steady fall, as electricity replaced gas for public illumination.[8] Gas lighting in Rathmines was replaced by electric lighting in 1900.[9]

Some gas lamp standards still survive, though converted to electricity. Perhaps the most prominent examples are the dolphin lamps around the base of the statue of Henry Grattan in College Green, which were erected in 1875 when the statue was installed.[10] Another set of dolphin lamps were erected on Grattan Bridge, which was completed and renamed in the previous year.[11]

With the introduction of electric lighting, many of the gas lamps were converted for electricity. As electric light was brighter and the lamps did not require the same maintenance, the lamps in the main streets were often set

Pl. 71—Sketches of electric lamp standards by Derry O'Connell. The standard on the left was a type used by Rathmines Urban District Council in the opening years of the twentieth century. The central example is a type used by Dublin Corporation in the 1890s, while the one on the right is a type produced by the corporation in the 1940s and 1950s.

higher to spread the light further, and this resulted in additional height being added to lamps. Some of the early electric lamp standards were also relatively short and were lengthened. Lamp standards could be moved, and comparison of photographs, even of relatively recent times, can show that the lamp standards have changed. Ontario Terrace, near the Grand Canal, is a short street with just three street lights, but these are of three different types. The one nearest to Mountpleasant Avenue Lower is possibly the oldest lamp standard still in use in Dublin, dating from the beginnings of the gas era in 1825. The second one along the street is a sugar-stick standard dating from about 1915, with a decorative base and a cast-iron creeper climbing up the pole. The third one, at the end of the street, is of a more common type produced by Dublin Corporation up to 1944 and probably dates from after 1930, when Ontario Terrace was subsumed into the city.[12]

The very tall and very ornate lamp standards on the principal streets of the city centre date from the period when electric lighting was first introduced. The first of these have a fluted base and a decorative swan-neck head and were erected from 1892. The second were the ones known as Scotch Standard, which had a fatter base bearing the Dublin Corporation arms and with a finial rising above the decorative swan-neck head. Both of these are still seen around the city and may be found in Harcourt Street, along with a few later replicas with narrower bases.[13]

In suburban areas the electric street lights were not so tall. These often had a fluted cast-iron base and still carried the projecting cross-bars on which ladders could be propped. Gas lights had these bars, to facilitate the lamplighter in lighting the lamps and trimming the wicks, but even in the electric age cross-bars were retained so that a ladder could be propped against the lamp standard for changing the bulb. Prior to 1930, when the southern townships became part of the city, some of the lamp standards carried the name of the local authority, while after that date they bore the three castles symbol of Dublin Corporation. Sometimes lamp standards were obtained from the adjacent local authority; the lamp standards in Ailesbury Gardens, Ballsbridge, carry the name 'Rathmines Urban District' and the date 1900, even though Ailesbury Gardens was in Pembroke Urban District and was not built until 1921. Dublin Corporation produced this type of lamp until 1944.[14]

WATER-SUPPLY

The original settlers who founded Dublin got their water from the rivers Liffey and Poddle, and there may have been wells in some parts of the city. An aqueduct was constructed from the Dodder at Firhouse to supplement the flow of the Poddle, pro-

Pl. 72—The Tongue, Mount Argus, which diverted water from the River Poddle into the city watercourse. It was designed so that one third of the water went into the left-hand channel to the city watercourse, while two thirds remained in the Poddle.

bably in the late twelfth century, and a branch watercourse was constructed from the Poddle at Mount Argus to a cistern near James's Street by the middle of the thirteenth century.[15] The triangular stonework that divides the waters at Mount Argus is known as the Tongue; the city watercourse then runs slightly to the west of due north to Dolphin's Barn, where it crosses beneath the Grand Canal on its way to the conduit. This system provided the only piped water system to the city for more than 500 years.

During the eighteenth century the expansion of the city and the enlargement of its population put a significant strain on the city's water-supply. The corporation's first move to address this problem was to enhance the existing system by providing new water storage, resulting in the construction of the city basin in 1721–2.[16]

The city continued to grow throughout the century and water-supply became a problem again. When the Grand Canal was constructed, the corporation agreed to pay the canal company for a supply of water for the city and this fed into the city basin. A further supply was negotiated and in 1806 a city basin was constructed on the northern side of the canal to the west of the Portobello Hotel. The canal water

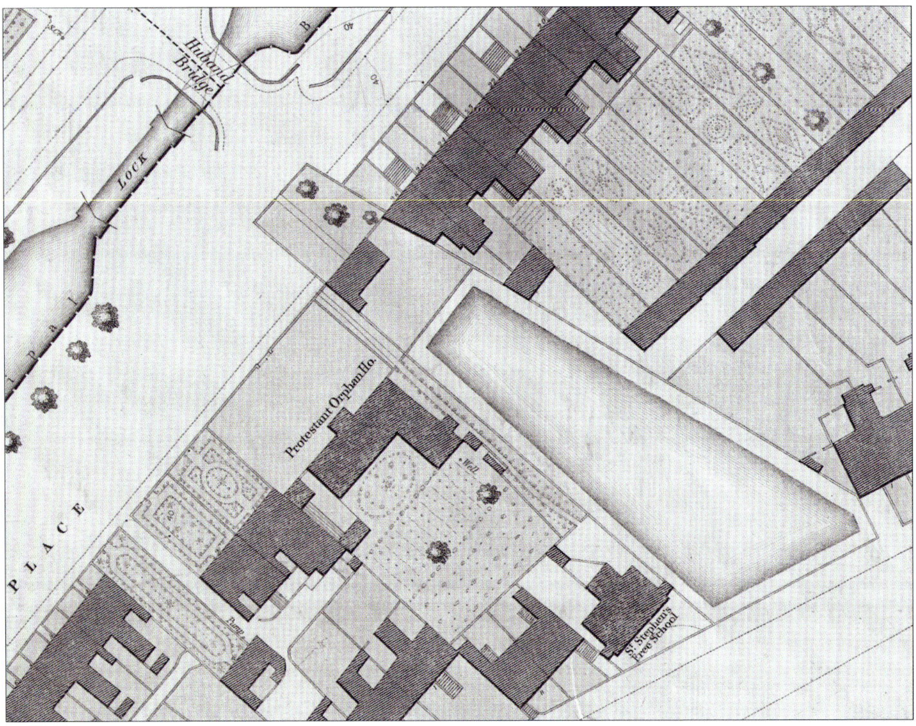

Pl. 73—Reservoir built by Aeneas Coffey in Haddington Road to supply his whiskey distillery. The reservoir used water from the nearby Grand Canal and subsequently supplied water to the Dublin & Kingstown Railway Company at Barrow Street.

was no longer needed after the introduction of the Vartry water-supply to the city; the Portobello Basin was made redundant in 1870 and was backfilled in 1883.[17]

A later supply from the canal was provided to Aeneas Coffey, who in 1833 developed a whiskey distillery in Barrow Street with a water-supply taken from the Grand Canal near Huband Bridge to a reservoir between Percy Place and Haddington Road. Coffey's distillery did not last long, though the reservoir served the successors on the distillery site following the construction of a railway works for the Dublin & Kingstown Railway later in the 1830s.[18]

Given that many houses and business premises did not have a water-supply, fountains were provided in various places around the city. These were not ornamental but drinking fountains, more akin to the cast-iron hydrants that were provided in various parts of the country in the early twentieth century and are still visible today. In 1899 the *Irish Builder* announced that drinking fountains would shortly be provided on Dublin's quays for the use of workmen and labourers.[19] The provision of fountains was provided for in legislation passed in 1783–4 and which gave the city's Paving Board the power to erect twenty fountains. This measure was successful and in 1786 the Paving Board was given further powers to provide 'such number of fountains or conduits for the supply of water, as they shall think necessary'.[20] The *Irish Builder* listed fifteen fountains erected in the south-east area, though it only included one in Merrion Square, while four are shown on the 1847 Ordnance Survey map, indicating that this was an underestimate.[21] Seven fountains were provided by Rathmines Town Council, which had also provided a pump on the western side of the street in the centre of Rathmines.[22]

There were some other fountains in the city, erected as one-off facilities. The earliest surviving example is the Rutland Fountain on the western side of Merrion Square. The Duke of Rutland was lord lieutenant between 1784 and 1787; he provided a fountain in Barrack Street, and it is believed that he had plans to provide another in Merrion Square, though this was prevented by his death in 1787. Instead, the fountain was erected in his memory on a grand scale to the designs of Francis Sandys and completed in 1791.[23] A figure of a river nymph reclining on an inverted urn was moved from Mary Street and fixed in the centre of the fountain, though this is no longer present.[24] Other fountains were provided in the nineteenth century, including the Crampton Memorial in College Street, erected in memory of Sir Philip Crampton to the designs of Joseph Kirk in 1862 and removed in 1959.[25] With the opening of Lord Edward Street in 1886, the eastern elevation of the former Newcomen's Bank was rebuilt and the opportunity was taken to provide a fountain, built into the wall. In 1880 Laura Grattan, widow of James Grattan, eldest son of Henry

Pl. 74—Rutland Fountain in Merrion Square, built to the designs of Francis Sandys in 1791 and named in memory of the late lord lieutenant, the Duke of Rutland, who had supplied drinking fountains in the city.

Grattan, erected a fountain on the northern side of St Stephen's Green and presented it to the city.[26] This consists of a central column with drinking fountains and two drinking troughs for horses and other animals. The fountain and its troughs were relocated further along the street during the construction works for the Luas. The Sheahan Memorial was erected in Hawkins Street in 1906 with a drinking fountain incorporated.[27] In addition to drinking fountains, some 22 ornamental fountains have been erected in the south-east area, some in the nineteenth century but the majority from the late twentieth century.[28]

The Ordnance Survey's large-scale map of Dublin city published in 1847 at the scale of 1:1,056 shows the routes of the water mains around the city and marks the locations of the drinking fountains. The map also shows the locations of wells within the grounds of various houses, indicated by the presence of pumps. The distribution is uneven; most of the houses on the southern side of Merrion Square are shown to have pumps in their stable yards, while there are few pumps at the rear of the houses on the other three sides of the square. The fountains and pumps were also shown on the large-scale Ordnance Survey maps of the 1860s and 1880s, providing an indica-

Pl. 75—Pipes carrying the Vartry water-supply into the city adjacent to Leeson Street Bridge. The pipes and the valves that sit on top of them carry the name of the engineer who designed the scheme, Parke Neville.

tion of which fountains had disappeared during the intervals between the maps.

Some of the eighteenth- and early nineteenth-century houses were built with cisterns to collect rainwater, and a few of these, built with sandstone or Portland stone slabs, survive in the basement areas to the front of the houses.

The big change in the water-supply came with the introduction of new systems in Rathmines township in 1863 and Dublin city in 1869. A proposal to obtain a water-supply from the Vartry River at Roundwood, Co. Wicklow, was put forward as a result of an inquiry, and in 1861 an act of parliament was obtained to allow the works to proceed.[29] The Rathmines Town Commissioners opened negotiations with Dublin Corporation for the township to avail of the Vartry supply, but in the absence of agreement they decided to go their own way.[30] An agreement was reached with the Grand Canal Company to obtain a supply from the canal, and a waterworks was constructed at Gallanstown, by the 8th Lock on the canal, completed in 1863. Work commenced on the construction of the Vartry scheme in 1862, and in 1869 the supply was made available in the city. Neither of these projects include much in the way of visible features within the south-east area, except for the substantial cast-iron water main that crosses over the Grand Canal on the eastern side of Leeson Street Bridge and which carries the name of the engineer, Parke Neville.

In the 1870s the Rathmines Town Commissioners realised that the water-supply from the Grand Canal was no longer sufficient, given the growth of the population. An alternative was suggested from the Dodder, based on a reservoir at Bohernabreena in the upper reaches of the river, and work commenced on the construction of the reservoir in 1881.[31] As with the earlier water schemes, the Bohernabreena works are outside the city boundary and have left little visible trace within the south-east area.

Drainage

In the early centuries the inhabitants of Dublin disposed of waste into the Liffey or the Poddle or consigned it to cesspits, and these remained the principal means of waste disposal until the eighteenth century. As the city expanded, it encompassed areas drained by other rivers and streams, including the River Dodder, the Muckross Stream, the Swan River, the Gallows Stream, the River Stein and the several tributaries of the Poddle, and all of these served as ways of disposing of waste. During the nineteenth century the smaller rivers were culverted, leaving only the Dodder and the Liffey visible. Long before the eighteenth century the rivers and streams had become heavily polluted. A great deal of rubbish and ordure was not thrown directly into the streams but left in the streets to be washed into the streams by the rain. The invention of the water-closet in 1775 made the situation worse, as those houses that fitted them discharged the effluent directly to streams or to cesspits that then polluted the streams and the city's wells.

The Paving Board, established in 1774, had some responsibility for drains, but mainly for keeping them clear rather than for laying new ones or improving the drainage system.[32]

Some new sewers were laid within the city area in the early to mid-nineteenth century, but the true situation is made clear in the 1847 Ordnance Survey map of the city, which shows the sewers and even the gullies at the sides of the road. It can be seen that there were no sewers in many of the smaller streets such as Chatham Street and Drury Street, nor even in thoroughfares such as Christchurch Place, Townsend Street, Westmoreland Street, Clanbrassil Street and South Circular Road. Unfortunately, the sewers were not depicted on the 1860s edition, so it is not possible to assess progress in the intervening years or to see what sewers were laid in the areas to the south of the Grand Canal.

In 1851 Parke Neville was appointed to the position of city surveyor and he set about the major task of laying new sewers in the city's streets. These sewers were built with stone sides and floors and were arched over with brick, and many of them are still fulfilling their function. The problem with this approach was that the waste matter that was removed swiftly and efficiently had nowhere to go other than to the rivers and streams.[33] Rathmines township suffered from the same problem, with much of the drainage from the area running into the Swan River, which had become an open sewer. A short-term solution was to culvert the river, which was done in 1867.[34]

The solution to the problem of river pollution was intercepting sewers, which would run alongside the rivers and collect the discharge from sewers before it entered the watercourse, carrying it downstream to discharge into the sea. Parke Neville had put forward this solution in 1853, but it was not taken up at that time. Proposals for such a scheme were put forward by Dublin Corporation in 1870 but, although government funds were made available, the cost proved to be more than the finance would cover.[35]

Rathmines and Pembroke Main Drainage

The first main drainage project in the Dublin area was implemented by a liaison between Pembroke and Rathmines townships and was facilitated by an act of parliament passed in 1877. The work was carried out between 1878 and 1881 and involved the construction of four sewers. The first ran along the Swan River from Harold's Cross via Rathmines, Ranelagh, Wellington Place and Ballsbridge to Londonbridge Road. The second came from the Pembroke Road and Shelbourne Road area to Londonbridge Road. The third ran alongside the railway from Sydney Parade to the Dodder at Lansdowne Road and along the east bank of the Dodder to Londonbridge Road. The fourth ran from Londonbridge Road to an outfall at the back of the South Wall, running on an embankment. At Londonbridge Road the sewers from the western side of the Dodder passed under the river by means of a siphon, with a siphon house on either side of the river. On the eastern side of the Dodder a pumping station was erected to pump the sewage to the outfall, and this raised the effluent up into a sewer above ground level on an embankment running from the pumping station to Irishtown Road, crossing to Chapel Avenue and then across what was the inner part of Dublin Bay to the South Wall. The latter section is now beneath a laneway beside Ringsend Park.[36] The pumping station had two horizontal high-pressure surface condensing steam engines and three boilers which operated until 1953, when they were replaced with diesel-powered pumps.[37]

Dublin Main Drainage

A Royal Commission was established in 1879 to examine the issue of Dublin's drainage. Having examined a number of options, it concluded that the interceptor sewer concept put forward by Parke Neville so many years before would be the best approach.[38] Nothing was done, however, until 1891, when Spencer Harty, Neville's successor, was given the opportunity to proceed. The scheme that he designed was almost identical to that put forward by Neville in 1853, except for the outfall. The project was the subject of a local government inquiry in 1892 and finally commenced in 1896. It involved the construction of major sewers beneath the streets along the quays to intercept the existing outfalls into the Liffey, including 32 outfalls on the southern side of the river.

The southern interceptor sewer increases in size as it travels eastward and is a cylindrical pipe 1.4m in diameter when it reaches Hawkins Street. Here it meets the northern interceptor, which has crossed in a siphon under the Liffey, and the two run southward along Hawkins Street in a tunnel 2.4m wide to Townsend Street. From there the tunnel runs along Hanover Street, Ringsend Road, Ringsend Park and Pigeon House Road to the main pumping station.

At Ringsend a pumping station was erected where the effluent was screened to remove rags and other non-sewage matter and then pumped up to a high-level tunnel

Pl. 76—Sir Joseph Bazalgette, designer of the London Main Drainage Scheme, who was involved in the early stages of the Dublin Main Drainage Scheme. The last of the sewage sludge-ships owned by Dublin Corporation and which brought the sludge out to sea to dump it was named in his honour.

that took it to the outfall works. The pumping station had four boilers supplying four vertical triple-expansion engines driving centrifugal pumps, three of which were available for use, while the fourth was in reserve. The steam engines were removed in 1923 and replaced by electric pumps. The pumping station was in use until 1985 and has since been demolished and replaced by a more modern pumping station.

Beyond the pumping station, the sewage travelled through a 2.4m-wide tunnel to Pigeon House Harbour, which had been acquired by Dublin Corporation from the military authorities in 1897 for the purpose of providing a sewage treatment station. Within the harbour eighteen settling tanks were constructed, each with a capacity of about 30 million litres. Lime had been added to the mix in the pumping station and the sewage was left to settle in the tanks for a period. Once settled, the water was drawn off and discharged into the Liffey, while the sludge was removed to a ship which took it out to sea and dumped it.

Even before the Dublin Main Drainage Scheme had been completed, legislation had been passed to extend the city boundaries. This included the annexation of the townships to the north and west of the city. The only part of the south-east area that was taken into the city at this time was the part of Dolphin's Barn and Goldenbridge that lay to the south of the Grand Canal. Dublin Corporation extended the Main Drainage Scheme to include its newly annexed lands, including this area south of the canal.

A number of ventilation stacks are to be seen in various places, marking the locations of these sewers, and these often bear the initials of the local authority responsible and a date.

Crumlin and Terenure

While the areas beyond the city boundaries were for the most part within the administrative area of one or other of the townships, by the end of the nineteenth century a large area that lay between the township of Rathmines and Rathgar and the former township of New Kilmainham lay in neither city nor township, comprising the area around Terenure, Kimmage and most of Crumlin and Drimnagh. In 1911 a sewer pipe was laid from Kimmage Road northward across the canal to join the sewer network at Dean Street, so as to drain the Terenure area. In the mid-1920s sewers were laid in Sundrive Road and Crumlin Road, crossing beneath the Grand Canal to join the city's drainage network, and in 1929 a sewer was laid to join Crumlin village to the existing sewers serving Inchicore.[39]

With these areas connected to main sewers, the entire south-east area was now served by either the city's main drainage system or that of Rathmines and Pembroke.

Dodder Valley

The Dodder Valley Drainage Scheme was a project undertaken by Dublin County Council in the 1970s to serve the rapidly expanding population of the area immediately to the south of the city, from Templeogue and Rathfarnham through Ballyboden, Churchtown and Goatstown. The sewer crosses the boundary into the city at Clonskeagh, through the grounds of UCD, before running down Nutley Lane to the shoreline on Strand Road. The amenity space between Strand Road and the sea was laid out at this time as an embankment over the twin pipes of the drainage project, running to the Ringsend pumping station. The work was completed in 1973.[40]

Grand Canal Scheme

Drainage of the new towns to the west of Dublin required a substantial new sewer and this was achieved in the 1970s and 1980s under the Greater Dublin Drainage Scheme. The project was announced in October 1972 and was in four parts.[41] The first involved boring a tunnel from Dolphin Road to Grand Canal Street, the second was a connecting tunnel from Grand Canal Street to the Ringsend pumping station, the third was the reconstruction of the pumping station and the fourth was the provision of a new treatment works at the Pigeon House. The tunnel was completed in 1975, commencing just to the west of Herberton Road and running beneath the road on the southern side of the Grand Canal. It has an internal diameter of 3.65m, divided into two compartments, one to take surface water and the other for foul, and it is located 6–14m below the surface.[42] This tunnel connected to a trunk foul sewer coming from the west, and along its route it intercepts sewers from Walkinstown, Drimnagh, Crumlin, Terenure and part of Rathmines and Pembroke, while also relieving flooding in Crumlin, Harold's Cross and Rathmines.[43]

At Maquay Bridge the surface water from the tunnel discharged into the Grand Canal Basin, while the foul water was brought via a tunnel 2.75m in diameter to the Ringsend pumping station. A new pumping station was erected with a capacity to pump 1.468 million litres a day, including the discharge from the Rathmines–Pembroke system, and this station was completed in 1985. The older treatment plant at Pigeon House Harbour was replaced with a new treatment plant, still for primary treatment only, and this was served by a new ship to transport the waste out to sea, appropriately named Sir Joseph Bazalgette after the engineer who designed the London main drainage system and worked on the early stages of the Dublin Main Drainage Scheme.[44]

In the late 1990s work began on a new treatment plant at Ringsend involving tertiary treatment, and this was completed in 2003, bringing to an end the dumping of sludge at sea.[45]

GAS

The concept of using some form of gas for lighting purposes was explored in the opening years of the nineteenth century, utilising either hydrogen or gas made from coal, with coal gas becoming the favoured fuel. Coal was heated in the absence of air, and this drove off carbon monoxide and hydrogen, leaving behind a solid residue known as coke, which could be used as a fuel in furnaces. The gas mixture also contained impurities such as sulphides, ammonia, oils and tar. To remove these impurities, the gas was bubbled through water and then over iron oxide. The gas was stored in large cylindrical tanks made of iron or steel, generally known as gasometers, though gas-holders was a more correct term. Early versions had an iron cylinder with a domed top, and this sat in a reservoir of water to ensure that there was a seal to retain the gas. The cylinder rose up as the tank was filled and descended during the day as the gas was used. The weight of the movable sections provided the pressure to send the gas through the network of pipes that ran beneath the streets. An improved version was telescopic, with more than one section. Some later gasometers were not telescopic but had a piston to regulate the pressure, and these became more common in the twentieth century. Gas production was not only for town gas but could also be produced on a smaller scale, and many industries and country houses in the mid-nineteenth century had their own gas-making apparatus with a small gasometer—these can often be seen on Ordnance Survey maps.

In 1815 proposals emerged for lighting Dublin with gas.[46] A bill went through parliament but was withdrawn. Some of the opposition to gas lighting in the city was based on objections not to gas lighting in itself but to the fact that it would be operated by the Paving Board, which was seen as being poorly run and inefficient.[47] In 1819 the Paving Board drafted a new bill to be submitted to parliament and once again there was opposition, with the city assembly submitting a petition against the bill on the basis that noxious vapours from the gas production were harmful and that the gas pipe network would pollute the water-supply in the streets.[48] The act was passed in July 1820, but instead of giving the responsibility for the supply of gas to the Paving Board it established a new company to be called the Dublin Gas Light Company, with power to acquire land and to lay pipes in the streets. The act allowed the Paving Board to enter into a contract with the company for the provision of street lighting.[49] In 1823 another act of parliament was passed to establish a second company, the Hibernian Gas Light Company.[50] Given that gas could also be produced from oil, a third company, to be called the Dublin Oil Gas Light Company, was established by act of parliament in 1824.[51]

In view of the delay in establishing companies to provide gas for the city at large, some businesses took to providing their own supply. In October 1819 Crosbie's public house at 22 South King Street was stated to have 'been for some time lit with gas' and had a gasometer in its rear yard.[52] In March 1819 the Theatre Royal, then located at Temple Bar, was fitted up with gas lighting.[53] The gas for this was generated in Westmoreland Street, where a woollen draper's had fitted up a gas-making apparatus for its own use, and a pipe was run across the street and down Fleet Street to the theatre. Although the pipe-laying had been carried out with permission, the gas plant in Westmoreland Street was deemed to constitute a nuisance and was required to close down. An alternative gas plant was established closer to the theatre on Wellington Quay, and this solved the problem.[54] The theatre advertised its gas lighting, but the gas lighting fitted in the public house and woollen draper's are only known because a problem arose. In 1821 new assembly rooms opened in College Green, and for the grand opening ball the premises were lit by gas by the Dublin Gas Light Company.[55] The presence of these isolated users suggests that there may have been many more premises in the city that provided their own gas supply for lighting purposes in the early years.

The Dublin Gas Light Company built its gasworks at North Wall, completed in 1822.[56] The other companies established their gasworks in Great Brunswick Street, now Pearse Street. The Hibernian Gas Light Company works was on the northern side of the street, adjacent to Grand Canal Dock, while the Patent Oil Gas Company for Ireland erected its works further to the west, adjacent to St Mark's Church.[57] The latter company built a fine frontage to Pearse Street, which still survives. After the demise of the company the building was converted for use as a theatre, known as the Antient Concert Rooms, and in 1920 it was converted to a cinema, operating under a succession of names—the Palace Theatre, the Forum, the Embassy and the Academy—before closing in 1981. After a fire and a period of dereliction, the building was reconstructed to provide office accommodation, opening in 2006.[58]

Over the next few decades from the 1820s, the history of gas supply in Dublin involves a lot of commercial politics. The first change was the agreement of the three companies to form a cartel, dividing the city amongst them to eliminate competition. Then, in 1834, a significant rise in the price of whale oil was enough to put the Patent Oil Gas Company out of business.[59] This was quickly followed by the acquisition of the remaining gas companies by English interests, and the Hibernian Gas Light Company, which had been founded by Daniel O'Connell and the most prominent merchants in Dublin, was taken over by the United General Gas Company, based in London.[60] In reaction to the monopoly, the Alliance Gas Company was founded in 1835, again with a significant English interest. The company acquired a site on Sir John Rogerson's Quay and by 1836 had completed the construction of its gasworks.[61]

Despite the existence of the Alliance company, the Paving Board seemed to favour the Hibernian/United General company in awarding contracts for street lighting. Moreover, the price of gas in Dublin was believed to be substantially higher than in other towns and cities, and it was pointed out that towns and cities in Britain and Ireland tended to control their own gas production rather than leaving it in private hands.[62]

In 1844 a group of Dublin residents, disillusioned by the monopoly of gas concerns in the city and the excessive prices, established the Dublin Consumers Gas Company to enter the market on behalf of the city's gas consumers. Shares were offered to gas consumers and the company's articles of association limited shareholders to the occupants of Dublin city and county, Meath, Kildare, Wicklow and Drogheda.[63] This company had not been long in existence before it amalgamated with the Alliance Gas Company in 1846, a move sanctioned by an act of parliament in 1847.[64]

A further company entered the field in 1864, when the Commercial Gas Company was established by businessmen based in the Kingstown and Blackrock area, though its initial intention was to provide a gas supply to Kingstown.[65]

In 1865 the United General Gas Company's twenty-year contract to supply gas for lighting Dublin's streets expired and the company failed to renew it, severely hampering the viability of its Dublin operations. Under legislation passed in 1866, restrictions on the amalgamation of gas companies was relaxed; the Alliance & Consumers Gas Company amalgamated with the Commercial Gas Company, while the United General company exited the Dublin market. The latter's gasworks were taken over by the amalgamated company, which still operated under the name Alliance & Consumers Gas Company, and it won the contract to light the city's streets.[66]

The changes to gas companies in 1866 marked the final step for the companies involved in the city's gas production. At this point there were two surviving gasworks in the city, at Sir John Rogerson's Quay and at Pearse Street, though in effect they were adjacent, separated only by the street at Misery Hill, and from this time the company operated them as a single unit. This was not an end to the expansion of the works, however, and adjoining plots of land were acquired to consolidate the site between the quays and Misery Hill, connected by a bridge below the street. The largest land acquisition was in 1870, when a plot extending to about 3.4ha, lying to

Pl. 77—Gas-holder at the corner of Sir John Rogerson's Quay and Cardiff's Lane, built in 1925 and demolished in the 1990s. It was a prominent landmark and could be seen in the view down Fitzwilliam Street, looming above the National Maternity Hospital building.

the north of the DART line and between Barrow Street and South Lotts, was acquired by compulsory purchase order. This land was not used as a gasworks but for gas storage. Initially the company erected a single gas-holder, this being a telescopic example, which was given the name 'Clayton' in honour of the discoverer of gas lighting. This was followed in 1885 by another telescopic holder, which was named 'Alliance' in honour of the company, and the framework of this one survives, with an apartment building erected within its circumference. A third one was added in 1925, named 'Dickens' in honour of the chairman of the company, and this was also telescopic, though guided by spiral runners. In 1934 an additional gas-holder of a newer type was erected on the Sir John Rogerson's Quay gasworks site; this was not telescopic but operated with an internal piston, avoiding the use of water as a sealant and hence averting the problem of the water freezing in winter.[67]

The gasworks were extensively modernised in the 1870s, and in 1879 an act of parliament allowed the company to construct tramways connecting the works to the quayside at Sir John Rogerson's Quay, to facilitate the movement of coal from the quay and coke from the works to the quay.[68]

As the townships of Rathmines and Pembroke were not part of the city until 1930, they arranged their own gas supply. Rathmines township was established in 1847, and its act of parliament gave it the power to provide its own gas for lighting the streets, but the township commissioners opted to contract a private supplier rather than generate their own gas. At that time there was little in the way of street lighting in the area, and the commissioners entered into an agreement with the Alliance company to provide that service.[69]

The Pembroke area was slower to seek township status, and it was public lighting that led to the decision to seek an act of parliament to establish a township. Up to that time, various parts of the Pembroke area were lit by private subscription, but some who had signed up for this facility failed to pay their share. Without legislation

Pl. 78—Gasworks on the western side of Grand Canal Dock, stretching from Pearse Street to Sir John Rogerson's Quay. The three ships belonged to the Alliance & Consumers Gas Company and delivered coal from Britain to the gasworks. The ship on the right is the *Glencree*, which was built in Dublin and scrapped in 1963.

there was no way of compelling them, and the solution, decided by the ratepayers, was to seek township status so that the township could provide street lighting; the resulting act was passed through parliament in 1863.[70]

The era of coal gas came to an end in Dublin in 1962, when the company changed to using fuel oil as the raw material, and in 1966 it changed again, using naphtha. This lasted just sixteen years until 1982, when the pipeline connecting to the Kinsale gasfield brought natural gas to the city.[71] This brought an end to the need for the gasworks, and the sites have since been cleared, decontaminated and redeveloped. The only surviving elements of the original gasworks are a chimney on the former Sir John Rogerson's Quay site and the frame of the gas-holder at South Lotts Road. Some railway track has been incorporated into the hard landscaping along Sir John Rogerson's Quay as a memory of the track that brought the coal from the quays to the gasworks.

Apart from the industrial heritage survivals, the building that was the headquarters of the gas company still stands in D'Olier Street. It was reconstructed in 1932 in an art deco style fronting on to the street, while the rear of the premises, backing on to Leinster Market, is in a half-timbered Tudor style. The D'Olier Street frontage is particularly fine.

Pl. 79—Rails on Sir John Rogerson's Quay. These facilitated the use of trains to haul heavy wagons of goods unloaded at the quays, such as the coal used in the gasworks.

ELECTRICITY

Experiments with the use of electricity to provide lighting had been under way since the beginning of the nineteenth century, but it was not until the later 1870s that a practicable system for lighting public streets was devised, using carbon arc lamps.

In November 1881 the Dublin Electric Light & Power Company offered to light some of Dublin's streets on a temporary basis to demonstrate the quality of the light. The company set up a generating station in Schoolhouse Lane, off Kildare Street, and this powered seventeen arc lamps installed in Kildare Street, Dawson Street and St Stephen's Green.[72] This demonstration did not produce the desired response from the corporation, and the Alliance & Consumers Gas Company responded by producing a more efficient gas light, which succeeded in winning over the Paving and Lighting Committee. A second experiment was carried out at the new South City Markets, where gas and electric lighting were both used, but the result was in favour of gas once again.[73] The electric company refuted the negativity, stating that its lighting had only been intended as a temporary demonstration and had been very successful.[74] Given that it had no power to dig up streets to lay cables and erect lampposts, the company sought an act of parliament to put it on a fully legal footing.[75] The *Freeman's Journal* pointed out that the members of the Paving and Lighting Committee of Dublin Corporation included several directors of the gas company and questioned its impartiality.[76]

Little progress was made over the next ten years, though the Electric Light company managed to install 114 street lamps and electricity had been installed in Jacob's biscuit factory and Pim's department store.[77] Some property owners adopted the system: the Gaiety Theatre erected a lamp outside the box office in 1882, while James Cleary, a wine and spirit merchant in Grafton Street, also had a light outside his premises and lit the interior with electric light.[78] The Dublin Electric Light & Power Company was wound up in 1883. [79] The Alliance & Consumers Gas Company invested in a power station of its own in Hawkins Street in 1888, providing power to Grafton Street, Henry Street and South Great George's Street. This did not progress and in 1890 the company announced that it was prepared to dispose of its power station, together with its engines.[80]

By this stage, Dublin Corporation had made the decision to establish its own power station, and it selected a site in Fleet Street. As construction progressed there, the streets were dug up to lay the underground cables and the first stage was to provide power to Westmoreland Street, College Green, Dame Street, Grafton Street and part of the north city. The Electrical Engineering Company of Ireland had the contract for laying the cables and connecting the system; this company also established its own supplies to clients, with lighting provided to Dublin Castle, the Royal College of Surgeons, the Gaiety Theatre and elsewhere by February 1892.[81] The Fleet Street power station was completed in July 1892 and the street lamps in College Green, Dame Street, Grafton Street and Westmoreland Street were lit for the first time.[82]

The Fleet Street power station ran two independent systems, each with three steam engines, two of which would provide the power while the third was on standby. The streets were lit by arc lights, which were powered by 60hp steam engines running three dynamos, while the steam engines to supply private premises with incandescent lighting were each 300hp, providing 2,000 volts AC operating at 160 cycles per second.[83] The venture was such a success that by November 1893 Dublin Corporation was seeking tenders for the extension of the buildings and plant.[84]

The cables laid in the streets for this system had been insulated with rubber and protected within iron pipes, and small transformers were provided outside houses to step down the voltage from 2,000V to either 100V or 50V.[85] Within five years, however, problems were occurring with cable failures and new cabling was to be laid, using paper insulation laid in wooden troughs and embedded in bitumen. At the same time, the system was modified to eliminate the individual transformers for each customer, replacing them with transformers at intervals feeding into a lower-tension network.[86]

With further demand for electric lighting, Dublin Corporation considered another expansion. With the acquisition by the corporation of the Pigeon House fort for use as part of the main drainage system, by 1896 consideration was being given to using it as the location for a new power station.[87] This location was accepted, and the new power station came onstream in September 1903, at which point the Fleet Street power station was shut down and became a distribution station.[88] The new power station employed four vertical steam engines, two at 800hp and two at 2,000hp, driving four alternators, two developing 500kW and two at 1,000kW, and twenty electricity substations were provided around the city.[89] In view of the distance of the power station from the area it was to supply, the current was delivered to Fleet Street on a three-phase system, this being one of the first times in the world that three-phase had been adopted.[90]

At the substations the voltage was stepped down to 1,000V for the arc lamps in the main streets, 200V for private lighting and 340V for powering machinery.[91]

The Fleet Street and Pigeon House power stations served only the city, while the townships opted to make their own arrangements. Pembroke township sought an

Pl. 80—Pigeon House power station, seen from the air in the 1950s.

act of parliament to this end in 1896, and in 1898 commenced the construction of a power station at South Lotts Road.[92] This also included a refuse-destructor, which burned refuse and used the heat to supplement the furnaces in the power station. While the power generation and refuse destruction are long gone, the use of this site as ancillary to the electricity network has continued, though it is now larger and is occupied by ESB Networks.

Rathmines township also opted to construct its own power station rather than use private companies, and its plant was constructed at the rear of the town hall on Rathmines Road on the site now occupied by the Swan Centre. This plant was brought into use on 31 August 1900 and employed two generators, one of 150kW and the other of 300kW, delivering direct current at 220V for lighting and 440V for powering machinery.[93] Three months later, Rathmines found that so many applications had been made for connections to the system that it would be necessary to extend the power station.[94] Conversely, Pembroke found that it had surplus power and, following an agreement between the two councils, a cable was laid from South Lotts to Rathmines to allow for the surplus to be utilised in the latter district.[95] In

Pl. 81—Ringsend power station and reclaimed land along the South Wall.

1907 Rathmines added a refuse-destructor to its power station.

In 1927 the Electricity Supply Board (ESB) was established as the national provider of electricity, and under the enabling legislation the power stations operated by Dublin Corporation and the Pembroke and Rathmines Urban District Councils were taken over by the ESB.[96] In view of the surplus power provided by the new hydroelectric plant at Ardnacrusha, the ESB mothballed the Pigeon House power station and it was only used as a backup, such as in a severe drought in 1932, when the water-levels in the Shannon were too low to allow for full production at Ardnacrusha. The station was modernised in the later 1930s, and its capacity increased to 95MW. In 1971 the Pigeon House B power station was commissioned, as a 240MW oil-burning power station, and after a period of use as a standby facility the original Pigeon House power station was decommissioned in 1976.[97]

Further expansion of the generating capacity on the Poolbeg peninsula came in the mid-1950s when the ESB commissioned the Ringsend A generating station, designed to run on pulverised coal or fuel oil, depending on the prevailing fuel prices.

Ten years later, Ringsend B was commissioned and designed to run on fuel oil. The combined output of the Ringsend facilities was 270MW.[98]

During the operation of the Pigeon House power station, the ash cleaned from its furnaces was deposited on the strand to the east. As the resulting reclaimed area grew, it was used for the storage of coal for the power station. In the 1960s the ESB planned to build a new power station on this land, while extending the area through reclamation to a total of about 36ha. The new power station was completed in 1971 and housed two 120MW oil-fired generators with a concrete chimney 207m high. These works included the provision of a jetty for the delivery of oil and a tank farm for its storage. The power station was expanded shortly afterwards and in 1978 the second phase was commissioned, with a second chimney and a 271MW turbine.[99] In the 1990s a combined cycle gas station was erected on the site, two gas turbines being commissioned in 1994 and a steam turbine in 1998. On 31 May 2010 the generating stations erected in the 1970s were closed.[100]

In the late 1920s, shortly after its foundation, the Electricity Supply Board moved into Nos 55–62 Mount Street Upper, and shortly afterwards its design department was installed in No. 13 Fitzwilliam Street. Over time the ESB increased its holdings in Fitzwilliam Street and by 1965 it was occupying Nos 13–30.[101] In that year it commenced the redevelopment of the site, erecting a new headquarters building from which the national grid was controlled. That building, completed in 1970, was demolished in 2018 and a new headquarters has been erected on the site.[102]

10.
Military installations

As the capital city of Ireland, Dublin needed to be defended against attack, whether casual and small-scale or military and large-scale. In the medieval period the city was defended by walls, commencing in the Viking period and continuing on a more substantial basis after the arrival of the Normans. Some elements of these walls survive in the south-east area, including parts of the medieval walls and towers of Dublin Castle and the bases of Isolde's Tower on Lower Exchange Street and Geneval's Tower to the north of Ross Road and at Cook Street and the Civic Offices..

City walls served not only military purposes but also an economic function. Cities and towns imposed tolls on goods being brought to market within the area of their jurisdiction, and the presence of walls with gates that closed at night served to prevent the illicit movement of goods. As the city expanded beyond its medieval walls, the

Pl. 82—The base of Isolde's Tower, which formed the north-eastern extremity of the medieval defences of Dublin, was found during archaeological excavations in 1993. It is now preserved in the basement below an apartment building.

need for this kind of enclosure led to the provision of an outer line of walls, and these were depicted on John Speed's map of 1610. The best-known element of this outer line of defences is St James's Gate, while there were other gates around the perimeter and Speed's map shows outer gates spanning Patrick Street and Stephen Street.

There have been later defences of the city, including barracks, forts and gun batteries, and these are examined here.

RINGSEND FORT

When a city needs to be protected against a maritime incursion, it is important that the first part of it to be encountered on approach should be a strong defensive position. In the medieval city Isolde's Tower occupied this position, similar to the location of Reginald's Tower in Waterford. With the expansion of the city, it became important to consider some form of defence further downstream; an obvious location would have been Ringsend, which was a sandy spit projecting out into the bay, extending close to the shipping lane in the estuary. In 1582 Dublin Corporation leased land at Ringsend to Nicholas Duffe and Nicholas Ball subject to a condition that they 'build a tower at Ringsend of such height and strength as shall be a perpetual continuance, like the tower of Drogheda' (spelling modernised)[1]—a reference to the tower on Millmount in Drogheda.

In 1656 Viscount Fitzwilliam was given permission 'to demolish the four bulwarks of the fort, undertaking to bring into the stores all the iron work belonging to the drawbridge upon demolishing the fort'.[2] The demolition does not seem to have been carried out immediately and the fort is still depicted on Bernard de Gomme's map of 1673, Thomas Phillips's map of 1685 and Grenville Collins's chart of Dublin Bay from around the same period.

TEMPORARY BARRACKS

With the increasing independence of the Irish parliament towards the end of the eighteenth century, followed by political tensions in the 1790s, the number of barracks in the city increased, and prior to the construction of additional permanent barracks a number of premises around the city were acquired for temporary use. The first of these within the south-east area was the former Custom House on what is now Wellington Quay. This building had become redundant with the opening of the new Custom House in 1791 and was converted for use as a barracks.[3] In 1795 Kerry House in St Stephen's Green, otherwise known as Shelbourne House, was vacant and was taken for use as a barracks for the Westmeath Militia.[4] The building became the Shelbourne Hotel in the 1820s. In 1803 eleven houses in South Great George's Street were converted for use as a barracks backing on to Dublin Castle. These barracks were shaded on Campbell's map of 1811 but not labelled. The map labelled other barracks, including one on the northern side of Lower Baggot Street and another on Mespil Road. Pigot & Co.'s directory for 1824 mentions a barrack depot on Townsend Street and this is marked as a recruiting depot on Campbell's map of 1811.[5]

No trace remains of any of these temporary barracks other than the much-altered Shelbourne Hotel.

Half-Moon Battery

In February 1793 Britain declared war on France, largely on account of the reign of terror in that country and, in particular, the execution of the French king.[6] This brought Ireland into the war. In response, particularly in the light of heightened political tensions within Ireland, in that same year the Board of Ordnance built a gun battery on the South Wall, 800m from the Poolbeg Lighthouse. The battery was armed with 24-pounder guns to control access to Dublin port and its approaches.[7] In 1906 the Poolbeg Bathing Club applied to the Port and Docks Board for a lease on the Half-Moon Battery for bathing purposes.[8] Although this was not granted initially, the battery became the base for the Half-Moon Swimming and Water Polo Club, which continues to this day.

Some remnants of the battery survive, including the half-moon-shaped projection on the seaward side of the South Wall and sections of granite ashlar walls in the swimming club's building.

Pigeon House fort

Another temporary barracks was located on the South Wall at the Pigeon House. Like the fort at Ringsend in the sixteenth century and Isolde's Tower in the medieval period, the fort at Pigeon House was intended to engage any attacking force sailing up the river. In the wake of the rebellion of 1798 the area around Pigeon House Harbour was fortified. It was surrounded by a wall, with drawbridges on the approach along the South Wall from the city, two gun placements facing downriver and stores, armoury, parade ground and soldiers' quarters. The Pigeon House Hotel was occupied as the officers' quarters.[9] Pigeon House Harbour continued in use as the mail

Pl. 83—Pigeon House fort. The view shows a troop of soldiers marching along the South Wall towards the barracks gate. On the left is Pigeon House Harbour and the former hotel building. Much of the fort has now gone, though significant elements survive, including part of the gate and the perimeter walls with musket loops.

packet station for the next twenty years despite the presence of the fort.

What distinguishes Pigeon House from the other temporary barracks is that its 'temporary' use lasted for nearly a century and it was only closed down in 1897. Its permanent status had become obvious by 1814, and the government bought the property from the Ballast Board, including sections of the South Wall to the east and west and an area of the strand to the south. The Ordnance Survey map of 1864 shows a gun store and various targets and artillery butts on the strand for target practice.

There are extensive remains of the former barracks at Pigeon House, including walls with gun embrasures at the western entrance on Pigeon House Road and facing into the harbour, and a circular gun emplacement at the north-east corner, where the gun battery faced downriver. Further remnants survive to the south of Pigeon House Road on an area of land at present overgrown. Three cannons were formerly displayed at the site but have been moved into the grounds of Poolbeg power station. These bear the royal insignia 'GR' surmounted by a crown, suggesting that they were amongst the original armaments at the fort.

CATHAL BRUGHA BARRACKS

Portobello Barracks was built as a cavalry barracks during the Napoleonic Wars; it was begun in 1810 and completed in 1815.[10] It is a substantial barracks, extending back approximately 360m from Grove Road on the Grand Canal and about the same width from east to west. It included two barrack squares and such buildings as a guardhouse and a riding school. A church was built near the northern gate in 1842, as well as a hospital, and a canteen was built in 1868. The barracks was extended eastward to Rathmines Road with the acquisition of Lissonfield House and southward towards Leinster Road in 1867. A number of other buildings were added in the later nineteenth century, including a sports hall and new barrack buildings; these later structures are distinguished by their red-brick façades, in contrast to the grey stone facing of the earlier structures. The cavalry moved out to the new Marlborough Barracks—now McKee Barracks—in 1888 and Portobello became an infantry barracks. It was handed over to the National Army in May 1922.

Most of the original buildings at Portobello Barracks survive. The most significant structure that is no longer extant was the long range of barrack buildings that ran east–west across the northern sides of the two barrack squares.

Pl. 84—The parade-ground in Portobello Barracks in the late nineteenth or early twentieth century. This is now Cathal Brugha Barracks.

BEGGAR'S BUSH BARRACKS

Beggar's Bush Barracks, on Haddington Road, was built in 1827 as a recruitment depot.[11] It is regular in plan, extending back about 240m from Haddington Road and about 160m in width. The plan is not rectangular, however, having bastions at the corners. While one of the later barracks, Beggar's Bush is the one that most closely resembles an earlier fortification, with its perimeter wall and bastions pierced by gun loops, and the effect is increased by the slightly higher elevation above both Shelbourne Road and Haddington Road. There were few buildings within the barracks initially and the number was increased significantly in the mid-nineteenth century, as may be seen from a comparison of the 1843 Ordnance Survey six-inch map with the larger-scale map surveyed in 1865. That map also shows that the barracks had been extended to Shelbourne Road by that time.

This was the first barracks to be handed over to the National Army of the Free State in January 1922. Many of the buildings survive, now converted to other uses, including the National Print Museum and formerly the Geological Survey of Ireland. Amongst the other artefacts to be seen are some cut-granite boundary marker stones

Pl. 85—Beggar's Bush Barracks in the late nineteenth or early twentieth century. Many of these buildings still survive, though with new buildings added.

in the perimeter walls, marked with the 'W D' insignia of the War Department. Across the front of the barracks is a railing consisting of a series of substantial cast-iron cannons set muzzle-up into the ground and with chains running between one cannon and the next. The origin of these is uncertain; some sources state that they came from a ship, while others say that they were from gun batteries and/or Martello towers. Another possibility is that they are some of the substantial number of cannons that were captured at Sebastopol during the Crimean War and brought back to these islands. The issue could be resolved if one of the guns were to be lifted to see whether there were identifying details cast into the breech, such as the Russian eagles found on many Crimean cannon. If they had been used on a ship, there could be marks of the breeching rope resulting from recoil of the cannon when fired. The 1865 Ordnance Survey map shows post-and-chain railings to the front of the barracks, and it is probable that this depicts the cannons.

SANDYMOUNT MARTELLO TOWER

During the Napoleonic Wars a number of measures were undertaken to protect Ireland's coastline from attack. When a brief period of peace broke down in 1803, the authorities began to consider the vulnerability of Dublin to attack from the sea. Napoleon had amassed a substantial army in northern France, particularly around Boulogne, in preparation of an invasion. This included some 1,400 boats, many of which were landing-craft to carry troops, while the forces amounted to 115,000 men and 4,000 cannons.[12] Intelligence sources suggested that Napoleon may have been planning to bypass Britain with his invasion force and to land on the east coast of Ireland. The response was to plan a line of defences along the Dublin coast, stretching from Bray to Balbriggan, and the most effective solution was a series of small gun towers, supplemented at vulnerable spots by gun batteries. The result was the construction of 26 Martello towers and nine gun batteries over an eighteen-month period in 1804 and 1805.[13]

Only one of these defensive positions is located within the Dublin city boundary and this is the Martello tower on Strand Road, Sandymount. The towers were numbered from south to north in two series, the southern series with sixteen locations and the northern series with twelve. There was no gun battery at Sandymount, but the Martello tower is a double tower, carrying two cannons instead of the single cannon that stood on most of the towers. Like all of the towers to the south of the Liffey, the Sandymount tower is built of granite ashlar, and it has a projecting machicolation over the original doorway, which is now a window. The other doors and windows in

Pl. 86—Sandymount Martello tower, built in 1804–5 as part of the defences to repel a possible invasion by Napoleon's forces. This was one of 26 Martello towers built along the Dublin coast, and one of only four that were bigger and designed to carry two cannon on the gun platform rather than just one.

Pl. 87—Boundary stone at the base of the Sandymount Martello tower, giving the distance to the boundary of the land controlled by the War Department. To the left of the stone is a benchmark, cut by the Ordnance Survey to assist surveyors in determining levels of land.

the tower are later insertions, some of them quite early, such as the doors on the northern and southern sides which bear the inscription 'J. Bennet, Church Street, Dublin, 1822'.[14] These were inserted as part of the alterations in the 1990s and were brought from the fort at Spike Island.[15]

In the later nineteenth century the Sandymount tower was acquired by the Dublin Tramways Company, and the ground floor was used as a waiting-room for tram passengers. The tower was later used as a shop, with buildings added on the south-eastern side. These were demolished in the 1990s and new buildings erected for use as a restaurant. The tower is currently vacant.

At the base of the tower on the western side is a cut-granite stone bearing the inscription

W↑D
No. 2
33FT 11INS
WEST

This is a boundary stone, delimiting the extent of the area controlled by the military authorities. The arrow denotes government property and 'WD' refers to the War Department. The boundary stones were numbered sequentially around the perimeter, so this is stone no. 2. The boundary itself is out in the road and, as the stone could not be located there, the numbers provide the distance that the boundary lies to the west of the stone.

Bibliography

Advice Series 2015 *Paving—the conservation of historic ground surfaces.* Department of Arts, Heritage and the Gaeltacht and Dublin City Council, Dublin.

Archer, J. 1801 *A statistical survey of the County Dublin with observations on the means of improvement.* Graisberry & Campbell, Dublin.

Ball, F.E. 1902–20 *A history of County Dublin* (6 vols). Gill & Macmillan, Dublin.

Benedetti, S. 1997 *The Milltowns—a family reunion.* National Gallery of Ireland, Dublin.

Berry, H.F. 1902 Sir Peter Lewys, ecclesiastic, cathedral and bridge builder and his company of masons, 1564–7. *Ars Quatuor Coronatorum* **15**, 4–22.

Black, A. and Barry, M.B. 2015 *Bridges of Dublin—the remarkable story of Dublin's Liffey bridges.* Dublin City Council, Dublin.

Bolton, J., Carey, T., Goodbody, R. and Clabby, G. 2012 *The Martello towers of Dublin.* Dún Laoghaire–Rathdown County Council and Fingal County Council, Dublin.

Bonar Law, A. and Bonar Law, C. 1999 *The Irish prints of James Malton.* The Neptune Gallery, Dublin.

Bonde, N. 1998 Found in Denmark, but where do they come from? *Archaeology Ireland* **12** (3), 24–9.

Branigan, G. 2014 *Fountains of Dublin.* The History Press Ireland, Dublin.

Butler, J.G., Ball, W. and Vesey, F. 1786–1801 *The statutes at large passed in the Parliaments held in Ireland* (20 vols). George Grierson, Dublin.

Carey, T. 2016 *Dublin since 1922.* Hachette Books Ireland, Dublin.

Casey, C. 2005 *The buildings of Ireland: Dublin.* Yale University Press, New Haven and London.

Clarke, H.B. 2002 *Irish Historic Towns Atlas No. 11—Dublin, part I, to 1610.* Royal Irish Academy, Dublin.

Condon, G. 2006 Telecommunications. In R. Cox (ed.), Engineering Ireland, 314–18. The Collins Press, Cork.

Corcoran, M. 2000 *Through streets broad and narrow—a history of the Dublin trams.*

Midland Publishing, Leicester.

Corcoran, M. 2005 *Our good health—a history of Dublin's water and drainage.* Dublin City Council, Dublin.

Cox, R. (ed.) 2006 *Engineering Ireland.* The Collins Press, Cork.

Cox, R. and Donald, P. 2013 *Ireland's civil engineering heritage.* The Collins Press, Cork.

Craig, M. 1952 *Dublin 1660–1860: a social and architectural history.* The Cresset Press, London.

De Courcy, J.W. 1996 *The Liffey in Dublin.* Gill & Macmillan, Dublin.

Delany, R. 1995 *The Grand Canal of Ireland.* Lilliput Press, Dublin.

Dublin Public Libraries 2000 *A directory of Dublin for the year 1738.* Dublin Corporation Public Libraries, Dublin.

Ferguson, S. 2009 *The Irish post box—silent servant and symbol of the State.* An Post, Dublin.

Ferguson, S. 2016 *The Post Office in Ireland.* Irish Academic Press, Newbridge.

Gilbert, Sir J. and Gilbert, Lady R. 1889–1944 *Calendar of Ancient Records of Dublin* (19 vols). Joseph Dollard, Dublin.

Gilligan, H.A. 1988 *A history of the port of Dublin.* Gill & Macmillan, Dublin.

Glancy, M. 1997 The rise and fall of the DuBedats of Dublin. *Dun Laoghaire Journal* **6**, 41–57.

Goodbody, M. 2015 The Pim family—a biographical genealogy (private circulation).

Goodbody, M. 2022 Clara's contribution to the birth of radio. *Offaly History* (https://offalyhistoryblog.wordpress.com/2022/11/05/claras-contribution-to-the-birth-of-radio-by-michael-goodbody).

Goodbody, R. 2014 *Irish Historic Towns Atlas No. 28—Dublin, part III, 1756 to 1847.* Royal Irish Academy, Dublin.

Goodbody, R. 2018 Regulating the growth of Dublin, 1750–1850. In T.R. Slater and S.M.G. Pinto, *Building regulations and urban form, 1200–1900*, 231–45. Routledge, London and New York.

Goodbody, R. 2023 *The Lead Mines—Ballycorus and Glendalough in the nineteenth century.* Wordwell, Dublin.

Griffith, R. 1847 *General Valuation of Ireland, County of Dublin, Barony of Dublin, South Dublin and Rathdown Unions. Valuation of the general parishes, townlands and tenements*. Dublin.

Griffith, R. 1848 *General Valuation of Ireland, County of Dublin, Barony of Dublin, South Dublin and Rathdown Unions. List of alterations made by the Sub-Commis-*

sioners of Valuation. Dublin.

Haliday, C. 1881 *The Scandinavian kingdom of Dublin* (ed. J.P. Prendergast). Alex. Thom & Co., Dublin. (Facsimile edition, with introduction by Breandáin Ó Ríordáin, Irish University Press, Shannon, 1969.)

Hammond, J.W. 1943 George's Quay and Rogerson's Quay in the eighteenth century. *Dublin Historical Record* 5 (2), 41–54.

Hamond, F. 2006 Survey of machinery at Boland's Mill, Ringsend, Dublin. Unpublished report.

Hamond, F. 2015 Industrial heritage survey of chimneys at ESB Power Station, Poolbeg, Dublin. Unpublished report.

Hamond, F. 2017 Survey of graving docks, Grand Canal Basin, Dublin. Unpublished report.

Hamond, F. 2019 The history of milling at Mount Argus, Harold's Cross, Dublin 6W. Unpublished report.

Harbison, P. 2004 *Beranger's rambles in Ireland.* Wordwell, Bray.

Harrison, R. 2002 Pim Brothers—merchants, manufacturers and entrepreneurs of nineteenth-century Dublin. *Journal of the Friends Historical Society* 59 (3), 236–56.

Harvey, R. 2006 *The War of Wars: the epic struggle between Britain and France, 1789–1815.* Constable, London.

Hayden, A. 1994 Werburgh Street, Dublin. *Excavations.ie: Database of Irish Excavation Reports,* 1994-087 (https://excavations.ie/report/1994/Dublin/0001696/).

Healy, P. 2004 *Paddy Healy's Dublin—archaeology, Early Christian remains and local histories.* South Dublin Libraries, Tallaght.

Healy, P. 2005 *Rathfarnham roads.* South Dublin Libraries, Tallaght.

Hearn, M. 2004 *Thomas Edmondson and the Dublin Laundry.* Irish Academic Press, Dublin.

House of Commons Papers 1821 *Grand Jury Presentments, Dublin.* London.

Johnston-Liik, E.M. 2002 *History of the Irish Parliament 1692–1800* (6 vols). Ulster Historical Foundation, Belfast.

Joyce, J. 1922 *Ulysses* (Bodley Head edn, London, 1986).

Kane, R. 1845 *The industrial resources of Ireland* (2nd edn). Hodges & Smith, Dublin.

Kearney, M. (ed.) 1996 *25 years of Poolbeg—a brief history of Poolbeg power station.* ESB, Dublin.

Kelly, D. 1995 *Four roads to Dublin—the history of Ranelagh, Rathmines and Leeson*

Street. The O'Brien Press, Dublin.

Kelly, M. 2019 Donnybrook Bus Garage, Stillorgan Road, Dublin 4, 1951. In E. Rowley (ed.), *More than concrete blocks: Vol. 2, 1940–1972*, 145–53. Dublin City Council, Dublin.

Kelly, T. 2009 The streets of Dublin. *Dublin Historical Record* **62** (2), 55–68.

Kilroy, J. 1996 *Irish trams.* Colourprint Press, Omagh.

Lennon, C. 2008 *Irish Historic Towns Atlas No. 19—Dublin, part II, 1610–1756.* Royal Irish Academy, Dublin.

Lennon, C. and Montague, J. 2010 *John Rocque's Dublin—a guide to the Georgian city.* Royal Irish Academy, Dublin.

Letterbox Study Group 2004 *Letter box listing.* Letter Box Study Group, Birmingham.

Lewis, S. 1837 *A topographical dictionary of Ireland* (2 vols). S. Lewis & Co., London.

Lunney, L. 2009 Aeneas Coffey. *Dictionary of Irish Biography*, 00. Royal Irish Academy, Dublin.

McAleese, M. (ed.) 2013 *Report of the Inter-Departmental Committee to establish the facts of State involvement with the Magdalene Laundries.* Department of Justice, Dublin.

MacAongusa, B. 2003 *The Harcourt Street Line—back on track.* Currach Press, Dublin.

McAteer, D. 1935 Suggested airport for Dublin. *Studies: An Irish Quarterly Review* **24** (93), 73–84.

McCabe, C. 1992 History of the town gas industry in Ireland, 1823–1980. *Dublin Historical Record* **45** (1), 28–40.

McCabe, D. 2011 *St Stephen's Green, Dublin, 1660–1875.* Stationery Office, Dublin.

McEntee, D. and Corcoran, M. 2016 *The Rivers Dodder and Poddle: mills, storms, droughts and the public water supply.* Dublin City Council, Dublin.

McManus, R. 2008 *Crampton built.* G. & T. Crampton, Dublin.

McParland, E. 1972 The Wide Streets Commissioners: their importance for Dublin architecture in the late 18th–early 19th century. *Quarterly Bulletin of the Irish Georgian Society* **15** (1), 1–31.

Mulryan, P. 2016 *The whiskeys of Ireland.* The O'Brien Press, Dublin.

Mulvihill, M. 2002 *Ingenious Ireland.* Town House, Dublin.

Murray, K.A. 1981 *Ireland's first railway.* Irish Railway Record Society, Dublin.

Myles, F. 2014 1–4 Windmill Lane, Dublin 2. *Excavations.ie: Database of Irish Ex-*

cavation Reports (https://excavations.ie/report/2014/Dublin/0026073/).

Nairn, R., Jeffrey, D. and Goodbody, R. 2017 *Dublin Bay—nature and history*. The Collins Press, Cork.

Neville, P. 1865 Dublin Waterworks. *The Civil Engineer and Architect's Journal* **28**, 266–7.

Ó Cionnaith, F. 2015 *Exercise of authority: surveyor Thomas Owen and the paving, cleansing and lighting of Georgian Dublin.* Dublin City Council, Dublin.

O'Connell, D. 1975 *The antique pavement—an illustrated guide to Dublin's street furniture*. An Taisce, Dublin.

O'Connell, K. 2006 Engineering in Radio Telefís Éireann (RTÉ). In R. Cox (ed.), *Engineering Ireland*, 319–27. The Collins Press, Cork.

O'Connor, C. and O'Regan, J. (eds) 1987 *Public works: the architecture of the Office of Public Works, 1831–1987.* Architectural Association of Ireland, Dublin.

O'Donnell, P.D. 1972 Dublin military barracks. *Dublin Historical Record,* 25 (4), 141–54.

O'Donoghue, B. 2007 *The Irish county surveyors 1834–1944.* Four Courts Press, Dublin.

O'Dwyer, F. 1981 *Lost Dublin.* Gill & Macmillan, Dublin.

O'Keeffe, P., Simington, T. and Goodbody, R. 2016 *Irish stone bridges* (2nd edn). Irish Academic Press, Newbridge.

Ó Maitiú, S. 2001 *W. & R. Jacob: celebrating 150 years of Irish biscuit making.* The Woodfield Press, Dublin.

Ó Maitiú, S. 2003 *Dublin's suburban towns, 1834–1930.* Four Courts Press, Dublin.

Ó Maitiú, S. 2021 *Irish Historic Towns Atlas: Dublin Suburbs No. 2: Rathmines.* Royal Irish Academy, Dublin.

O'Sullivan, C.J. 1987 *The gasmakers—historical perspectives on the Irish gas industry.* The O'Brien Press, Dublin.

O'Toole, S. 2019 ESB HQ, Fitzwilliam Street, Dublin 2, 1970. In E. Rowley (ed.), *More than concrete blocks: Vol. 2, 1940–72*, 368–77. Dublin City Council, Dublin.

Page, Sir T.H. 1800 Report of Sir Thomas Hyde Page on the improvement of Dublin Bay and Dalkey Sound. In *Accounts to be Presented to the House of Commons Relating to the Inland Navigation of Ireland and to the Port of Dublin*, House of Commons Papers, 1806 (292)(293)(294).

Pembroke Estate Papers (n.d.) Research guide to private sources at the National Archives. National Archives, Dublin.

Pigot & Co. 1824 *City of Dublin and Hibernian Provincial Directory.* J. Pigot & Co., London and Manchester.

Price, L. 1942 *An eighteenth century antiquary: the sketches, notes and diaries of Austin Cooper (1759–1830).* Falconer, Dublin.

Reynolds, M. 1983 *A history of the Irish Post Office.* MacDonnell Whyte Ltd, Dublin.

Roundtree, S. 2010 Brick in the eighteenth-century Dublin town house. In C. Casey (ed.), *The eighteenth-century Dublin town house—form, function and finance*, 73–81. Four Courts Press, Dublin.

Roundtree, S. 2023 *Brickmaking in Ireland—a gazetteer.* Wordwell, Dublin.

Rutty, J. 1772 *An essay towards a natural history of the county of Dublin* (2 vols). Dublin.

Rynne, C. 2006 *Industrial Ireland 1750–1930: an archaeology.* The Collins Press, Cork.

Sanctuary, A. 2008 *Rope, twine and net making.* Shire Publications, Gosport.

Sandymount Community Services 1993 *A local history of Sandymount, Irishtown, Ringsend.* Sandymount.

Sexton, M. 2005 *Marconi—the Irish connection.* Four Courts Press, Dublin.

Shepherd, E. and Beesley, G. 1998 *The Dublin & South Eastern Railway.* Midland Publishing, Leicester.

Simington, R.C. 1945 *The Civil Survey, 1654–1656, Vol. VII: County of Dublin.* Stationery Office, Dublin.

Simpson, L. 1996 Cecilia Street West. In I. Bennett (ed.), *Excavations 1995: summary accounts of archaeological excavations in Ireland*, 21. Wordwell, Bray.

Stafford Johnson, J. 1942 The Dublin Penny Post: 1773–1840. *Dublin Historical Record* 4 (3), 81–95.

Standage, T. 1998 *The Victorian Internet—the remarkable story of the telegraph and the nineteenth-century pioneers.* Walker & Co., New York.

Stillman, C. and Sevastopulo, G. 2005 *Classic geology in Europe, 6: Leinster.* Terra Publishing, Harpenden.

Sweeney, P. 2010 *Liffey ships and shipbuilding.* The Mercier Press, Cork.

The Dublin Almanac and General Register of Ireland (various dates, 1834–49). Pettigrew & Oulton, Dublin.

The Gentleman's and Citizen's Almanack (compiled by J.W. Stewart) (various dates, 1760–1832). Dublin.

Thom's Directory (various titles, various dates, 1847–2012). A. Thom, Dublin.

Townsend, B. 1999 *The lost distilleries of Ireland.* Neil Wilson Publishing, Glasgow.

Tweedy, R. 1999 *The story of the Court Laundry.* Wolfhound Press, Dublin.

Valuation 1828 *New Valuation of the City of Dublin.* House of Commons Papers,

1835 (5).
Wallace, P.F. 2016 *Viking Dublin: the Wood Quay excavations.* Irish Academic Press, Newbridge.
Warburton, J., Whitelaw, J. and Walsh, R. 1818 *History of the City of Dublin* (2 vols). Cadell & Davies, London.
Wilkinson, G. 1845 *Practical geology and ancient architecture of Ireland.* J. Murray, London.
Wilson's Dublin Directory (various dates, 1783–1832). Dublin.
Zimmerman, M. 2007 *The history of Dublin cinemas.* Nonsuch Publishing, Dublin.

ONLINE SOURCES

Archaeological excavations: https://excavations.ie/.
Census of population, 1901 and 1911: http://www.census.nationalarchives.ie/search/.
Dictionary of Irish Architects: https://www.dia.ie/.
Dictionary of Irish Biography: https://www.dib.ie.
Down Survey maps: https://downsurvey.tchpc.tcd.ie/down-survey-maps.php.
Dublin bridges and tunnels: https://en.wikipedia.org/wiki/List_of_Dublin_bridges_and_tunnels#Bridges_on_the_Grand_Canal.
Dublin City Industrial Heritage Record: https://experience.arcgis.com/experience/4caa2648489044e08a656bd2ad5a512a/page/Viewer---English?views=Industrial
Historical maps: https://maps.archaeology.ie/HistoricEnvironment/.
Irish Newspaper Archives: https://www.irishnewsarchive.com/.
Irish Times Archive: https://www.irishtimes.com/archive.
National Archives of Ireland: https://www.nationalarchives.ie/.
National Library of Ireland: https://www.nli.ie/.
Offaly History: https://offalyhistoryblog.wordpress.com/2022/11/05/claras-contribution-to-the-birth-of-radio-by-michael-goodbody/; accessed 6 November 2022.
Old Dublin Town: http://www.olddublintown.com/dublin-buses.html; accessed 6 December 2022.
Williams, J. 2009 Richard Turner. *Dictionary of Irish Biography*: https://www.dib.ie/biography/turner-richard-a8681

MAPS (IN CHRONOLOGICAL ORDER)

John Speed, *Dublin*, 1610.

Down Survey, *Dublin*, 1655–6.

Bernard de Gomme, *The city and suburbs of Dublin*, 1673.

Thomas Phillips, *An exact survey of the city of Dublin and part of the harbour*, 1685.

Charles Brooking, *A map of the city and suburbs of Dublin and Earl of Meath's Liberties*, 1728.

John Rocque, *An exact survey of the city and suburbs of Dublin*, 1756.

John Rocque, *A survey of the city, harbour, bay and environs of Dublin*, 1757.

John Rocque, *An actual survey of the county of Dublin*, 1760.

Bernard Scalé, *An accurate survey of the city and suburbs of Dublin*, 1773.

John Taylor, *The environs of Dublin*, 1816.

William Duncan, *The county of Dublin*, 1821.

Ordnance Survey, six-inch survey, fair plans, 1837–9.

Ordnance Survey, six-inch survey, Dublin sheet 18, unpublished, 1837.

Ordnance Survey, five-foot survey, manuscript maps, 1838–43.

Ordnance Survey, six-inch survey, Dublin sheets 18 and 22, first edition, 1843.

Ordnance Survey, five-foot survey, Dublin city, first edition, 1847.

Ordnance Survey, five-foot survey, Dublin city, second edition, 1864–5.

Ordnance Survey, 1:2,500 survey, parishes of St Peter's, Donnybrook and Rathfarnham, first edition, 1865.

Ordnance Survey, five-foot survey, Pembroke, first edition, 1865.

Ordnance Survey, six-inch survey, second edition, sheets 18 and 22, 1871.

Ordnance Survey, five-foot survey, Rathmines and Rathgar, 1870s.

Ordnance Survey, five-foot survey, Rathmines and Rathgar, 1882.

Ordnance Survey, five-foot survey, Dublin city, 1886–92.

Admiralty, Dublin Bar and River Liffey, 1889.

Ordnance Survey, 1:2,500 survey, second edition, 1907.

Ordnance Survey, six-inch survey, fourth edition, sheets 18 and 22, 1936.

Endnotes

Chapter 2

[1] Wilkinson 1845, 244.
[2] Stillman and Sevastopulo 2005, 91.
[3] Gilbert and Gilbert 1889–1944, vol. II (1891), 328.
[4] Roundtree 2010, 77.
[5] *Ibid.*, 78.
[6] Rutty 1772, vol. II, 28.
[7] John Rocque, *A survey of the city, harbour, bay and environs of Dublin* (1757).
[8] 11 Geo. III, c.6.
[9] Wilkinson 1845, 249.
[10] See https://artsandculture.google.com/asset/dolphin-s-barn-brick-1910/jAHiDvCBwYUKPA; Roundtree 2023, 103–4.
[11] Berry 1902, 6.
[12] Gilbert and Gilbert 1889–1944, vol. VI (1896), 370.
[13] NLI, call number PD AD 3217.
[14] Rutty 1772, vol. II, 116–17.
[15] *Ibid.*
[16] *Ibid.*, 110–11.
[17] *Ibid.*, 113.
[18] Simpson 1996, 21.
[19] Lennon 2008, 30; Wide Street Commissioners maps 367, 616.
[20] *Wilson's Dublin Directory* (various dates, 1798–1832); *The Dublin Almanac and General Register of Ireland* (various dates, 1834–47); *Thom's Directory* (various dates, 1847–1971).
[21] Rutty 1772, vol. II, 136–7.
[22] Harbison 2004, 46–7.

Chapter 3

[1] Wallace 2016, 138.
[2] Gilbert and Gilbert 1889–1944, vol. II (1891), 457–8.
[3] *Ibid.*, vol. IV (1894), 87.
[4] De Courcy 1996, 392.
[5] Gilbert and Gilbert 1889–1944, vol. VI (1896), 453–5, 458, 467–8.
[6] *Ibid.*, vol. VII (1898), 77–80, 84–5; Nairn *et al.* 2017, 141.
[7] Gilbert and Gilbert 1889–1944, vol. VI (1896), 485–6, 491–3.
[8] Nairn *et al.* 2017, 141.
[9] De Courcy 1996, 407.
[10] Sandymount Community Services 1993, 96.

Chapter 4

[1] Kane 1845, 71–117.

[2] Clarke 2002, 26.
[3] Ball 1902–20, vol. II (1903), 100, 110.
[4] Lennon 2008, 28.
[5] *Wilson's Dublin Directory* (various dates, 1818–28); Pigot & Co. 1824; *Freeman's Journal*, 20 November 1830, 2.
[6] *The Dublin Almanac and General Register of Ireland* (various dates, 1834–47); *Thom's Directory* (various dates, 1847–1909).
[7] *Irish Independent*, 4 October 1926, 7; *Belfast Newsletter*, 11 August 1928, 1.
[8] *Irish Independent*, 24 August 1928, 8; *Westmeath Independent*, 29 June 1929, 6.
[9] *Drogheda Independent*, 13 October 1934; *Sunday Independent*, 16 April 1939, 14.
[10] *Thom's Directory* (various dates, 1938–2011); *Irish Farmers Journal*, 24 October 1987, 20.
[11] *Thom's Directory* (various dates, 1846–52).
[12] Hamond 2006, 4.
[13] *Freeman's Journal*, 4 August 1877, 3, and 2 August 1882, 8.
[14] *Irish Times*, 10 February 1888, 3, and 4 June 1888, 7.
[15] Hamond 2006, 6.
[16] Myles 2014.
[17] Valuation 1828, 59.
[18] *Wilson's Dublin Directory* (1818 and 1822).
[19] Pembroke Estate Papers, NAI, 2011/2/2/6; Rocque's map of Dublin Bay, 1757.
[20] Archer 1801, 209.
[21] *Ibid.*, 205–7.
[22] The descriptions of the mills on the Dodder are largely based on information from the Registry of Deeds and the Valuation Office.
[23] There were mills on the southern side of the Dodder at Milltown and Clonskeagh, though these are outside the present city boundary and hence beyond the scope of this volume.
[24] *Irish Builder*, 1 November 1885, 290.
[25] *Freeman's Journal*, 4 November 1857; *Thom's Directory* (1857), 1182.
[26] *Irish Builder*, 1 November 1885, 290.
[27] *Freeman's Journal*, 8 March 1819, 3.
[28] *Ibid.*, 19 April 1792, 1.
[29] *Belfast Newsletter*, 6 August 1802, 1.
[30] *Thom's Directory* (1850), 827; *ibid.* (1851), 895.
[31] *Freeman's Journal*, 2 December 1889, 5.
[32] *Irish Independent*, 17 August 1988, 2.
[33] *Irish Press*, 26 November 1988, 9.
[34] *Evening Herald*, 27 February 1989, 1.
[35] *Thom's Directory* (1857), 1165.
[36] McEntee and Corcoran 2016, 138.
[37] Hamond 2019, 2–4.
[38] Valuation house book, National Archives of Ireland; http://census.nationalarchives.ie/reels/vob/IRE_CENSUS_1821-51_007246799_00094.pdf.
[39] Hamond 2019, 6.
[40] *Ibid.*, 8.
[41] Valuation Office cancelled books, Haroldscross West, 1855–99.
[42] Valuation house book, National Archives of Ireland; http://census.nationalarchives.ie/reels/vob/IRE_CENSUS_1821-51_007246843_00351.pdf.
[43] *Freeman's Journal*, 10 September 1877, 3; Valuation Office cancelled books, Haroldscross West, 1870s, plot 6.1.
[44] Warburton *et al.* 1818, 975.

[45] Harrison 2002, 241.
[46] *Ibid.*, 242.
[47] Lewis 1837, vol. II, 2.
[48] Valuation house book, National Archives of Ireland; http://census.nationalarchives.ie/reels/vob/IRE_CENSUS_1821-51_007246843_00535.pdf.
[49] Harrison 2002, 244.
[50] Valuation Office cancelled books, 1855–62, Haroldscross, plot 19.
[51] Harrison 2002, 244.
[52] *Irish Independent*, 14 June 1922, 6.
[53] *Belfast Newsletter*, 29 September 1921, 6.
[54] *Ibid.*, 8 October 1921, 8.
[55] *Freeman's Journal*, 13 May 1922, 6.
[56] *Ibid.*, 10.
[57] *Irish Independent*, 14 June 1922, 6.
[58] *Ibid.*, 23 September 1922, 10; *Freeman's Journal*, 16 November 1922, 4.
[59] *Irish Press*, 15 June 1936, 10, and 21 June 1937, 7.
[60] *Ibid.*, 11 June 1948, 2.
[61] *Cork Examiner*, 19 October 1965, 1.
[62] *Irish Press*, 19 July 1969, 11.
[63] *Irish Times*, 18 November 1873, 2.
[64] *The Irish Builder*, 15 February 1874, 57.
[65] *Belfast Newsletter*, 29 May 1880, 1.
[66] *Irish Press*, 21 April 1936, 9.
[67] Simington 1945, 292.
[68] *Freeman's Journal*, 24 September 1832, 1.
[69] *Ibid.*, 6 September 1850, 4.
[70] Valuation house book, National Archives of Ireland; http://census.nationalarchives.ie/reels/vob/IRE_CENSUS_1821-51_007246799_00153.pdf.
[71] *Freeman's Journal*, 9 July 1883, 6.
[72] *Ibid.*, 3 April 1886, 2.
[73] *Ibid.*, 5 March 1879, 1.
[74] *The Dublin Almanac and General Register of Ireland* (1844), 784.
[75] Valuation house book, National Archives of Ireland; http://census.nationalarchives.ie/reels/vob/IRE_CENSUS_1821-51_007246799_00161.pdf.
[76] *Freeman's Journal*, 8 January 1857, 1.
[77] *Ibid.*, 2 June 1866, 1; *Thom's Directory* (1877), 1517.
[78] *Evening Herald*, 19 September 1894, 3; *Thom's Directory* (1895), 1592.
[79] *An Claidheamh Soluis*, 25 February 1905, 6.
[80] *Freeman's Journal*, 8 January 1906, 16.
[81] *Thom's Directory* (1911), 1496; *ibid.* (1917), 1497; *ibid.* (1924), 1522.
[82] *Ibid.* (1927), 401.
[83] Delany 1995, 9–10, 21.
[84] *Freeman's Journal*, 28 June 1831, 1.
[85] Valuation house book, National Archives of Ireland; http://census.nationalarchives.ie/reels/vob/IRE_CENSUS_1821-51_007246799_00159.pdf.
[86] *Freeman's Journal*, 8 January 1857, 1; *The Nation*, 5 February 1859, 15; *Freeman's Journal*, 21 November 1859, 2.
[87] *Thom's Directory* (1868), 1572; Glancy 1997, 43.
[88] *Thom's Directory* (1877), 1517.
[89] *Freeman's Journal*, 29 June 1891, 8.

[90] *Thom's Directory* (1909), 1497.
[91] *Ibid.* (1911), 1496; *ibid.* (1917), 1497; *ibid.* (1924), 1422; *ibid.* (1927), 401.

Chapter 5

[1] Warburton *et al.* 1818, vol. II, 975.
[2] Census of Ireland 1871, Part 1, Vol. 1, Province of Leinster; Census of Ireland 1891, Part 1, Vol. 1, Province of Leinster.
[3] Clarke 2002, 26.
[4] Lennon 2008, 29.
[5] *Dublin Directory* (1738), 219.
[6] *The Dublin Almanac and General Register of Ireland* (1837), 683.
[7] *Thom's Directory* (various dates to 1990).
[8] Ó Maitiú 2001, 1, 24, 27, 102.
[9] *Thom's Directory* (various dates, 1895–1941); *Irish Press*, 2 March 1936, 2.
[10] *Thom's Directory* (various dates, 1890–1910).
[11] *Irish Daily Independent*, 19 December 1894; *Thom's Directory* (various dates, 1910–24).
[12] *Irish Independent*, 20 December 1947; *Thom's Directory* (various dates, 1960–71).
[13] *Evening Echo*, 26 June 1971; *Irish Independent*, 28 February 1972.
[14] Clarke 2002, 26.
[15] Lennon 2008, 29.
[16] Benedetti 1997, 1.
[17] Johnston-Liik 2002, vol. V, 74.
[18] Registry of Deeds, Book 100, p. 189, no. 70122.
[19] *Wilson's Dublin Directory* (various dates, 1790–1804); *Freeman's Journal*, 3 October 1793.
[20] Goodbody 2014, 55–6.
[21] *Wilson's Dublin Directory* (various dates, 1783–1832); Pigot & Co. 1824; Valuation 1828.
[22] *Wilson's Dublin Directory* (various dates, 1804–32); Pigot & Co. 1824; *The Dublin Almanac and General Register of Ireland* (various dates, 1834–46).
[23] *Wilson's Dublin Directory* (various dates, 1783–1832); *The Dublin Almanac and General Register of Ireland* (various dates, 1834–47); *Thom's Directory* (various dates, 1847–68); *Freeman's Journal*, 24 March 1853, 1, and 7 January 1856, 1.
[24] *Wilson's Dublin Directory* (various dates, 1791–1832); *The Dublin Almanac and General Register of Ireland* (various dates, 1834–44).
[25] Goodbody 2015, 79, 27, 31; *Wilson's Dublin Directory* (various dates, 1798–1814); *The Dublin Almanac and General Register of Ireland* (various dates, 1834–44).
[26] Mulryan 2016, 19–21.
[27] Lennon 2008, 29.
[28] Goodbody 2014, 59–60.
[29] *Ibid.*, 59–60.
[30] Mulryan 2016, 27–30; Townsend 1999, 2; Pigot & Co. 1824, 69.
[31] *Wilson's Dublin Directory* (various dates, 1824–32).
[32] Mulvihill 2002, 187–8.
[33] *The Dublin Almanac and General Register of Ireland* (various dates, 1834–40); Lunney 2009.
[34] Townsend 1997, 146; Murray 1981, 220.
[35] *Freeman's Journal*, 8 May 1843, 1.
[36] *Ibid.*, 28 April 1890, 7; *Belfast Newsletter*, 18 February 1905, 10; 24 June 1905, 1; 23 January 1908, 10.
[37] *Thom's Directory* (various dates, 1908–24); *Freeman's Journal*, 8 June 1921, 3; *Irish Times*, 5 March 1925, 4.
[38] Lennon 2008, 29.

[39] Kelly 2009, 67–8.
[40] Goodbody 2014, 60–2.
[41] Sanctuary 2008, 10–13.
[42] Goodbody 2014, 62.
[43] Hearn 2004, 4–8.
[44] *Ibid.*, 30, 105.
[45] *Irish Independent*, 1 June 1983, 3.
[46] *Irish Press*, 22 January 1968, 1.
[47] Kelly 1995, 195–6; *Evening Herald*, 15 December 1994, 8.
[48] Tweedy 1999, 15, 27.
[49] *Freeman's Journal*, 13 October 1902, 1; *Irish Times*, 16 September 1904, 1.
[50] *Irish Independent*, 24 September 1975, 4.
[51] McAleese 2013, 27.
[52] *Saturday Herald*, 23 November 1912, 1.
[53] *Irish Times*, 9 June 2004, 38.
[54] Kelly 1995, 181; Mulvihill 2002, 85–6.
[55] Casey 2005, 461–2.
[56] *Thom's Directory* (1945), 971, 1168.

Chapter 6

[1] Lennon 2008, 30.
[2] Dublin Public Libraries 2000, 156; Lennon 2008, 30; Goodbody 2014, 62.
[3] 23 & 24 Geo. III, c.35.
[4] *Dublin Evening Post*, 17 February 1798.
[5] *Wilson's Dublin Directory* (1822), 61.
[6] Pigot & Co. 1824, 71.
[7] *The Dublin Almanac and General Register of Ireland* (1834), 43, 67, 140.
[8] *Thom's Directory* (various dates).
[9] *Ibid.* (various dates, 1868 onward).
[10] *Evening Herald*, 25 May 1892, 2; *Freeman's Journal*, 4 November 1893, 2.
[11] *Freeman's Journal*, 14 December 1898, 7; *Thom's Directory* (various dates, 1890–1930).
[12] Hayden 1994.
[13] Lennon 2008, 30.
[14] *Ibid.*
[15] *Thom's Directory* (1880), 1485.
[16] *Wilson's Dublin Directory* (various dates, 1783–1832).
[17] *The Dublin Almanac and General Register of Ireland* (various dates, 1834–47); *Thom's Directory* (various dates, 1847–84).
[18] *Cork Examiner*, 8 July 1886, 4.
[19] *Thom's Directory* (various dates, 1902–84).
[20] *Wilson's Dublin Directory* (various dates, 1812–32).
[21] Williams 2009, 40.
[22] *Thom's Directory* (1877), 1744.
[23] McManus 2008, 8.
[24] Bonde 1998.
[25] Gilligan 1988, 246.
[26] Sweeney 2010, 9.
[27] Hammond 1943, 51.
[28] Sweeney 2010, 12.
[29] Gilligan 1988, 247.

[30] *The Dublin Almanac and General Register of Ireland* (various dates, 1834–47); *Thom's Directory* (various dates, 1847–1960).
[31] Delany 1995, 178; *Freeman's Journal*, 26 February 1883, 3.
[32] Sweeney 2010, 13.
[33] Delany 1995, 178.
[34] Sweeney 2010, 144–5.
[35] Murray 1981, 161.
[36] *Ibid.*, 220–2, 227.
[37] Goodbody 2023, 130–1, 138; *Irish Independent*, 12 May 1993, 19.
[38] *Freeman's Journal*, 20 November 1830, 2.
[39] Valuation Office cancelled books, Haroldscross.
[40] Lewis 1837, vol. I, 121; Griffith's Valuation.
[41] *Thom's Directory* (1880), 1494.

Chapter 7

[1] See https://www.dublinport.ie/about-dublin-port/about-us-2/.
[2] Clarke 2002, 1.
[3] 3 Geo. III, c.36; 15 & 16 Geo. III, c.28, and 17 & 18 Geo. III, c.10; Gilbert and Gilbert 1889–1944, vol. XII (1905), 537–8.
[4] Goodbody 2018, 236–7.
[5] Goodbody 2014, 2.
[6] Gilbert and Gilbert 1889–1944, vol. XII (1905), 285–8.
[7] 13 & 14 Geo. III, c.22.
[8] Ó Cionnaith 2015, 27.
[9] *Irish Builder* (1886), 72.
[10] *Ibid.* (1869), 199.
[11] Advice Series 2015, 17.
[12] *Irish Builder* (1882), 242; Advice Series 2015, 17.
[13] *Irish Builder* (1886), 109–10.
[14] *Cork Examiner*, 2 February 1886, 2.
[15] *Irish Builder* (1868), 244; *ibid.* (1872), 335.
[16] *Ibid.* (1872), 299.
[17] *Ibid.* (1885), 165, 250; *ibid.* (1889), 15iii; *ibid.* (1895), 274.
[18] Black and Barry 2015.
[19] O'Keeffe *et al.* 2016, 248–52.
[20] *Ibid.*, 250; plaque on bridge.
[21] Healy 2005, 3, 5.
[22] House of Commons Papers 1821, 477, *Grand Jury Presentments, Dublin*, 7, 11; *Freeman's Journal*, 29 July 1831, 2.
[23] *Freeman's Journal*, 8 November 1834, 3.
[24] *Dublin Builder*, 15 December 1863; Ordnance Survey six-inch map, Dublin sheet 22, 1843.
[25] *Irish Times*, 16 March 1972, 9, and 24 June 1972, 9.
[26] O'Donoghue 2007, 176.
[27] *Freeman's Journal*, 17 April 1807, 4.
[28] *Belfast Newsletter*, 9 January 1807, p. 2.
[29] House of Commons Papers 1821, 477, *Grand Jury Presentments, Dublin*, 7, 11; *Freeman's Journal*, 22 October 1807, 2.
[30] House of Commons Papers 1821, 477, *Grand Jury Presentments, Dublin*, 7, 11; *Dublin Journal*, 7 September 1809, 3; *Freeman's Journal*, 18 June 1810, 3, and 22 June 1810, 2.
[31] *Freeman's Journal*, 23 June 1812, 1.

[32] O'Keeffe *et al.* 2016, 189.
[33] Casey 2005, 337.
[34] See https://www.dublinport.ie/about-dublin-port/about-us-2/; accessed 15 October 2022.
[35] Wallace 2016, 154–68.
[36] Gilbert and Gilbert 1889–1944, vol. VI (1896), 371.
[37] 6 Anne, c.XX.
[38] 26 Geo. III, c.XIX.
[39] Gilbert and Gilbert 1889–1944, vol. VI (1896), 516.
[40] *Ibid.*, 533–4.
[41] Nairn *et al.* 2017, 191–2.
[42] De Courcy 1996, 374.
[43] Gilbert and Gilbert 1889–1944, vol. IX (1902), 263–4.
[44] *Ibid.*, vol. X (1903), 363.
[45] *Ibid.*, vol. IX (1902), 264, and vol. X (1903), 364.
[46] *Ibid.*, vol. X (1903), 363.
[47] *Ibid.*, vol. XI (1904), 85.
[48] *Ibid.*, 332.
[49] Gilligan 1988, 38.
[50] Gilbert and Gilbert 1889–1944, vol. XI (1904), 453.
[51] Gilligan 1988, 59.
[52] Nairn *et al.* 2017, 230.
[53] *Freeman's Journal*, 3 February 1870, 4, and 11 June 1888, 5.
[54] *Cork Examiner*, 27 October 1964, 6.
[55] Gilligan 1988, 244.
[56] *Ibid.*, 57.
[57] *Ibid.*, 60–1.
[58] *Freeman's Journal*, 19 October 1793, 3.
[59] Page 1800, 49.
[60] *Freeman's Journal*, 9 June 1818, 2.
[61] Corcoran 2005, 94–5.
[62] Gilligan 1988, 137.
[63] *Irish Independent*, 5 February 1959, 8; *Irish Press*, 3 November 1960, 15.
[64] Delany 1995, 61.
[65] *Irish Independent*, 30 November 1928, 6.
[66] *Drogheda Independent*, 11 December 1937, 13.
[67] Delany 1995, 61.
[68] *Ibid.*
[69] See https://en.wikipedia.org/wiki/List_of_Dublin_bridges_and_tunnels#Bridges_on_the_Grand_Canal, accessed 28 October 2022; Delany 1995, 72, 74.
[70] Delany 1995, 61.
[71] *Freeman's Journal*, 8 August 1856, 1.
[72] *Irish Daily Independent*, 16 April 1898, 2; *Freeman's Journal*, 25 April 1900, 4; *Evening Herald*, 11 March 1933, 1.
[73] *Irish Independent*, 11 December 1947, 2; *Irish Press*, 4 March 1948, 3.
[74] *Irish Press*, 21 January 1948, 10; *Irish Independent*, 2 February 1963, 14.
[75] *Irish Independent*, 31 May 2008, 4.
[76] Delany 1995, 51–5.
[77] Sweeney 2010, 143.
[78] Delany 1995, 177–8.
[79] Murray 1981, 13–16.

[80] *Ibid.*, 26.
[81] *Ibid.*, 142–3.
[82] Shepherd and Beesley 1998, 154.
[83] Murray 1981, 220–1.
[84] *Ibid.*, 155–60.
[85] MacAongusa 2003, 102.
[86] Shepherd and Beesley 1998, 10.
[87] *Ibid.*, 154.
[88] *Ibid.*, 44–5.
[89] Cox and Donald 2013, 163.
[90] Corcoran 2000, pl. 8.
[91] Kilroy 1996, 18.
[92] Corcoran 2000, 9.
[93] Kilroy 1996, 18–21.
[94] Corcoran 2000, 22.
[95] *Ibid.*, 36.
[96] Kilroy 1996, 49.
[97] *Freeman's Journal*, 21 July 1877 and 22 July 1881.
[98] Corcoran 2000, 32.
[99] *Ibid.*, 32–5.
[100] *Ibid.*, 38.
[101] *Evening Herald*, 19 May 1897; Corcoran 2000, 41.
[102] Corcoran 2000, 101.
[103] *Ibid.*
[104] *Ibid.*, 42–3, 48; *Evening Herald*, 7 April 1899, 1.
[105] The figures for the numbers of tram cars accommodated in each depot in 1910, as given below, are quoted from Corcoran 2000, 80.
[106] *The Gentleman's and Citizen's Almanack* (1798), 160–1.
[107] *Ibid.* (1812), 80–2.
[108] *Ibid.* (1818), 83–6.
[109] *Belfast Newsletter*, 20 May 1806, 3.
[110] *Moore's Irish Almanack* (1850), 43; Corcoran 2000, 8.
[111] *Thom's Directory* (1868), 1553, 1610, 1617, 1658.
[112] Old Dublin Town website, accessed 6 December 2022.
[113] Kelly 2019, 144–53, 438.
[114] McAteer 1935.
[115] *Evening Herald*, 14 May 1935, 7.
[116] *Irish Times*, 18 May 1974, 11.
[117] Clarke 2002, 14.
[118] Ó Cionnaith 2015, 33.
[119] Goodbody 2014, 25, 31, 32, 42.
[120] Joyce 1922, 46.

Chapter 8

[1] Lennon 2008, 27, 31.
[2] Reynolds 1983, 18.
[3] 23 & 24 Geo. III, c.117.
[4] 5 Geo. III, c.25 (UK).
[5] Reynolds 1983, 24, 26.
[6] Stafford Johnson 1942, 84–5.

[7] *The Gentleman's and Citizen's Almanack* (1798), 153.
[8] *Ibid.* (1804), 145.
[9] Reynolds 1983, 26.
[10] *The Gentleman's and Citizen's Almanack* (1812), 79–80.
[11] Stafford Johnson 1942, 93–4; *The Dublin Almanac and General Register of Ireland* (1837), 55.
[12] *The Dublin Almanac and General Register of Ireland* (1837), 55.
[13] Ferguson 2016, 206.
[14] *Ibid.*, 326.
[15] *Thom's Directory* (1847), 406; *ibid.* (1857), 775.
[16] O'Connor and O'Regan 1987, 49.
[17] *Irish Times*, 5 March 1925, 4.
[18] Ferguson 2009, 10–14.
[19] *Thom's Directory* (1868), 1092.
[20] Ferguson 2009, 15–19.
[21] *Ibid.*, 41.
[22] Letterbox Study Group 2004, 9.
[23] Ferguson 2009, 17.
[24] *Ibid.*, 42–3.
[25] Carey 2016, 12; *Irish Independent*, 16 March 2022.
[26] Ferguson 2009, 50.
[27] Standage 1998, 25–56, 71–4.
[28] Bolton *et al.* 2012, 151.
[29] Ferguson 2016, 195, 197.
[30] *Ibid.*, 198, 250; *Thom's Directory* (1876), 1353.
[31] Ferguson 2016, 159–67; *Thom's Directory* (various dates to 1955).
[32] Ferguson 2016, 290.
[33] Mulvihill 2002, 45.
[34] Ferguson 2016, 269–70.
[35] O'Connor and O'Regan 1987, 49.
[36] *Irish Times*, 28 April 1925, 5; Ferguson 2016, 285.
[37] Ferguson 2016, 290.
[38] *Irish Times*, 9 May 1925, 1.
[39] *Irish Independent*, 12 December 1985, 5.
[40] Condon 2006, 318.
[41] Goodbody 2022; Sexton 2005.
[42] O'Connell 2006, 322–5.

Chapter 9

[1] Gilbert and Gilbert 1889–1944, vol. III (1892), 72.
[2] *Ibid.*, vol. VI (1896), 180–1; 9 Will. III, c.17.
[3] 4 Geo. I, c.11.
[4] Ó Cionnaith 2015, 90–1.
[5] Bonar Law and Bonar Law 1999, 9–19.
[6] Ó Maitiú 2021, 62–3.
[7] Rynne 2006, 425.
[8] McCabe 1992, 36.
[9] Ó Maitiú 2003, 103.
[10] *The Nation*, 27 November 1875, 1.
[11] Black and Barry 2015, 122.
[12] O'Connell 1975, 18–19.

[13] *Ibid.*, 16.
[14] *Ibid.*, 18.
[15] Clarke 2002, 28.
[16] Gilbert and Gilbert 1889–1944, vol. VII (1898), 151, 153–5, 204.
[17] Delany 1995, 138, 191.
[18] Murray 1981, 220.
[19] *Irish Builder* (1899), 178.
[20] Ó Cionnaith 2015, 89; 23 & 24 Geo. III c.57; 26 Geo. III c.61
[21] *Irish Builder* (1899), 104.
[22] Ó Maitiú 2021, 62–3.
[23] Corcoran 2005, 14; McParland 1972, 21.
[24] *Freeman's Journal*, 24 September 1791, 4, and 5 June 1792, 2.
[25] O'Dwyer 1981, 24.
[26] *Freeman's Journal*, 18 September 1880, 6.
[27] Branigan 2014, 67–8.
[28] *Ibid.*, 41–68.
[29] Neville 1865, 266.
[30] Ó Maitiú 2003, 87–8.
[31] *Ibid.*, 95–6.
[32] 13 & 14 Geo. III, c.22.
[33] Corcoran 2005, 39, 73.
[34] Ó Maitiú 2003, 99.
[35] Corcoran 2005, 76.
[36] *Ibid.*, 79–81.
[37] *Ibid.*, 80.
[38] This section is based on Corcoran 2005, 91–103.
[39] Corcoran 2005, 114.
[40] *Ibid.*, 149–51.
[41] *Cork Examiner*, 26 October 1972, 20.
[42] *Irish Press*, 8 July 1975, 3.
[43] Corcoran 2005, 152.
[44] *Ibid.*,154, 155.
[45] *Irish Independent*, 1 July 2003, 9.
[46] *Belfast Newsletter*, 5 December 1815, 4.
[47] *Freeman's Journal*, 14 May 1818, 2.
[48] Gilbert and Gilbert 1889–1944, vol. XVII (1916), 289, 316–17.
[49] 1 Geo. IV, c.lv.
[50] 4 Geo. IV, c.xxxviii.
[51] 5 Geo. IV, c.xlii.
[52] *Freeman's Journal*, 4 October 1819, 3.
[53] *Ibid.*, 15 March 1819, 2.
[54] National Archives of Ireland, CSO_RP_1820_446.
[55] *Freeman's Journal*, 16 February 1821, 4.
[56] *Ibid.*, 1 January 1822, 3.
[57] *Wilson's Dublin Directory* (1824), 229.
[58] Zimmerman 2007, 130–1.
[59] McCabe 1992, 34.
[60] *Freeman's Journal*, 17 October 1826, 2.
[61] *Ibid.*, 20 July 1835, 1, and 9 June 1836, 1.
[62] O'Sullivan 1987, 39–40.

[63] *Freeman's Journal*, 19 September 1844, 2.
[64] *Ibid.*, 23 September 1846, 3; O'Sullivan 1987, 56.
[65] *Freeman's Journal*, 12 February 1864, 1.
[66] O'Sullivan 1987, 56–8.
[67] McCabe 1992, 32.
[68] *Ibid.*, 36.
[69] Ó Maitiú 2003, 103.
[70] *Ibid.*, 39.
[71] McCabe 1992, 39–40.
[72] Rynne 2006, 428.
[73] *Belfast Newsletter*, 9 November 1881, 5.
[74] *Ibid.*, 14 November 1881, 3.
[75] *Freeman's Journal*, 19 November 1881, 3.
[76] *Ibid.*, 21 November 1881, 5.
[77] Rynne 2006, 428.
[78] *Freeman's Journal*, 19 March 1882, 5.
[79] *Ibid.*, 23 January 1883.
[80] *Ibid.*, 23 January 1888; Rynne 2006, 430; *Irish Builder*, 1 July 1890, 164.
[81] *Evening Herald*, 13 February 1892, 2.
[82] *Ibid.*, 27 July 1892, 2.
[83] *Freeman's Journal*, 19 November 1892, 5.
[84] *Irish Daily Independent*, 9 November 1893, 8.
[85] *Freeman's Journal*, 19 November 1892, 5.
[86] *Evening Herald*, 21 September 1897, 1.
[87] *Ibid.*, 19 October 1896, 1.
[88] *Irish Times*, 15 September 1903, 5, and 26 September 1903, 11.
[89] *Ibid.*, 8 January 1903, 7.
[90] Rynne 2006, 430.
[91] *Irish Times*, 18 July 1903, 14.
[92] *Freeman's Journal*, 20 May 1896, 6; *Evening Herald*, 2 December 1898, 2.
[93] *Freeman's Journal*, 31 August 1900, 6.
[94] *Evening Herald*, 7 November 1900, 4.
[95] Ó Maitiú 2003, 167.
[96] *Ibid.*, 210.
[97] Kearney 1996, 9–10.
[98] ESB (n.d.), *Ringsend Generating Station*.
[99] Kearney 1996, 15–20.
[100] *Evening Herald*, 31 May 2010, 16.
[101] *Thom's Directory* (various dates, 1927–65).
[102] O'Toole 2019, 368–77.

Chapter 10

[1] Gilbert and Gilbert 1889–1944, vol. II (1891), 168.
[2] Haliday 1881, 228–9n.
[3] Craig 1952, 94.
[4] Price 1942, 114–15.
[5] Pigot & Co. 1824, 118.
[6] Harvey 2006, 117–18.
[7] De Courcy 1996, 185.
[8] *Freeman's Journal*, 6 June 1906, 16.

[9] De Courcy 1996, 299–301.
[10] O'Donnell 1972, 150.
[11] *Ibid.*, 152.
[12] Harvey 2006, 413–15.
[13] Bolton *et al.* 2012, 21.
[14] *Ibid.*, 145.
[15] *Irish Independent*, 10 October 1995, p. 33.

List of illustrations

Pl. 20—'[Greenmount and Boyne Linen Company, Harold's Cross, Co. Dublin]', April 1956. Photograph by Alexander Campbell Morgan (1919–58). (Morgan Aerial Photographic Collection. © National Library of Ireland.)
Pl. 21—Greenmount Brewery label. (© Laois Local Studies, Laois County Library.)
Pl. 22—Haig's Dodder Bank Distillery, *c.* 1795. (© Unknown. Every effort has been made to trace the source of this watercolour. The author would be grateful to be informed of the ownership so that due acknowledgement can be included in future editions.)
Pl. 23—Tara Street Baths. ([DD032] Courtesy of Dublin City Library & Archive.)
Pl. 24—Francis Danby (1793–1861), *Ringsend from Beggar's Bush*. (BELUM.U2095. Ulster Museum Collection. Courtesy of National Museums NI.)
Pl. 25—'[Cropped fragment of an engraved bill-head (presumably cut from a larger sheet of paper or receipt) for the Turner Hammersmith Iron Works, Balls Bridge [Ballsbridge], Dublin, featuring an image of the entrance into Turner's Iron Works]'. Engraved by John Kirkwood. (© National Library of Ireland.)
Pl. 26—Aerial view of Hammersmith Works. 'Hammersmith Works, Ballsbridge', held by G. & T. Crampton. (© Unknown. Digital content by Assoc. Prof. Joseph Brady. Published by UCD Library, University College Dublin.)
Pl. 27—Frontage of the Hammersmith Works on Pembroke Road. 'Hammersmith Works, Ballsbridge', held by G. & T. Crampton. (© Unknown. Digital content by Assoc. Prof. Joseph Brady. Published by UCD Library, University College Dublin.)
Pl. 28—The middle dry dock at Grand Canal Dock. (Photograph by Rob Goodbody.)
Pl. 29—Grand Canal Street, *c.* 1920. (Harold Fayle Collection. Archives of the Irish Railway Record Society
Pl. 30—Bernard de Gomme, *The citty and suburbs of Dublin from Kilmainham to Rings-End, wherein the rivers, streets, lanes, allys, churches, gates &c are exactly described*, 1673 (detail). (© National Maritime Museum, Greenwich, London.)
Pl. 31—Construction of Butt Bridge. ([Chan001] Courtesy of Dublin City Library & Archive.)
Pl. 32—The Samuel Beckett Bridge under construction. (© Dublin City Council.)
Pl. 33—'Dodder Bridge, Milltown, Co. Dublin'. Photograph by Fergus O'Connor. (Fergus O'Connor Collection. © National Library of Ireland.)
Pl. 34—'The Bridge, Dodder River, Rathfarnham, Dublin City, Co. Dublin'. (Eason Photographic Collection. © National Library of Ireland.)
Pl. 35—Francis Place (1647–1728), *Dublin from Donnybrook Bridge*, 1698. Ink and watercolour on paper, 12.5cm x 39.5cm, NGI.7521. (National Gallery of Ireland Collection. Photo © National Gallery of Ireland.)
Pl. 36—George Victor du Noyer (1817–69), *Old London Bridge, on the River Dodder, Dublin*, 1841. Graphite and watercolour on paper, 27.8cm x 27.2cm, NGI.2500. (National Gallery of Ireland Collection. Photo © National Gallery of Ireland.)
Pl. 37—Ringsend Bridge. (Photograph by Rob Goodbody.)
Pl. 38—John Rocque, *A survey of the city, harbour, bay and environs of Dublin on the same scale as those of London, Paris & Rome* (Dublin, 1757). (Courtesy of Trinity College Dublin.)
Pl. 39—James Walker (1748–1808), after George Holmes (fl. 1789–1802), *Poolbeg Lighthouse, South Wall, Dublin Bay*, 1801. Line, 14.6cm x 23cm, NGI.11689. (National Gallery of Ireland Collection. Photo © National Gallery of Ireland.)
Pl. 40—James Malton (1761–1803), *The Marine School, Sir John Rogerson's Quay, Dublin*, 1795. Ink and watercolour on paper, 52.4cm x 78.2cm, NGI.2704. (National Gallery of Ireland Collection. Photo © National Gallery of Ireland.)
Pl. 41—Sir John Rogerson's Quay in the 1980s. [Gasometer, Sir John Rogerson's Quay.] (Courtesy of Dublin City Library & Archive.)

Index

About the author

Rob Goodbody is a building historian. His primary degree included the study of geology, archaeology and historical geography, and he holds masters' degrees in building conservation and local history. He was a founding member of both the Mining Heritage Trust of Ireland and the Industrial Heritage Association of Ireland and has been on the committee of the Rathmichael Historical Society since 1984.

Previous books include *The lead mines, Sir Charles Domvile and his Shankill Estate*; *The Metals—From Dalkey to Dun Laoghaire*; *Irish Historic Towns Atlas, Dublin, Part III—1756–1847*; and *On the Borders of the Pale—A History of the Kilgobbin, Stepaside and Sandyford Area*. He has also co-authored a number of books, including *The Martello Towers of Dublin* and *Dublin Bay—Nature and History*, and edited the second edition of *Irish Stone Bridges* by Peter O'Keeffe and Tom Simington.